"**Wonderfully** [...]
[an] important and high[...]
—*Santa Barb*[...]

"Daniel Botkin shows us riches we never dreamed of. As a lifelong biologist, with abundant experience in the field (including the area Lewis and Clark explored), he is uniquely qualified to reveal to the present generation the rich environmental meaning of this glorious page of American history."
—Garret Hardin, author of
Living Within Limits

"With scores of natural ecosystems endangered in at least half of the contiguous forty-eight states, the pertinent scientific question is 'How can they be saved?' Botkin provides a bag of clues and a map."
—*Sierra* magazine

"Intriguing...Botkin describes the American West as seen by Lewis and Clark in 1804–06 and compares it with today's West as shaped by industrial civilization...The records of Lewis and Clark are valuable for helping us understand what nature was like before we changed it."
—*Publishers Weekly*

"We can only hope that books like this will steer us toward a more respectful and environmentally sound way of life."
—*Booklist*

"Everyone who shares an interest in the environment and the economic future should read this book...He has a view of the environment that is both practical and deeply rooted in history and fundamental science, and he emerges with important and innovative things to say about the perceived tension between ecology and competitiveness. Centering these approaches on the journals of the Lewis and Clark expedition provides great continuity with the American West as it existed shortly after the United States became a nation."
—Harold J. Morowitz,
Director, Krasnow Institute for Advanced Study,
George Mason University

to rocks. the shell is thin and consists of some ... small circular apperture is formed in the center of the under shell. the animals is soft & tonuless.—

The white salmon Trout which we had previously seen only at the great falls of the Columbia has now made its appearance in the creeks near this place. one of them was brought us to day by an Indian who had just taken it with his gig. this is a likeness of it; it was 2 feet 8 Inches long and weighed 10 lb. the eye is mo- derately large, the pupil black with a small admixture of yellow and iris of a silvery white ... a little ... a yellowish border near its position ... of the fins brown, the position ... the drawing, may be seen from ... in proportion they are small ... are boney but in to the fish the fins ... tail and back fin pointed except the ... little so, the prim which are a ... ventral ones, con back fin and ... ten rays; those of the tain each ... thirteen, that of the tail ... and the small fin placed louble ... tail above has no bony neor the ... is a tough flexable substance rays, but ... smooth skin. it is thicker in covered with ... to its width than the salmon. proportion ... is thick and from beset on each border the longer ... small subulate teeth in a single series. with ... the ... of the mouth are as before ... neither this fish nor the salmon are caught with the hook, nor do I know on what they feed. ———

Our Natural History

The Lessons of Lewis and Clark

Daniel B. Botkin

OXFORD
UNIVERSITY PRESS

OXFORD
UNIVERSITY PRESS

Oxford New York
Auckland Bangkok Buenos Aires
Cape Town Chennai Dar es Salaam Delhi Hong Kong Istanbul
Karachi Kolkata Kuala Lumpur Madrid Melbourne Mexico City Mumbai
Nairobi São Paulo Shanghai Taipei Tokyo Toronto

Published as an Oxford University Press paperback, 2004
198 Madison Avenue, New York, New York 10016
www.oup.com

Oxford is a registered trademark of Oxford University Press

Library of Congress Cataloging-in-Publication Data
Botkin, Daniel B.
Our natural history : the lessons of Lewis and Clark /Daniel Botkin
p. cm.
Originally published : New York, NY : Putnam, c1955.
Includes bibliographical references.
ISBN 0–19–516829–1 (pbk.)
1. Natural history—West (U.S.)
2. Botkin, Daniel B.—Journeys—West (U.S.)
3. Lewis and Clark Expedition (1804–1806)
4. Nature conservation—Philosophy.
5. Human ecology.
I. Title.

QH104.5.W4B682004
508.73—dc22   2003061171

Permission granted by Gary Moulton, editor of The Journals of the Lewis and Clark Expedition,
to quote extensively from the published volumes of the new edition.
Use of the drawing of "White Salmon Trout" from the Lewis and Clark Journals
is used by permission of the American Philosophical Society, Philadelphia, PA.
Use of Woody Guthrie prose is by permission of WOODY GUTHRIE PUBLICATIONS, INC. NEW YORK, NY.
LUMBER IS KING. *Words by Woodie Guthrie, music by Pete Seger. Copyright © 1988 by* WOODY GUTHRIE PUBLICATIONS, INC.
All rights reserved. Used by permission.
ROLL, COLUMBIA, ROLL *(The Grand Coulee Dam). Words and music by Woodie Guthrie* TRO *Copyright © 1958*
(Renewed) 1963 (Renewed) 1976 Ludlow Music Inc., New York, NY. Used by permission.
COLUMBIA TALKING BLUES *(Talking Columbia). Words and music by Woody Guthrie* TRO *Copyright © 1961 (Renewed) 1963*
Ludlow Music, Inc., New York, NY. Used by permission.

1 3 5 7 9 10 8 6 4 2
Printed in the United States of America
on acid-free paper

For Erene,
my inspiration for eighteen years

Acknowledgments

Many people helped me as I sought to understand the expedition of Lewis and Clark and to visit locations along their path. These contacts and the experiences that followed created a network that is in itself an interesting story. Gary Moulton, editor of the new edition of the Lewis and Clark journals, discussed the expedition with me and offered invaluable suggestions of places to visit and people to see. He suggested I speak with Ty Harrison, the botanist who identified the vegetation described by Lewis and Clark, for the new edition of their journals, and whom I also thank for helping me to find representative natural areas of prairie and woodlands along the Missouri River and suggesting people to visit as well. Ty Harrison suggested I meet Tom Bragg and Gary Garabrandt. Tom Bragg, botanist at the University of Nebraska, Omaha, pointed out prairie lands to visit; Gary Garabrandt, Chief Ranger of the Fontenelle Forest Association, Bellevue, Nebraska, gave me many hours of pleasant and insightful discussion and tours of the prairies, wildlife refuges, and woodlands along the Missouri. Gary Garabrandt, in turn, introduced me to Neal and Izen Ratzlaff, whom I thank for their hospitality during a visit to Omaha and for our long discussions about the conservation of prairie. Dr. David C. Glenn-Lewin and Tom Jurik of Iowa State University gave me a wonderful field trip through natural areas of Iowa and provided important references concerning the geological and natural history of that state. I thank them all.

During my work in Oregon, many people and organizations helped me understand the issues that concern the Pacific Northwest, the natural history of the forests and fish of Oregon and Washington, the status of the environment, and the state of our knowledge about that environment. In particular, I thank Phil Cogswell, an editor of the *Oregonian*, for many delightful discussions about Oregon's history and environmental controversies, and for providing me with useful references as well. I also wish to acknowledge how much I gained from discussions with staff of the Oregon Department of Forestry, especially state forester Jim Brown and Janet McLennan, chair of the Oregon Board of Forestry, with the staff of the Oregon Department of Fish and Wildlife, and members of the Oregon Coastal Zone Management Association, especially its Director, Jay Rasmussen; with non-governmental environmental organizations, especially Oregon Trout, Ecotrust, and Oregon chapters of the Audubon Society and the Wilderness Society. I thank the staff of the Fontenelle Forest Association and of the Fort Clatsop National Monument for their courteous assistance during my visits. The World Forestry Center provided office space for our project on salmon and their habitats, and their Director, John Blackwell, provided a great deal of help.

Many of my scientific colleagues have played important roles over the years, and the results of my discussions and work with them are reflected throughout this book. Dr. Thomas Dunne of the University of Washington taught me about the geomorphology of the Columbia and the role of geological processes in the lives of salmon, and provided important references about the geological history of the Missouri. Dr. Kenneth Cummins of the South Florida Water Management District educated me about the life history of salmon and the dependence of these fish on forested habitats. I am deeply indebted to Dr. Matthew Sobel of the State University of New York, Stony Brook, who over many years has helped me analyze and understand the role of chance and uncertainty in nature. Similarly, I am indebted to Dr. Lee Talbot, former Director of the International Union for the Conservation of Nature, for many thoughtful discussions about biological conservation, and who kindly reviewed my discussion in this book about endangered species. Dr. Harold Morowitz of George Mason University has been a continuing source of inspiration on the subject of innovation in science and on the need for clear thinking and clear writing about it; I thank him also for reviewing early drafts of this manuscript. I thank Dr. Charles Beveridge, historian and Director of the Olmsted Papers, Washington, D.C., and Roderick Nash, historian and Professor Emeritus of the University of California, Santa Barbara, for many discussions over the years about environment and society.

The writing and rewriting of this manuscript benefited especially from the help of Joan Melcher, a screenwriter and professional editor who read and reread drafts of the manuscript, advising me about its structure and providing helpful editing. I would especially like to thank Jane Isay, my editor and publisher at Grosset Books, who, in the course of many drafts, provided an excellent perspective on what worked and what did not, who helped me with the level of discussion, the balance of personal, historical, and scientific material, and with suggestions about the overall structure of the book. I thank Betty Ann Oakes for help with notes and permissions, and Dorothy Rosenthal for discussions about the scientific method and for useful references and citations.

Since this book presents aspects of my research over many years, it represents the products of many specific research projects, some of whose support came from government agencies and some from private foundations. The government agencies include: the Department of Agriculture U.S. Forest Service, NASA, the National Oceanographic and Atmospheric Administration, the National Science Foundation, and The Woodrow Wilson International Center for Scholars. The private foundations include: The Andrew W. Mellon Foundation, Pew Memorial Trust, and W. Alton Jones Foundation. The project on salmon and their habitats, discussed in Chapters 9 and 10, was supported by a contract to the Center for the Study of the Environment, Santa Barbara, California, through Oregon Legislative Bill 1125 (1991), and with funds from the Oregon Department of Forestry, the U.S. Department of Agriculture Forest Service, the Bureau of Land Management, and the California Department of Forestry and Fire Protection.

Finally, I thank the staff of The Center for the Study of the Environment for assistance of many kinds and for bearing with me during the production of this book, especially Susan Day, Dr. Lloyd Simpson, and Angela Magness.

Contents

CONTENTS

Preface

In a time when environmentalism has become so well accepted that it may seem a fad, we forget how central and ancient is our human concern with our surroundings. It is both a burden and a luxury of our era that we make the conservation of nature and wilderness a goal of our society: a burden because we have done so much damage to the environment; a luxury because we appear to have complete power over wilderness.

As important as the environment is, we continually fail to solve major environmental problems, and the situation is growing worse. As a professional scientist involved in attempts to deal with environmental problems, I am confronted with these failures daily. Some make the headlines repeatedly, such as the conflict between those who would protect old-growth forests and loggers in the Pacific Northwest. Many others are less well known but equally persistent. They range from disputes over an off-the-road motorcycle trail and a single pond where a little-known species of toad breeds, to disagreements among nations as to how to act in response to a possibility of a global warming.

A recent survey suggests that 82 percent of voters place the environment among the top three or four issues. If required, 72 percent would sacrifice economic growth for environmental quality, but 82 percent believe creating a cleaner environment will increase jobs and income levels. It is hard to find a politician who does not claim to be an environmentalist.

With this widespread acceptance of the need to solve environmental problems, why do we continually fail to find solutions? For the past twenty-five years I have been involved in many different kinds of environmental issues, from conservation of endangered species, such as the bowhead whale and the whooping crane, to regional issues, such as seeking sustainable forest practices and conserving old-growth forests, to global issues, such as global warming. And I have found from my experiences that, although we have the scientific and technological know-how sufficient to improve our environment greatly (and to do this while improving our economic condition as well), we have a faulty understanding of how nature works, and so we are doomed to failure.

Puzzled by our inability to use our environmental sciences well, I took a year off from my scientific work and spent it at the Woodrow Wilson International Center for Scholars in the Smithsonian Institution in Washington, D.C., reading about what people had said in other times about environment and nature, from the ancient Greeks to the eighteenth century. And I discovered that writers in the Western tradition have framed their thinking on this subject around three questions:

· What is the character of nature undisturbed by human influence?
· What is the influence of nature on us?
· What is our influence on nature?

Each age has had at the same time a complete answer and no answer at all. But it became clear from the continual concern of our ancestors that the idea of nature had, and continues to have, a deeper meaning than a collection of facts, a single threatened species, or a single polluted stream. In the ancient Anglo-Saxon epic *Beowulf*, the word "wilderness" retained its original meaning as a place of wild creatures. The world was viewed as a dark and dangerous place, and the community of people seemed no more than a small group huddled around the light of a fire in a damp shelter, trying to keep out the cold and away from the creatures. A hero was a person, like Beowulf, who went out into that darkness and killed the dangerous wild beasts. As my friend John Perlin has taught me in his *A Forest Journey: The Role of Wood in the Development of Civilization*, Gilgamesh was a typical hero, one who cleared the forests, replacing darkness with light, bringing wood for fuel and buildings back to his city for use by those who feared the darkness.

The result of my year in Washington and later work was a book, *Discordant Harmonies: A New Ecology for the Twenty-first Century*, which suggests that our present approach to environmental issues—our present natural history—is based on faulty beliefs, mythologies, and religious convictions. It may seem strange that a scientist would focus on these aspects of culture, but I have come to recognize that culture has a major influence on how we conserve and manage our environment. So today we are still answering questions about nature much as the Babylonians had in the *Gilgamesh Epic*, and the ancient Britains in *Beowulf*.

In recent years, I have been approached by a wide variety of organizations, each of which has asked me to help solve a specific environmental problem. Each told a similar story: a failure of perceptions and ideas, not of science and technology. A consulting firm from Los Angeles was hired to create land-use plans for two rapidly growing cities in the Los Angeles Basin. Every sector of society in both cities, they said, genuinely wanted to create a good environment, but all the sectors hated the environmentalists. The firm was stymied for two reasons: obstructionism of the environmental groups, and the firm's inability to understand how to find innovative concepts for the new plans. Their approach to planning did not work, and they saw in *Discordant Harmonies* a possibility for new, innovative solutions.

Two years ago I spoke to the annual meeting of the Society of American Foresters of New York State. Forest conservationists at the meeting told me that a conflict between landowners and conservationists over the future of the Adirondacks was on the verge of being resolved when representatives of a major national environmental organization came into the area, made extreme pronouncements, and drove the opposing groups apart. The organization made it seem as if the world were black and white, one realm of "nature" and another of "people." The two were in conflict and nature should be allowed to win out. This dichotomy is false and destructive, but it forms the basis for much of what is said and done about the environment.

My first reading of the Lewis and Clark journals in 1970 formed one basis for my thinking about wilderness. A few years ago, I decided to return to Lewis and Clark and their journals. Perhaps better than anyone else, those two had explored a wilderness, gathered information, and wrote carefully about what they saw, heard, felt, hunted, and retreated from.

As I sat on an airplane rereading the experiences of Lewis and Clark, I decided that there was one more path to take in my own search for an understanding of our environment: to understand the character of nature when first seen by Lewis and Clark and to compare that with the environment of the American West today. So I began to retrace their journey myself, to explore our real wilderness heritage as reported by Lewis and Clark, and to revisit that wilderness and see how it had changed.

The result is this book, which describes the wilderness of the American West as seen by Lewis and Clark during their journey of 1804–1806, and compares it to today's American West as shaped by industrial civilization. Lewis and Clark saw the land as people of European descent would never see it again, traveling (by their own reckoning) 4,134 miles on their outward journey, 3,555 miles by a shorter route on their return. It was America's greatest odyssey, beginning in St. Louis, navigating up the Missouri River and through the prairies, enduring a winter with the Mandan Indians in North Dakota, reaching the summit of the Rocky Mountains and then going down to the Columbia River, and down that river to the Pacific. Their journey has been called America's national epic of exploration, conceived by Thomas Jefferson, wrought by Lewis and Clark.

I learned much from their journals, and learned even more in the process of comparing my experiences with theirs. I was surprised to discover how rich their notes about nature were. As an example, I discovered that I could make an estimate of the presettlement density and abundance of grizzly bears simply from the expedition's encounters with these fierce animals. I discovered that the geology and geomorphology of the Missouri River had been relatively little studied—compared to the Mississippi, the Columbia, and the Amazon—and that it took a lot of digging through obscure reports to reconstruct why the Missouri flows where it does and how it has interacted with and affected the landscape.

When European settlers came to the New World, they brought with them not only their technology, their religions, and their social attitudes, but also their ancient natural history, a view of environment that can be traced back to the Greeks and Romans and is the product of age-old dependencies on nature. Joseph Campbell, the great interpreter of the relationship between myth and civilization, said that one of the keys to human existence is nature-knowledge, which forms the basis of our philosophies and religions. But—and this is the dilemma of our time— our nature-knowledge is 4,000 years old, inconsistent with what we actually understand, through science, about the environment. He argues that we must reconcile these two experiences if we are to find new interpretations for the meaning of our lives.

Today, with the advantages of modern environmental scientific knowledge and with the opportunity to take a fresh look at nature as it was before Western technology, we can uncover a new natural history, a natural history that is consistent with our scientific understanding and our modern relationship with the environment. Solutions to environmental problems are not simply matters of facts and improved techniques. They will not form the basis for a sustainable environment unless we come to a new understanding of the texture and weave of nature and of our relationship with it. If we begin to understand the true nature of our natural heritage, we will learn what we have and have not done to it, and we can become the stewards of our environment, conserving and using wisely our natural resources, for ourselves, for the betterment of our cultures and societies, and for all life on the Earth. In reliving Lewis and Clark's experiences, we can see the mirror of nature in the snows of the Rockies and in the waters of the Missouri and the Columbia. In those reflections we can better understand where people fit into the puzzle of nature and how we can solve our environmental problems in a way that suits our humanity as well as the needs of other living things. We can come to know our natural history.

CHAPTER ONE

A Road Through the Wilderness

Lewis was blessed with those qualities most important in a naturalist: an unquenchable curiosity, keen observational powers, and a systematic approach to understanding the natural world.

GARY E. MOULTON

It was the greatest wilderness trip ever recorded. Captains Meriwether Lewis and William Clark led an expedition from Missouri through parts of what are today Kansas, Iowa, Nebraska, South and North Dakota, Montana, Idaho, Washington, and Oregon, traveling along the Missouri and Yellowstone rivers, over the Rockies, down the Kooskooskee and the Columbia. The

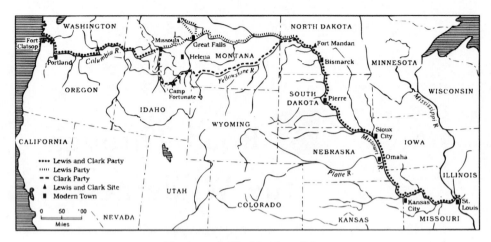

Lewis and Clark's Expeditions

trip lasted from May 14, 1804, to September 23, 1806, a total of 863 days (approximately two years and four months). From April 1805 through August 1806 "all communication with the world was suspended," and in this sense they were truly in the wilderness.

Their journey divides into seven stages. It began with the first summer on the Missouri, lasting from May 14 to October 16, 1804. From October 16, 1804, until April 7, 1805, the expedition wintered with the Mandans near Mandan and Hidatsa villages in what is now North Dakota, near the present town of Washburn. The third stage was the continuation of the journey to the headwaters of the Missouri, which lasted from April 7, 1805, until July 27, 1805. The fourth stage was the difficult western ascent of the Rockies, across the great Continental Divide on the Montana-Idaho border, then over the rugged Bitterroot Range, which lasted from July 27, 1805, when the expedition reached the Three Forks of the Missouri, about 100 air miles south of Great Falls, Montana, to October 16, 1805, with the sighting of the Columbia

2

River at its confluence with the Snake and Yakima rivers at what is now Richland, Washington. In the fifth stage the expedition traveled down the Columbia, from October 16, 1805, to December 7, 1805. In the sixth stage, the expedition spent its second winter near the Pacific Coast at Fort Clatsop, near to modern Astoria, Oregon. The final, seventh stage was the return, which lasted from March 23, 1806, when the expedition left Fort Clatsop, to September 23, 1806, when the expedition returned to St. Louis.

Lewis and Clark were careful and accurate observers. With President Jefferson's assistance, Lewis was introduced to experts of the time who trained him in natural history and in the methods of collecting samples of animals and plants. He and Clark were instructed to record the conditions of the countryside. President Jefferson wrote to Lewis: "Record the mineral productions of every kind . . . Volcanic appearances . . . Climate, as characterized by the thermometer, by the proportion of rainy, cloudy, and clear days, by lightning, hail, snow, ice; by the access and recess of frost; by the winds prevailing at different seasons; the dates at which particular plants put forth or lose their flower or leaf; times of appearance of particular birds, reptiles, or insects." These instructions they followed, recording the condition of the rivers, prairies, forests, mountains, and wildlife without dogma, without romanticism, without fantasy. They were leaders of a small band traveling by foot, riverboat, canoe, and horseback through unknown and often harsh terrain. Needing to survive, they could not afford the luxury of a glamorized utopian vision of nature. Because of this they are our best contact with the reality of nature.

A   C A R E F U L L Y   P L A N N E D
A N D   M E A S U R E D   E X P E D I T I O N

"Accept no soft-palmed gentlemen dazzled by dreams of high adventure," Lewis had told Clark when they were interviewing people to make up the crew. "We must set our faces against all such applications and get rid of them on the best terms we can. They will not answer our purposes," he wrote. He had planned the expedition with great care. To succeed, the expedition required careful selection of equipment, careful planning of the route and method of exploration, and great leadership of the small band of men who were to cross the wilderness.

Lewis was occupied for months with the selection and invention of devices to take on the journey. His scientific and surveying equipment included quadrant, compass, hydrometers, a theodolite, and thermometers to record air temperature. Lewis invented a lead, watertight container to hold gun powder that could be melted down, when empty, to make bullets. He brought 52 of these, and they worked exceedingly well. Twenty-seven were used on the outward journey and only five of the remaining ones had cracked and allowed water to reach the powder by the time they were ready to return home. He purchased only the best imported gunpowder, since at that time American-made powder was of inferior quality. He also designed a rifle especially for the expedition, a design that became the model for the first mass-produced rifles of the U.S. Army. In addition to these new rifles, Lewis brought three cannons, which were mounted on the boats, small flintlock pistols, muskets, blunderbusses, one new kind of air rifle, tomahawks, and scalping knives.

He purchased the best clothing available for the members of his

4

expedition, along with blankets, hooded coats, some clothing of a water-repellent material, 30 yards of flannel to be carried to make new clothing, and needles and awls to make the clothing. So that everything that was needed could be repaired or made on the way, he brought adzes, augers, and axes; chisels, and files; knives, nails, rasps, rope, saws, vises, and spades.

His medicine chest included the best available pharmaceuticals of the day, most of which were derived from plants or were simple minerals: balsam; borax; calomel, a mercury compound used as a purgative; camphor, a plant product used to treat pain and itching; cloves, which relieves toothache; cinnamon; copperas, which is iron sulphate, used to treat anemia; ipecac, a dried root of a South American shrub, used as an emetic, jalap; laudanum, which is a solution of water and alcohol containing opium; niter, which we call saltpeter, an ingredient in gunpowder used to treat many diseases, especially asthma; and nutmeg. He brought bandages, lancets, syringes, and tourniquets.

On the Missouri, the expedition traveled on a 55-foot keelboat, called a bateau, (Lewis also tested an iron-framed canoe, but it did not work.) and a large wooden dugout, called a pirogue. For these, he brought boathooks, chains, and padlocks. In all, the equipment for the trip weighed 3,500 pounds. He and President Jefferson had carefully planned the expedition, and Lewis had spent months choosing equipment and purchasing it. His trip was meant to be as unadventurous as possible.

A HUNGRY NIGHT

On Tuesday, June 17, 1806, Captains Meriwether Lewis and William Clark and their expedition of 29 men, one woman and her baby approached the summit of the Rocky Mountains in an attempt to return home after more than two years travel that had taken them up the Missouri, over the Rockies, and down the Columbia River, from St. Louis to the Pacific Coast. They had fulfilled most of the goals of their journey. They had found a path across the continent, had met the tribes of Indians along the way and told them of the Louisiana Purchase signed in 1803, granting all of this land to the new United States of America and giving the Indians their new "father" in Washington. They had noted the customs of these tribes, as President Jefferson had asked them to do, and rendered what they could of their languages into written script. They had observed the animals and plants of the countryside and written about the conditions of the soils, rivers, mountains, and minerals. Now they were trying to find their way back to bring their news to the new nation. At the summit they found snow 12 to 15 feet deep, and no clear way through. For the first time, the greatest of all American odysseys, perhaps the greatest expedition ever made into a wilderness, and certainly the most carefully and accurately recorded by its participants, was forced to retreat.

Turning back, "melancholy and disappointed," the members of the small band retraced their hard-won steps downslope, westward. Lewis had directed each of his three sergeants to keep a journal during the expedition. That evening, Sergeant Gass, one of the hardiest and most important members of the group, wrote "there was not the appearance of a green shrub, or anything for our horses to subsist on, and we know it cannot be better for four days march, even"—he continued most curiously—"could we find the road," a task which appeared "almost impossible, without a guide."

On that far-off June day high in the cold mountains of the Idaho-Montana border, the Lewis and Clark expedition was lost in a wilderness that was threatening, dangerous and challenging, a real outdoors far different from what most of us imagine today. And what were they doing searching for a road in the wilderness? And what was a road doing in the wilderness at all? Weren't Lewis and Clark, explorers of almost mythical proportions in America's heritage, supposed to be on the ultimate hike of a backpacker's dream, a 7,000-mile trek through wilderness untrammeled by human beings, undivided by roads?

And why did they turn back "melancholy?" Wasn't the essence of wilderness the chance for adventure, the excitement of danger, and the challenge of new threats? If Lewis and Clark voluntarily confronted wilderness, why did they need or want a guide? Were they not, like Bob Marshall of our century, out to test themselves against the challenges of nature without the aid of any other human being? Wasn't wilderness what Aldo Leopold was to call it more than 100 years after Lewis and Clark had experienced it: a place you could walk—and wanted to walk —for two weeks without crossing your own footsteps?

Americans have a special fascination with wilderness. In part, it is a fascination with the land as seen by the pioneers and explorers, a land of romantic appeal, open and free, uncluttered in our imagination by the middens of main street, clean and pure, spotless and without poverty; democratic, without status; a place where all are equal before the challenges of grizzly bears and mountain blizzards. It is a fascination with the romance of adventure, with Daniel Boone and Davy Crockett. It is a fascination with the apparent stillness and permanence of the natural lands of our imagination, a bedrock of firmament that seems preferable to the constant changes, the vagaries and fashions of cities, wars, clothing styles, the modern world; it is the lure of the life we cannot lead.

I believe that in the answers to these questions lies an important message to us today, a message that concerns the essence of the reasons we often fail to solve environmental problems, fail as a society to agree on approaches to environment, and fail at a personal level to come to terms with ourselves within our surroundings. The answers to these questions have to do with the real character of nature undisturbed by human influence and the role and effects of human beings on their environment over centuries.

After their discussions on the lonely summit on Tuesday, June 17, 1806, the expedition began its retreat toward their camp of the day before, at a place Lewis and Clark had named Hungry Creek, in what is now Idaho. Reaching that creek, they traveled two miles upstream until they found "some scanty grass" for their horses and camped for the night. The grass was "so scant" that their horses wandered far in the night looking for forage, and some were lost "a considerable distance among the thick timber on the hillsides."

On that June day when the expedition turned back for the first time, Lewis and Clark were searching for the road they had taken on their westward travel, an Indian road that had brought them through one of the crucial parts of the entire trip, the traverse of the mountains between the Missouri and Columbia rivers. It was there, in the mountains, that travel was most difficult and dangerous, and where their success depended on the experiences and aid of the Indians and on the changes that the Indians had wrought on the landscape. Lewis and Clark were traveling in *their* wilderness, but they were also traveling in the Indians' backyards, in the Indians' hunting and gathering grounds, along paths familiar to Native Americans, paths that took them from their homes for one season to their homes for another, and from the lands of one tribe to another's. In that wilderness was a road familiar to the Indians, and on which the success of the expedition ultimately depended.

Although the Lewis and Clark expedition took place almost two centuries ago, their approaches to the problems that confronted them are familiar and strangely modern: familiar because they make use of the methods of observation that are an integral part of our scientific and technological approach to problem solving; modern because, when it comes to solving environmental problems, Lewis and Clark seem sometimes to apply these methods in advance of ourselves.

THE PASSAGE THROUGH

The next morning, June 18, the expedition did not find all the horses, though they searched from dawn until 9:00 a.m. Lewis and Clark sent two of the men to find the Nez Perce Indians, who had promised to provide a guide through the mountains, offering a rifle as a reward. The rest of the members of the expedition began the upward journey once again. They crossed Hungry Creek, where the rocks and water caused them great difficulty. One horse fell and threw its rider onto the rocks. Another man cut a vein in his leg "and we had great difficulty in stopping the blood." Food was scarce and difficult to hunt in the "thick underbrush and fallen timber."

They camped again after traveling only two miles uphill from where they had been on the 15th. They were low on food, and could find little to eat, for fish and deer were scarce—and they were bothered by mosquitoes. The next day, they retreated downhill once again. "The mortification of being obliged to tread back our steps rendered still more tedious a route always so obstructed by brush and fallen timber that it cannot be passed without difficulty," a difficulty that again badly wounded a horse. Thus they struggled until June 23.

G U I D E D   O V E R   T H E   M O U N T A I N S

But on that day, they found three Indians who agreed to guide the expedition over the mountains. The next day, June 24, 1806, the expedition began its second major attempt to find a way back across the Rockies. By June 26, Lewis and Clark had only reached the point from which they had turned back nine days before. Going onward, through snows still 10 feet deep, they "crossed abruptly steep hills . . . near tremendous precipices, where, had our horses slipped, we should have been lost irrecoverably." They camped above the headwaters of streams, on a south slope where the snows had melted, finally finding grass for their horses.

On June 27, the expedition reached a summit where there was a cone-shaped stone about six feet high, with a pine pole on top, a cairn made by the Indians to mark the height of land. From this location, Lewis and Clark recorded that they had "a commanding view of the surrounding mountains, which so completely inclose us that, though we have once passed them, we almost despair of ever escaping from them without the assistance of the Indians." In what they called "this trackless region" their guides never hesitated and were so accurate in the travel that "wherever the snow has disappeared . . . we find the summer road" of the previous year.

Two days later, they descended below the snows, found a good camp for their horses to graze, deer for themselves to eat, and warm springs, where they and their Indian guides bathed; they had crossed the main divide of the Bitterroot Mountains, passing from what is now Idaho to what is now Montana. Although the great divide of the Rockies lay ahead, they had left behind their greatest ordeal. Soon after, on July 1, 1806, they agreed to divide into two groups and explore different routes eastward, and by July 3, Lewis's group found a route "so well beaten that we could no longer mistake it," and left their Indian guides. Two days later, they found themselves in "an extensive, beautiful, and well-watered valley nearly 12 miles in length," and on Monday, July 7, they reached the divide between the Columbia and the Missouri. The danger was over. They had been led on the road through their wilderness by Indian guides and had succeeded.

From Lewis and Clark's experiences in the high mountains, we learn two lessons about environment. First, the countryside of the American West, prior to the great changes wrought by modern technology, was not much like the idyllic, static scenery we view from our cars in Yosemite and the Grand Canyon. Theirs was as much a social and personal journey, with human and humanitarian consequences, as it was an exploration of the unknown. Second, often what we appreciate about environment and believe to be unaffected by human beings is actually the product of long, human-induced changes in the landscape.

We have few cases where travelers through that kind of nature kept accurate notes and were comparatively objective in their observations. Lewis and Clark were sent by Jefferson to record what they saw, not what they imagined or believed. This they did, with comparatively little overlay of the prejudices and fashions of their time. Their experiences in the wilderness are invaluable, important far beyond sheer adventure or the bare facts of what they accomplished. Their experiences can help us understand what nature was really like before it was changed by modern civilization and technology, help us understand how we have really changed nature. Their experiences can help us develop *our* natural history, one that is consistent with our knowledge of nature, both in the experience of that nature in the New World and in our new scientific understanding.

MYTHS AND NATURE

Underlying modern environmental conflicts is the belief in the classic balance of nature, the idea that nature, undisturbed by human influences, is constant and that this constancy is desirable and good—and the best possible condition for all life. This classic idea has several historic origins that are deeply imbedded in our culture. Most important of these are the ancient myth of a divine order in nature and the industrial-age concept of nature as a machine.

The divine-order myth begins with the sense of wonder at the beautiful and complex order in the universe, especially the amazing adaptations of each creature to its needs—the trunk of the elephant, the fins of a fish, the curious symbioses between animals. In the words of Cicero written in first century B.C., "Who cannot wonder at this harmony of things, at this symphony of nature which seems to will the well-being of the world?" This order seemed too perfect to have arisen by chance. It must have been created by gods, or The God. As perfect beings, they could only have made a perfect world. To question the perfection of nature was to question the existence of God.

But the belief in a divine order leaves an important question unanswered. If the world must be perfect, why do we find imperfections? Traditionally, two answers have been given, both of which point the finger at us. One says that we have done too little, the other that we have done too much. The first explanation is that we were put here to be the Earth's stewards, to be the final cog in the machine that creates

12

perfection, and we have not done our job. The second is that nature is perfect without our actions, and that anything we do in our arrogance destroys the balance of nature, and is bad. The latter is the view that has dominated the twentieth century, although lip service is given occasionally to the idea that we should be stewards of nature.

Prior to the industrial and scientific revolution, the explanation for the *origin* of order in nature was based on the idea of divine creation, but explanations about *how nature worked* were derived from analogies with entities familiar to people: their own bodies and the bodies of animals. This is the basis of the organic myth, the myth of Mother Nature. Nature was a companion creature, which, like us, passed through life's stages. People believed that there had been a long past golden age of nature's youth, and the lack of perfection in nature observed in civilized times was the result of the aging of Mother Earth: mountains were wrinkles on her skin, volcanoes her warts. While these may seem fanciful to us, explanations based on the bodies of animals were the only ones available, and were taken quite literally. Rivers were spoken of as the Earth's veins; underground passages of upward-moving waters were Earth's arteries. The existence of these two currents implied an Earth heart.

With the beginning of the Industrial Revolution and the rise of modern science and engineering, people no longer viewed the Earth as a living creature; instead, it operated like a machine, following the newly discovered Newtonian laws of motion. This led to the more recent, but very important, myth of nature as the machine. The science of ecology arose and underwent its early development during the flowering of the machine age and therefore is loaded with associated misconceptions.

The machine myth grossly oversimplifies how nature works. Put simply, nature functions as a perfect machine, and undisturbed nature operates at a constant rate of speed and output, like a well-made steam engine. In this way, the machine-age myth reinforced the idea of the balance of nature. But the myth of the machine added two important notions. One is that nature can be maintained at a maximum power output, so that we can manage wildlife, forests, and other living resources at a point of maximum yield. The other is that nature is completely malleable, and that we can change it and improve it in any way we like to achieve the balance of nature and whatever other economic or social goals we may have.

If the divinely created, perfect balance-of-nature-without-people were true, then all human actions that lead to change would cause undesirable conditions. Thus the solution to all environmental problems is simply to get human beings out of the way and let nature take its course. Management of the environment is simple: remove people. Knowledge about nature is unnecessary: Nature knows best. God is on our side and no one can argue with us.

Not only is the classic balance of nature a false solution to environmental problems but it alienates human beings from their surroundings. If everything we do must be wrong for nature by definition, then we have no place within nature. A false dualism is set up, one that is both untrue and psychologically uncomfortable.

Nature is never constant. Left alone the environment shifts continuously among many conditions. What is natural? Rates of changes and kinds of changes that have existed on the Earth over life's history and to which life has evolved and adapted. Lewis and Clark, like modern rivermen, were confronted hour by hour, day by day, with the reality of a changing, unpredictable, and harsh nature. It is these rates of change and kinds of changes that must be our guide to finding solutions to environmental problems.

14

A REVOLUTION IN OUR
UNDERSTANDING OF THE
ENVIRONMENT

During the past twenty years there has been a revolution in our scientific understanding of the environment, especially in the science of ecology, the science that deals with the relationship between living things and their environment. But related sciences—atmospheric chemistry, climatology, geology, paleontology—have also experienced tremendous leaps in knowledge. Today scientists can reconstruct the history of the Earth's temperature and the concentration of carbon dioxide in the Earth's atmosphere for the past 160,000 years. Through the study of tiny pollen grains buried in the muds of ponds and bogs, scientists have reconstructed the history of the distribution of our forests and prairies in much of Europe and eastern North America. Every piece of these remarkable sets of evidence tells us that nature has always changed, and that the history of life on the Earth has been a story of continual waxing and waning.

There are two key lessons in this remarkable history. First, nature, never having been constant, does not provide a simple answer as to what is right, proper, and best for our environment. There is no single condition that is best for all of life. Some creatures are adapted to disturbed environments, like the Kirtland's warbler, an endangered bird that nests only in forests that have recently burned. The warbler became endangered because of the Smokey the Bear policy of our century to suppress all fires as unnatural and undesirable. Other species, like sugar maple, are adapted to relatively undisturbed conditions. An environment that is "best" has many different conditions at different locations at the same time. The nature that is best is not a single, idyllic scene from a Hudson River School of painting, but a moving picture show, mosaics on a video screen, many different conditions distributed in complex patterns across the landscape.

Second, life has influenced the environment at a global level, and this influence extends back more than three billion years. Our environment is as much a product of what life has done as it is the result of physical and chemical factors in the history of our planet. Furthermore, we see that our own actions have begun to change the environment at a global level. Like it or not, we must accept that nature provides no simple, absolute answers, and that the destiny of our environment is in our hands.

THE VALUE OF EXPERIENCING THE NATURAL HISTORY OF OUR WILDERNESS

When I was teaching at the Yale School of Forestry and Environmental Studies, I joined my colleague Peter Jordan, a wildlife biologist, in a study of the wonderful wilderness at Isle Royale National Park. Little visited by Native Americans before the time of European exploration, and little visited and settled afterwards, Isle Royale represents one of the best examples left anywhere in the world of a nature undisturbed by human influence, of a natural ecological system, with wolves, moose, forests, and lakes, that has not been altered either over the centuries or in our century by human beings. There we hiked cross country with map and compass through bogs and over fallen logs. As I walked, I came

16

to realize that every twig on the ground, every tree in the forest, was a story—how it got where it was, why it persisted and prevailed. Each leaf, each twig, each tree was there as a result of causes that posed an intriguing puzzle to solve. How did a cedar tree, which was supposed to survive only in cold bogs, grow well on the top of an otherwise barren rocky outcrop, with its roots snaking nakedly down the boulders? Why did a big bull moose come out of the woods in the midst of a great storm and choose that moment to swim a quarter mile across a channel? Stupidity? Great strength? Knowledge that this was a time when there would be little danger from wolves? These questions intrigue those who love natural history, but the process of answering them would be pleasant to few people.

I suspect that most people would not like the true wilderness if they were given the chance to experience it. Wilderness is fascinating and sometimes beautiful, but it is uncomfortable, demanding, threatening, like the snows in the Rockies on a June day. There isn't much to eat. The ground is hard to sleep on.

Great storms are exciting in the wilderness, when you have the luxury to enjoy them from a sound building or read about them. Once, on Isle Royale, the wind was so strong that the trees along the shore stretched almost horizontally. Walking along that shore, I felt intensely alive. That night the wind continually blew my tent like a loose sail on a ship so that I had to choose between keeping my head inside, out of the rain, and becoming almost seasick with the continual motion of the canvas roof, or putting my head outside in the fresh air and getting cold and soaked. This is not such an uncommon experience in the wilderness, nor was this a particularly difficult or dangerous one.

Later, hoping to help develop methods to project when species might become extinct, I traveled to East Africa as part of a study of elephants. With my colleague Rick Miller and his wife, Jane, I visited Sengwa National Park in what is now Zimbabwe, a national park set aside solely for scientific research, to learn ways to manage wildlife in parks. The rule at Sengwa was that no one carried a gun, but anyone was free to walk anywhere he wanted—quite different from the protection and the transportation afforded most tourists on their African safaris. One afternoon, the three of us walked for several hours through the woodlands and savannahs in an area that we knew we shared with elephants and lions. It was a special experience. We grew alert and observant. We spoke little. We experienced directly a nature in which people were visitors who left little sign of their passing, and in which we did not flaunt our dominion and our dominance, having left behind in our camp the means to assert those qualities. Should the need arise, we were left with our wits and our feet.

From these and other experiences I recognized the value of careful observations of nature, and therefore the value of the records of Lewis and Clark. If we do not understand what nature was like before we changed it with mass settlement and modern technology, we cannot evaluate what we have done to it. A prerequisite to lasting solutions to environmental issues is a new world view that includes a realistic understanding of what nature is like without human influence. Only with that understanding in hand do we have a basis upon which to judge our actions. Achieving that perception is not simple. We have few ways to view the nature of our past. Most of the methods are highly technical and scientific and not of interest to the public. But there are a few remarkable sets of records—observations by early explorers of North America—that describe vividly and personally the character of the environment before the effects of industrial and technological society. The best of these is the Lewis and Clark journals. With Lewis and Clark as our guides, we can learn much about the environment of our past, our environment today, and what our environment might be in the future.

Through their hungry nights, their encounters with grizzly bears, their travels up the Missouri and down the Columbia, their winters with the Mandans in the plains and with the Clatsops on the Pacific Coast, we can find a beginning for a new natural history that will help us trace the elusive relationship between ourselves and nature.

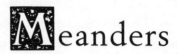eanders

Nature and the Missouri River

I spent a year putting the bridge over the [Missouri]
river; I've spent my time ever since, keeping
the river under the bridge.

ATTRIBUTED TO A CIVIL ENGINEER

Going up that river was like traveling back to the earli-
est beginnings of the world, when vegetation rioted on
the earth . . . An empty stream, a great silence . . .
And this stillness of life did not in the least resemble
peace. It was the stillness of an implacable force brood-
ing over an inscrutable intention.

JOSEPH CONRAD, *HEART OF DARKNESS*

THE EVER-CHANGING
RIVER

The Missouri River, the easiest way west for Lewis and Clark, was not easy at all: it was treacherous and challenging, fickle and unpredictable. The river was continually changing its channel, cutting away its banks, depositing sand in new places, and acting in ways that were generally dangerous to the expedition. Its channel meandered, and the depth of the river varied greatly; the pattern of the river was complex and required considerable knowledge to navigate it rapidly, knowledge the expedition had to gather on its way. There were buried snags—dead trees with one end stuck in the river bottom and the other end at the surface or near enough to rip the bottom out of a boat. Unpredictability and complexity were constant companions on the river.

On Saturday, August 11, 1804, the expedition followed a big bow of a meander of the Missouri River, traveling 18 and three-quarters miles by Clark's measurements, then camping on the shores of the river about 20 miles south of the present location of Sioux City, Iowa, near the boundaries between Monona and Woodbury counties. The next morning, Sunday, August 12, 1804, Lewis and Clark sent one of the men inland to find the place where they had stopped the day before. He had only to walk in a direct line a half mile, or to be exact, 974 yards as he measured it, straight across the bottom of the bow of the meander, from one shore to another, to find himself at the place the expedition had camped the previous night.

A similar thing had happened the week before on Sunday, August 5, 1804, when Clark set out in the evening to hunt. They were camped northeast of the present town of Blair, Nebraska. He had traveled only 370 yards east as he paced it when he found himself at the place on the river that they had measured as 12 miles downstream, as a fish swims, from the expedition's present location. The men had hauled boats and equipment upstream those 12 miles to gain only a fifth of a mile toward the Pacific Ocean.

These two occurrences and many others persuaded Lewis and Clark that the river meandered frequently in great arcs through its floodplain and that, over longer periods, the meanders themselves moved across the countryside. Meanders are a part of the wild river's dynamics over time and space. Variability, uncertainty, risk, and complexity are features of the environment in general, epitomized by this wild Missouri.

Understanding these attributes is essential if we are to find long-lasting solutions to environmental issues. We learned this the hard way in 1993 in the Midwest when heavy rains caused major floods. We had come to believe, having forgotten since the last major period of floods, that we could engineer the problem away. We may forget this lesson again if we do not make it part of our cultural heritage.

THE RIVER'S MEANDERING

A river on a wide and generally smooth floodplain does not flow in a straight line—or if it does, it does not maintain that straight line for long, especially if it is carrying a heavy load of sediments, as does the Missouri. Meanders are a natural form of a river, in part because the meander form keeps an even slope as the water flows downhill, mini-mizing the energy used by the river. In addition, even in a straight path eventually some chance occurrences cause a difference in where material is deposited; and other material is eroded—a log catches on the bottom, a pebble is pushed into the riverbed by the whirling white water and catches hold. If the riverbed and its borders have been smooth, they will be so no longer. Because flowing water takes the path of least resistance, it begins to assume a sinuous shape around small obstacles, and the river begins to form a meander, creating shapes something like the reaction of spring steel that has been pulled straight and then released.

Although scientists can be sure that a river like the Missouri will meander, the exact location of any meander is influenced by chance events and cannot be predicted with complete accuracy. That is to say: the river wanders. It is also to say that the river is neither completely chaotic nor completely fixed.

Geologists who study rivers and how they affect the land tell us that, over time, the arc of a meander becomes sharper and sharper so that the river forms a shape like a wishbone of a chicken or a sharply curving bow, usually called an oxbow. Always seeking the path of least resistance, the flowing water will cut across the bottom of the bow, when conditions allow.

Lewis and Clark came to understand this process as they navigated their way upstream. On August 4, 1804, when they were a little north of the present location of DeSoto National Wildlife Refuge north of Omaha, Nebraska, they wrote that the river banks "are washing away, the trees falling in, and the channel is filled with buried logs," so that "judging from the customary and notorious changes in the river . . . a few years will be sufficient to force the main current of the river to cross and leave the great bend dry."

Oxbows abandoned by the Missouri are scattered on the landscape. An oxbow cut off by the river sometimes remains as an isolated lake that persists for a long time. Lewis and Clark State Park in Iowa, a few miles west of the town of Onawa, is on one of these old oxbows. An aerial view of the lake shows it to be a dramatic wishbone shape providing a place for swimming and boating today.

THE   NATURALNESS   OF   CHANGE

In our minds, we have an idea of nature undisturbed by human influence as constant, fixed, and permanent. This idealized nature forms the basis of our environmental laws and policies, of our conservation and management of our living resources, from the conservation of biological diversity in tropical rain forests to the harvesting of ocean fish. It is this image of nature that dominates our idea of our own relationship with the environment. But that was hardly the character of the wild Missouri River that obstructed the travel of Lewis and Clark. If the romantic, nineteenth-century painting *Sunset in Yosemite* by Bierstadt, a static formation of rocks and trees, is *our* ideal of nature, then the Missouri River is *nature's* reality, an environment of risk and uncertainty, not stability and permanence. When you think of nature undisturbed by human beings, think of the Missouri, the longest river in the United States, as it was seen by Lewis and Clark in 1804.

The treachery of the Missouri was apparent from the beginning of the trip. On July 18, 1804, the expedition passed just south of the present location of Nebraska City, Nebraska, when they saw that a part of a cliff "nearly three-quarters of a mile in length, and about 200 feet in height" had fallen into the river, an event that must have happened rapidly and, if the timing had been different, could have wiped out the expedition.

The dangerous changeability of the river continued almost to the headwaters. "Set out this morning at an early hour, the current strong; and river very crooked; the banks are falling in very fast," wrote Lewis on May 11, 1805, as they were on their way toward the headwaters of the river. They had just survived their first winter in crude shelters they had built near the villages of the Mandan Indians, not far from what is now Bismarck, North Dakota. They were downstream from the river's Great Falls, near the present location of Fort Peck Reservoir in Montana, when Lewis wrote, "I sometimes wonder that some of our canoes or pirogues are not swallowed up by means of these immense masses of earth which are eternally precipitating themselves into the river . . . We have had many hair breadth escapes from them." The Missouri underwent continual changes as it deposited newly transported material on one side and cut away the banks on the other. "The banks of the Missouri are constantly falling, and the river is changing its bed," they wrote.

The Platte River, which they had passed early in the trip and explored briefly, left Lewis with an impression similar to that of the Missouri, of great power and motion and therefore of dynamic change. It was a river in which sand boiled up and was "hurried by this impetuous torrent," so that the sand collected and formed bars that appeared in a few hours and just as suddenly "dissipated to form others and give place perhaps to the deepest channel of the river."

Changes took place at many different intervals, from hour to hour, from day to day, from season to season. On August 31, 1804, Lewis noted that there had been rain the night before and the river had risen during the night.

After their winter with the Mandans, the expedition set out westward on April 7, 1805, continuing up the Missouri. On April 14, Lewis and Clark noted that they had reached a point never before traveled by Europeans. On May 7, when the expedition was a few miles south of the present town of Frazer, Montana, Lewis noted that driftwood began to come down the river as a result of the water level rising with the spring runoff.

As these experiences make clear, variations over time were the norm, and random events persisted throughout the time the men were on the river. We tend to refer to incidents such as a cliff falling into the river or a bank washing away as "accidental" events, with at least two connotations: that these are bad and that they could be and should be avoided. But the reality is that variation over time and random events are inherent in the workings of a natural system such as the Missouri River. They may appear good or bad, beneficial or harmful, depending on our needs and uses of the river, but they are the natural character of the river.

While the exact occurrence of any of these chance events cannot be predicted with complete accuracy, we do know that they will occur at some time. Equally important, as we learn more, we can say with what frequency they will occur and with what strength. We can characterize the amplitude of each kind of change and its probability of occurrence.

THE PATH OF LEAST RESISTANCE

Meanders in the rivers are natural, produced as the river seeks the path of least resistance across its floodplain. Over the years, the meanders themselves migrate back and forth across the river valley. Meanders of the Missouri have been measured to migrate across the floodplain at an average rate of about 250 feet a year. Over much longer times—thousands of years—the river has wandered across the plains, eroding and depositing, like an artist working his oils over and over again on his canvas. On this sculptured, painted landscape, Lewis and Clark pushed the small river craft upstream, through the meanders, through the fallen sands, through the snags. The Missouri had changed before Lewis and Clark passed its way, it kept changing under their feet, and it changed after they left. The countryside, as a result, was also always changing. It was not a permanent structure, not so permanent as the famous paintings of the Missouri made in the 1830s by Bodmer as he and Prince Maximilian followed the trail of Lewis and Clark up the river. The countryside of the Missouri River Valley is more like the sand paintings of the dry country Indians, more a process than a structure, more a coming and going than a being. At any one time the Missouri is a river that flows through a certain channel in the prairies. But over time the Missouri has moved across the prairie, touching and changing all of it.

With its tributaries, the Missouri is not simply *in* the Great Plains, it *is* the Great Plains. Lewis and Clark, hiking across country to find a place to hold a council with the Indians, hauling their ton and three-quarters of equipment against a six-mile-an-hour current, saw the connection between the countryside and the streamside. Today, as we speed over the interstates in our cars and RVs, as our engineers channel the river so that it lies where we want it to be, we fail to see these processes, and we begin to imagine that the river and the landscape are as fixed as the snapshots we take of it.

When confronted with the stories of Lewis and Clark as they traveled up the Missouri and met with one kind of chance event after another, we see these events as part of the adventure, but not as part of ordinary life—and we ignore them. However, when we sit down to work out how the environment should be, when we set down plans to manage and conserve nature, we get ourselves into trouble because we forget about the naturalness of change—we leave the risk and uncertainties to the movies, and we revert to our belief in the constancy of the environment. We mistake chance for adventure and unpredictability for accident. We assume and we act from the assumption that nature undisturbed by human influence is constant, deterministic, and stable. This has been the case with the massive civil engineering projects that have taken place on the Missouri since the end of the Second World War.

A HUNGRY RIVER

The variability and fickleness of the Missouri had social consequences that were well known throughout the nineteenth and early twentieth centuries. "Some people would think it was just a plain river running along in its bed at the same speed; but it ain't," said a river man who raced boats on the river a century after Lewis and Clark had traveled up it. "The river runs crooked through the valley; and just the same way the channel runs crooked through the river . . . the crookedness you can see ain't half the crookedness there is." The Missouri became known as the hungriest river ever created, "eating all the time—eating yellow clay banks and cornfields, eighty acres at a mouthful."

As the land along the Missouri River was settled, the social consequences of this instability could be seen. Late in the nineteenth century, there was a saloon near the river on the Kansas side, where drinking was legal. The boundary between Kansas and Missouri, where drinking was illegal, was defined in the law as the center of the navigable channel of the Missouri River "as it runs." In 1881, a flood shifted the channel of the river overnight so that the saloon that had been to the west of the river and therefore on the Kansas side was suddenly located to the east of the river and therefore, according to the law, moved from a drinking state to a dry state. The owner was arrested and convicted by the circuit court in Platte City, Missouri, for selling intoxicating liquor. The conviction was challenged and overturned by a court of appeals, which, in effect, decided against the river's short-term shiftiness, concluding that the boundary would be at the center of the channel as long as changes occurred "gradually and imperceptibly," but that "sudden avulsion" left the boundary where it had been, in the now dry channel. The records suggest that the decision was welcomed by the citizens of Missouri, who no longer had to cross the river to buy a drink. The vote for constancy of the river and its bed—a vote for a fixed form of the environment, opposing the digressions and deviations of the natural channel, foretold ominously what we would do to the wild Missouri in the twentieth century.

As in the case of the saloon that was moved by the Missouri from one state to another, the frequent changes, the fickleness of the river, were seen as merely a problem, disrupting navigation and threatening settlements. Obstacles created to navigation became more and more apparent as the river was developed, which happened rapidly after Lewis and Clark had passed this way. The *Independence*, the first steamboat to navigate the Missouri, moved up her waters on May 28, 1819, only 12 years after Fulton's steamboat on the Hudson and only 13 years after Lewis and Clark returned to St. Louis. In spite of meanders, eroded banks, rapidly building sandbars, and logs hidden under the water, that steamboat traveled 200 miles in 84 hours, a tremendous change in the rate of travel compared to the Lewis and Clark expedition, which struggled 18 miles upstream on a good day. Steamboat traffic peaked in 1858 and lasted only four decades, when the railroad took the cargo traffic away from the river. Yet so treacherous was the Missouri that more than 450 steamboats were lost on the river during that time—a rate of about 11 wrecks a year.

LEGISLATING NATURE

We not only believe that nature undisturbed is constant, but that where it isn't, we can make it so, to our benefit and to nature's. This has been the case with the Missouri River as well as with the Mississippi River, whose wild meanderings and abrupt changes were contrary to the desires of settlers and travelers in the nineteenth century. Attempts to tame these rivers using machine-age technology began, from a federal legislative point of view, in 1879, when the U.S. Government created the Mississippi River Commission, whose purpose was to build levees to protect surrounding lands from flood waters.

The natural processes of change continued for more than a century after the Lewis and Clark expedition. Then in 1927, after disastrous floods, Congress passed laws that directed the Army Corps of Engineers to build dams, locks, levees, retaining walls, and dikes. However, modification of the Missouri did not really get going until 1944, when the U.S. Congress authorized a vast program for flood control and irrigation, involving the construction of 100 dams and reservoirs. Another federal enterprise, the Missouri Basin Program, added more dams and reservoirs and more straightening of the channel in 1953. The ambitiousness of this legislation is reflected in the area of the Mississippi-Missouri River basin, which covers one and a quarter million square miles—41 percent of the land area of the lower 48 states—and involves the drainage of 35 of these 48 states.

Among the largest dams constructed as part of these programs are Fort Peck Dam near Glasgow, Montana; Garrison Dam in North Dakota; Gavin's Point, Fort Randall, and Oahe in South Dakota. At first, these dams and reservoirs seemed to have only benefits, providing electric power as well as flood control and irrigation. The vast Missouri River system began to water farms in much of the Midwest, from Denver and Fort Collins in Colorado to Nebraska and Iowa. Today these states are part of America's great agricultural strength. Eight of the Great Plains states are among the major U.S. producers of wheat: Kansas, North Dakota, Texas, Montana, Nebraska, Colorado, Oklahoma, and South Dakota. They owe much of that production to water that comes from the Missouri drainage system. The Army Corps of Engineers estimated that $8 billion spent on these structures saved $145 billion in property damage and loss over the years. It was a simpler time, when the power of civil engineering appeared to bring only good and it seemed natural to use our technology to remove the undesirable variations of the river. We believed that we could make that river run like clockwork, like a steam train timed to the conductor's watch, and we could see no downside to those changes.

But when these projects were in place, the dams built, the reservoirs full, the river ceased to be the sculptor of scenery. It was no longer the agent that transported great fertile soil from the mountains and hills to the farmable plains. Channelized and dammed, it could no longer flood. The river was tamed—for a while. Now the soil, eroded from the Rockies and once deposited on the plains, enriching them, is lost to the Gulf, where it builds unwanted deltas. So great is the burden of sediments the Missouri brings downstream that at St. Louis, where the rivers meet,

31

the Mississippi is forced to the far side of its valley. The river's structure appears fixed and permanent, but this seeming permanence has destabilized the Great Plains landscape. The building of banks, the cutting away of banks, the deposition and erosion had their natural benefits. Over thousands of years, the Missouri's meandering had deposited a rich soil over a wide floodplain. In the river's variability was the land's permanence.

THE LOST MESSAGE OF
THE MISSOURI

On July 22, 1804, the expedition camped just north of the confluence of the Platte River and the Missouri, where they saw the kind of woodlands that grew along the lowlands at that time. "The low grounds on the south near the junction of the two rivers are rich, but subject to be overflowed . . . opposite our camp the first hills approach the river, and are covered with timber."

One of the easiest places to see the effects of the channelization of the Missouri is at DeSoto National Wildlife Refuge just north of Omaha, Nebraska, which I visited with three other ecologists, Tom Jurik and David Glenn-Lewin, professors of botany at Iowa State University and experts on the vegetation and the environment of this Iowa countryside, and one of David's graduate students. We saw the Missouri very much tamed—an Army Corps of Engineer's canal, with broken rocks set along the shores, like an ocean breakwater, and the sides cut away and made uniform. The wonderful and wild Missouri of fact and folklore was dead. In its place was a placid, tamed stream. My reaction was not so much sentimental as it was a recognition that we had made a

Faustian bargain with the river—trading short-time stability, a chance to build and live on the floodplain, to farm that floodplain year after year, without worrying about the dreadful floods, in exchange for a loss of the renewing sediments that had created the fertile farmland in the first place.

The straightening and channelization of the Missouri has had many consequences for natural ecological systems of the river valley. The structure of the vegetation communities on the floodplain has changed. The wetlands back from the shore contained large willows—larger than I was familiar with—and other floodplain species, such as cottonwoods. There was a dense understory of flowering dogwood. David Glenn-Lewin suggested that such an understory would never have existed with the natural flooding of the river, which would have killed the dogwood. He believed that the presettlement floodplain forests would have had a "cathedral" aspect—tall trees and little understory, but that there would have been many dead logs on the bottomland. Elsewhere, the elimination of flooded areas is eliminating trees adapted to those conditions, such as cottonwoods and ash.

Viewing the channelized Missouri at the wildlife refuge, caged within straight lines of broken rocks, made our beliefs about nature seem all the more ironic, because the Missouri we had created was the realization of what we believed nature was like before we altered it. The dominant belief about environment today is that all changes in nature are the result of human action, and that a wild nature is a constant environment. But when we altered the Missouri River we made it as fixed a structure as our engineering allowed. As I said earlier, when you think of nature, of the essential character of nature undisturbed by human influence, think of the wild Missouri as it was seen in 1804 by Lewis and Clark. To this we can add: when you think of what we have

33

done to nature in most cases, think about the Missouri in 1991 at DeSoto National Wildlife Refuge.

The true nature of the Faustian bargain became evident in late June 1993. At St. Louis, near the meeting of the Missouri and Mississippi, the rivers rose to 49.6 feet, more than 19 feet over flood stage and six feet higher than ever recorded. Heavy rains continued through July. At Papillion, Nebraska, a suburb of Omaha, an inch fell in six minutes on July 26, 1993. To the north, the Red River rose four feet in six hours. As much as 17,000 square miles were inundated. Nine midwestern states suffered an estimated $10 billion in destruction from the combined flooding of the Missouri and Mississippi, with hundreds of bridges washed out, more than 50,000 square miles of farmland flooded, and estimates of tens of thousands of houses damaged or destroyed. "This summer's war against the water has changed life along these rivers—and people will be living with its effects for months and years. In some ways, forever," journalist Richard Price wrote in *USA Today*.

The U.S. Army Corps of Engineers, along with state and private efforts, had spent $25 billion on a system of levees, walls, and other flood control measures on the Missouri-Mississippi River system over the previous 50 years. These were supposed to tame the river. They created the vision of a calm and peaceful river, with straight channels and smoothly flowing waters. But the greater the apparent control over the Missouri, the greater the faith people had in their own effectiveness —and the less alert they were to possible dangers.

Over the years, people had been lulled by their confidence in engineering structures. While about 7 percent of the nation's 2.3 billion acres lie within a 100-year flood area, less than 15 percent of the properties in these areas had flood insurance in 1993.

Attitudes had changed as well. Experiences with the effects of levees and dams during floods had accumulated and were being compared. Geology Professor George C. B. Belt, Jr., of St. Louis University, compared two floods of similar strength, one in 1908 and one in 1973. The 1973 flood rose eight feet higher because of levees and retaining walls that confined the waters to a smaller area, forcing the water higher. Newspaper reporters recognized the problem. The *Los Angeles Times* reported that the nation's $25 billion system of flood-control structures may "have proved to be the salvation of many communities" but that ironically "it is possible that those same feats of engineering may have aggravated the natural disaster in other areas." It was becoming clear that a confined river, unable to spread its waters over the flood plain, flowed faster and more violently against the artificial borders of its narrow, straightened channel. Overflowing from these conditions could lead to worse damage than along an untamed river.

Environmental groups led the charge against the artificial structures. The organization, American Rivers, called on the White House and Congress to discourage floodplain development, protect wetlands, reform flood insurance programs, and promote water and soil conservation on farms. "It's time to prevent a repeat of this tragedy," said Bill Redding of the Sierra Club, in Madison, Wisconsin. "We need to provide future hope and safety for the region's farmers and urban residents."

Government officials were beginning to get the message. "People have created the flood problem," said Bill Dieffenbach, assistant chairman of the Missouri Department of Conservation's planning division. "We have spent billions on flood control, but it doesn't work with these kinds of floods. And we've had four or five of these in the last 40 or 50 years."

The Army Corps of Engineers also began to recognize the reality of natural change, and the need to manage with nature, not against it. "We have the opportunity to make decisions in favor of preserving the ecological and cultural value of the nation's flood plains and flood-prone areas," Brig. Gen. Stanley G. Generga, the Corps of Engineers director, wrote in a letter in 1993 to *USA Today*.

"Locating homes, businesses and industry out of harm's way is the most practical, common-sense approach to avoiding flood loss, as is limiting development in flood-prone areas to parks, greenways, recreation areas, wildlife habitat and other uses not susceptible to flood damages," Generga added. Richard E. Stuart, chief of Army Corps of Engineers Flood Plain Management Services division, said in September of 1993 that "it probably does not make economic sense to try protecting a community from a flood of such magnitude."

But rhetoric aside, the government moved slowly. Congress cut back a presidential proposal to provide $370 million in 1994 to reimburse farmers who would restore farmland to natural wetland status, providing only $22 million, in spite of the fact that the requests from farmers exceeded the budget in the first year of the project, 1992, when $42 million were allocated and farmers enrolled 50,000 acres. Ironically, no funds were available from Congress for this program in 1993. "Instead of paying farmers to restore wetlands, Congress will end up flooding the Mississippi Valley with disaster payments," said Wendy Hoffman, an official with the Washington-based Environmental Working Group. The disaster payments are "badly needed, but they will only set farmers and taxpayers up for another disaster by not allowing major rivers to regain their natural flood-carrying capacity," she said.

While human structures and society fared poorly along the Missouri in 1993, wildlife and vegetation, which evolved in the presence of persistence changes, did better where engineering structures did not prevent these creatures from responding as they always had. I returned to DeSoto National Wildlife Refuge in November 1993, after the great flood. The neat, straight banks were gone, washed away, the even line of boulders a jumble of rocks. Strong prairie winds carried an unusual cold spell to the river; snow flurries sped across our line of vision, moving almost horizontally. As the winds blew stiffly in the cold, frosty, snow-scattering air, I watched snow geese settle on the oxbow backwaters, then, startled, rise as a flock and circle widely overhead. They had returned on their migration, just as they had in years before.

Chuck Theiling, a river ecologist with the Illinois Natural History Survey, was out in his boat during and after the floods of 1993 observing effects on wildlife. "The flood did not set off mass migrations of animals fleeing the high water, nor did it present any serious threat to native plants and animals, except perhaps for a species or two already endangered by environmental destruction. The flooding generally had a positive impact on native floodplain species," a report on his observations concluded. Most native species thrived. Of course, deer, raccoons, skunks, possums, quails, and their associates fled to higher ground, but most made it. In some cases, it was artificial structures that threatened their survival during the flood. The levees and retaining walls made these animals' escape from the flood waters more difficult, and when levees broke the waters moved with unusual violence, threatening the fleeing wildlife.

On July 8, 1993, a levee broke and flooded a wetland that had been the subject of a restoration project, covering the area with 10 feet of water. There was debris everywhere, from tree branches to bottles and boards. Although a dead fawn and some dead birds were seen, observers also spotted a field mouse clinging to a floating twig, with a gray spider and a katydid holding onto its fur.

. . .

Since the time of Lewis and Clark, the Missouri has been teaching the same lessons, but rarely have we listened, rarely have we learned. There is a rational approach we can take to living with the river, benefiting from its waters, conserving its living resources, enabling it to fertilize and help restore the land.

People who live on flood plains should be educated about the risks they face. Those who choose to live on these flood-prone areas should be required to carry their own insurance against damage, or, with compensation, be moved off the land. Thus can we begin to live with the river, to manage with nature, and to accept the Missouri and the nature it represents for what they really are, changeable and only partially predictable. Then we can recognize the Missouri of Lewis and Clark, not a river fixed in time and space, but a changing, fluid source of both benefits and peril.

CHAPTER THREE

Wet and Dry Mud

Chance, Uncertainty, and the River's Source

When something is suggested, or some evidence is produced, the first response [of scientific colleagues] is, "It can't possibly be true." And then, after a bit, then the next response is, "Well, if it's true, it's not very important." And then the third response is, "Well, we've known it all along."

DR. JONAS SALK

We were cut off from the comprehension of our surroundings . . . We could not understand because we were too far and could not remember, because

*we were traveling in the night of first ages, of those
ages that are gone, leaving hardly a sign—and no
memories.*

JOSEPH CONRAD

*Did I have any adventures? Heck No! An adventure
is either the result of foolhardiness or bad planning.*

JIM LARSEN, BOTANIST, *SPEAKING ABOUT HIS
EXPERIENCES DOING RESEARCH IN THE
WILDERNESSES OF NORTHERN CANADA*

On June 3, 1805, when the expedition was camped at what we know now as the mouth of the Marias River, Lewis wrote, "This morning early we passed over and formed a camp on the point formed by the junction of two large rivers." Like a detective trying to solve a mystery, Lewis continued, "An interesting question was now to be determined: which of these rivers was the Missouri."

The Missouri begins where the Gallatin, Madison, and Jefferson rivers—rivers named by Lewis and Clark—come together, at what is now Missouri Headwaters State Park near the town of Three Forks, Montana. From its origin, the Missouri flows north near the modern towns of Helena and Great Falls after which it begins a turn to the northeast. About 50 miles downstream from Great Falls, and considerably northeast, the Marias River flows into the Missouri, draining waters from the north. It was at this junction that Lewis and Clark confronted the problem of which fork to take.

A mistake—choosing the wrong river and following it—would have serious consequences for the expedition. "To mistake the stream at this period of the season, two months of the traveling season having now elapsed, and to ascend such stream to the Rocky Mountains or perhaps much further before we could inform ourselves whether it did approach the Columbia or not, and then be obliged to return and take the other stream would not only lose us the whole of this season but would probably so dishearten the party that it might defeat the expedition altogether," Lewis wrote.

As if he were a scientist sitting in a comfortable laboratory office, rather than at a rough camp in bad weather, Lewis pursued the problem with a seeming academic curiosity, writing, "To this end an investigation of both streams was the first thing to be done." Equally important to us is that he saw the need to measure things about the river, making observations quantitative, to "learn their widths, depths, comparative rapidity . . . and thence the comparative bodies of water furnished by each," and by these means to attempt to infer which was the main stream.

Like a modern scientific team, the camp divided into two groups, each examining the available evidence and each proposing what we would refer to today as an hypothesis. Most of the men believed the north fork was the main river and therefore the one to follow. Lewis reviewed the evidence on their side: the north fork was deeper but not as swift. However, its waters ran "in the same boiling and rolling manner which has uniformly characterized the Missouri throughout its whole course." The waters were brown, thick, and turbid—the big muddy, so it seemed. The bed of the river was also mainly mud, so that the "air and character of this river" seemed "precisely that of the Missouri below." For these reasons, most of those on the expedition were convinced that the north fork was the Missouri. On the other side were Lewis and Clark who, Lewis wrote, were "not quite so precipitate."

They decided to explore both forks, testing the two hypotheses. The next morning, Clark led a group up the left fork, while Lewis took a group on the right. The rest of the expedition remained at the base camp where the two forks joined. Lewis traveled up the north fork from June 4 to 6. He found that this fork continued northward toward what is now the border between Montana and Alberta, Canada, and he became convinced that this direction was too far to the north to be the route to the Pacific. After taking time to attempt a reading of the latitude and longitude (which failed because of cloudy weather), he began his return on June 7 to go back to the junction of the two forks and rejoin the main body of the expedition. Lewis was correct; the north fork was a small tributary which they named the Marias River. By waiting a few extra days on the Marias River to try to take measurements to determine his latitude and longitude, he was trying to reduce the uncertainty about the position of the expedition. But a change in the weather, a bit of bad luck he could not have predicted, prevented him from making the measurements.

Lewis and Clark were uncertain about what to do and wanted to avoid making a crucial error. The error they faced at the junction of the two rivers was what scientists call *an error of uncertainty of the first kind—a problem about the facts of a situation that already exist, or, given present conditions, must occur.* They simply lacked information. One of the channels was the main river. That fact was not going to change during the time of the expedition. There was only one correct river to take. There was something direct and simple to do to resolve this uncertainty—explore the two rivers and determine by direct observation which was the correct one.

It was a problem different from whether the cliffs on the side of a channel might fall in on their boat—an event that could happen at any time. This is *an uncertainty of the second kind—uncertainty of the occur-rence of an event that has some probability of happening, but whose occur-rence involves inherent uncertainty.* Unlike the first kind of uncertainty, the second kind cannot be resolved so directly and simply. We cannot necessarily reduce the uncertainty of a future event by studying it. We can, however, learn much about the kind of chances we face, and whether we want to accept the odds that confront us.

Our modern environmental problems confront us with both kinds of uncertainty. We do not have trouble accepting the idea of our own errors—that, like Lewis and Clark, we might not know which river to take. But we have a great difficulty understanding and accepting the second kind of uncertainty—that there may be some inherent chance in nature. We want to believe that nature undisturbed is constant, but as we learned in the last chapter, nature is, like the Missouri, always changing.

When we speed past the Missouri in a car, crossing over it on a bridge at sixty miles an hour, the river bed appears fixed in time. Push-ing up the river in a slow-moving boat against a six-mile-an-hour cur-rent, sleeping on its banks, studying the countryside through which it flowed, Lewis and Clark saw a very different river. It is a matter of relative time scales. They spent more than a year on the Missouri, a time as long or longer than some of the actual variations of the river's shape. In this day of satellite and aircraft observations, automobile travel, and vacations made up of quick stops, observation time is shorter than the time of natural variation. While the Missouri's refusal to stay put and stay constant was the source of many a good story and pithy saying, it interfered with society and with commerce. A steady, con-stant river is what we wanted and what we created.

Our methods of conserving and managing most environmental factors assume the constancy of nature—except for human intervention. But the reality is the other way around. We assume a fixed natural environment, believing that our interventions are the causes of variations in an otherwise static structure of environment. But like the fickle Missouri, all of nature changes on many scales of time and space. Still, we long for and try to create an environment that is fixed, like the bridge over the Missouri or like the channelized Missouri at DeSoto National Wildlife Refuge. Having lost our heritage about the river and the prairie, we ignore its important message.

A LITTLE LUCK AND SOME CLEAR THINKING BY LEWIS SAVES WINDSOR

On Lewis's return, following the Marias River downstream, it began to rain, and the peculiar clay soil of the floodplain turned into a slippery mess, difficult to traverse. After a "most disagreeable and restless night" camped in the rain, Lewis and his small band set off downriver to join the rest of the expedition. The clay soil prevented the rain from soaking through and became so slippery that it was like "walking over frozen ground which is thawed to small depth." We know today that they were walking on a clay derived from glacial till and shale, commonly called gumbo, a clay that turns into a plastic and sticky material when wet.

Lewis slipped on this soil while walking on a bluff above the river but managed to save himself from falling 90 feet to the waters. Just after he had saved himself, he heard one of his men, Windsor, cry out "God, Captain, what shall I do?" Lewis saw that Windsor had slipped on the clay and slid so that his right arm and leg hung over the bluff and he was holding on to the edge with his left arm and leg. "I expected every instant to see him lose his strength and slip off," Lewis wrote, but "I disguised my feelings and spoke very calmly to him and assured him that he was in no kind of danger." Lewis then astutely told Windsor to take his knife out of his belt with the hand that was hanging over the precipice, and dig a hole in the bank for his right foot, and by such a practice work his way up, which Windsor did, and in that way he was saved.

Searching for the right fork is an inherently different problem from trying to avoid slipping on wet clay and falling into a river, or avoiding banks of the river falling onto their boats and capsizing them, or dealing with floods or sudden changes in water levels. These *uncertainties are referred to today as problems of risk, because the event has not yet happened and its occurrence has to do with inherent chance, or with processes whose causes, for all practical purposes, we cannot distinguish from true chance events.* Translated into human events, risk becomes a matter of prediction, forecasting, luck, and fortune, the latter two of which were also constant companions of the expedition, as Lewis and his men discovered on their trip exploring the Marias River.

CHANCE AND PREDICTABILITY

The problems the Missouri River caused Lewis and Clark, as well as settlers who followed them in the nineteenth and twentieth centuries, bring up a fundamental problem about chance events and predictability. When Lewis and Clark were exploring a river previously unknown, chance events might have seemed completely unpredictable. It is wrong to think that just because there is an element of chance in the environment that it must be completely chaotic. For example, the clay along the Marias River posed different risks of danger when it was dry and when it was wet. Knowing about this kind of clay today, we would know that it would be unwise to walk along the bluff by the Marias when it was raining, and much safer if it had been dry for a long time. The probabilities of slipping actually do change with the weather in a predictable way, so we can attach different probabilities to that danger depending on the weather. This is the kind of knowledge we can obtain about the second kind of uncertainty. And this understanding is one key to find long-lasting solutions to our environmental problems.

Suppose you and I wanted to hike along the Marias River this year so that we could retrace the path that Lewis and Windsor took. We have modern scientific knowledge about the kind of clay and its dangers. We know that there is some risk of falling over the bluff onto the river below, but that the risk is much less if we go during dry weather than during rain. And so we can check the weather forecasts, which we know are often wrong but which are better than no forecast, and choose a day when we can expect the clay to be dry. The probability of slipping on the clay changes with the environmental conditions. We can make some kinds of predictions about events that involve chance.

The notes of Lewis and Clark do not seem to suggest that they thought the river was completely predictable or completely unpredictable in the sense of complete chaos. They had had too much experience in nature to believe either extreme.

The one aspect of nature that we have accepted as involving chance and probabilities is weather forecasting. We are all familiar with weather forecasts that fail, and weathermen now phrase their forecasts in terms of probabilities. We need to apply that concept to the rest of the phenomena in nature.

The Great Plains through which Lewis and Clark were passing is a country of great variability in climate. There are few cases for the Great Plains where we have recorded weather long enough to have great confidence in our predictions of weather in the future simply based on past observations. On average over the time that records have been kept, 10 times a year the temperature rises or falls 45 degrees Fahrenheit or more within 24 hours in the Nebraska Sandhills. Montana and North Dakota are also states of extremes. The average annual low temperature is 130 degrees Fahrenheit colder than the average summer maximum. Within the Missouri Basin we find the record low temperature recorded in the lower 48 of the United States—minus 66 degrees Fahrenheit in Yellowstone National Park in 1933. In Glendive, Montana, the temperature reached 47 degrees below zero in February 1893 and the following July rose to 117 degrees above zero.

This is a countryside of wind; in the afternoon the average wind on the Great Plains is 12 to 14 mph. Before the Missouri was dammed and channelized, the worst floods occurred when intense warm winds called chinooks melted heavy snowpacks on frozen soil, as happened in April of 1881, 1943, and 1952, producing huge runoffs in a short time.

The weather varies enough from place to place to cause many problems. Storms over the prairie can be like squalls on the Pacific—sudden, intense, but local. As an example, two towns eight miles apart, Mitchell and Scottsbluff, Nebraska, had very different years in 1929 and 1930. For the two years, both towns received a total of 34 inches of rain, but Scottsbluff enjoyed this rain benignly as 17 inches each year, while Mitchell received 14 inches the first year and 20 inches the second. That three-inch difference in a semiarid countryside was enough to ruin crops.

The television weatherman usually compares today's weather with "normal" weather but "normal" weather is a misnomer. There is aver-

age weather—an average temperature and an average precipitation—
because an average is a simple mathematical calculation. No matter
how much something varies, there is always an average value, because
an average is defined as the sum of all the values divided by the number
of values. But normal implies much more—a characteristic condition
that persists and is correct, proper, and in the case of the environment,
natural.

The idea of normal makes sense for the temperature of the human
body, because we, like all mammals, have an automatic temperature
control system which keeps us within a range of temperatures (usually
expressed as a single temperature, 98.6 degrees F, but actually a larger
range) at which our body functions best. When our temperature rises
out of this range—somewhere into 99 degrees F or higher—then we can
correctly say that our temperature is above normal and we have a fever.
We can't legitimately say the same thing about the weather, although
we do. Real weather is always changing, and the length of time that
people have been recording the weather is not long enough to characterize a "normal" condition, if one ever did exist. In trying to explain
the weather, the weatherman is struggling with both horns of the environmental dilemma—uncertainty and risk: uncertainty is involved because the time over which the average has been measured is short; risk
is involved because the exact weather for a certain day is a matter of
probabilities.

The insistence on believing in a normal climate gets us into practical
trouble. Here's the question. Look at the weather records or water flow
records, which are a result of weather conditions, anywhere in the Missouri Basin and ask: for what period of years is the normal calculated? In
1933 the Army Corps of Engineers produced what has been called "the
most exhaustive study ever made of the hydrology of the Missouri
River," a 1,245-page document used as a basis for the Missouri River

plan of development of dams and channels. In that report, the average flow of the river where it enters the Mississippi was given as 96,300 cubic feet per second. That number was based on four years of measurements in what later turned out to be a series of comparatively wet years. Sixteen years later, with the experience of the Great Drought included, the U.S. Geological Survey reported the average flow much lower—70,290 cubic feet per second. These differences in what was considered normal greatly affected planning and developing dams, calculations of amounts of water that could be removed for irrigation, and building levees to control floods.

My experiences with weather forecasting make me familiar with the chances and probabilities attached to them. I have a pilot's license with an instrument rating, and have experienced both kinds of errors—uncertainty and risk—during my flying time. One summer day my wife and I flew from Santa Barbara to San Jose, California. I checked the flight weather forecast, which called for scattered clouds but otherwise good weather. I filed an instrument flight plan, taking no chances, I thought. This plan indicated the map of the route I was asking the air traffic controllers to allow me to follow from one radio beacon to another, known as "VORs." It gave me a safe, but comparatively short, route, keeping me away from the highest mountain peaks. With this flight plan successfully filed, we took off in a Cessna 182 and began flying north. I followed the planned route so that both I and the controllers knew where I was. I constantly checked maps to make sure I was following the planned route—to eliminate uncertainties of the first kind—about the facts of the terrain and my route over it. However, there is always some variation in the position of an airplane because of updrafts and downdrafts, changes in winds, and variations in the pilot's precision in controlling the airplane. Acknowledging these kinds of error, the air traffic system provides a protected space—a volume—

around any airplane on an instrument flight plan. This is a protection against an error of the second kind—that inherent chance variations lead to unpredicted variations in the exact position and velocity of the airplane.

But chance events continued to affect the flight. As we flew north, the forecasted scattered clouds became broken (taking up 50 percent or more of the sky, but not forming a continuous cloud layer) and there were occasional big buildups, the beginning of thunderstorms. We were flying at 10,000 feet when the air traffic controller called and told me to make a temporary adjustment in my direction of flight, which put our plane directly on a course that led into one of the larger buildups. The instant we were inside the cloud we were bombarded by freezing rain and hail; the windshield froze over in about 30 seconds. We were experiencing an inherent variation in weather prediction due to the second kind of uncertainty—risk in the environment.

Relying on my training, I turned on the carburetor heat, checked that the plane was in smooth and level flight, and then, like Lewis talking to Windsor, I called the air traffic controller on the radio and said in my best professional voice—disguising my feelings and speaking very calmly—that I would like to request a lower altitude. We got one immediately—down to 8,000 feet, which put us under the cloud and out into the sun. In a minute or so, the ice melted off the windshield, and I could see that the wings also were clear of ice; all seemed well. But up ahead were more clouds. These were smaller than the one we had just been through, higher than 8,000 feet but not up to 10,000 feet. I called the controller back and requested a higher altitude so I could get over those clouds, and not have to fly inside them, fearing more freezing rain and hail. Not aware that I had just experienced unexpected icing—an error of the risk kind—the controller replied, "You just requested a lower altitude; now you want a higher one—

please make up your mind." Like Lewis, I had experienced both kinds of errors—both kinds of uncertainty—but the second one sent chills through me, just as slipping on mud and almost falling over a cliff had done for him.

As I write this chapter, I am directing a study for the states of Oregon and California about the effects of forest logging and other forest practices on salmon and their habitats in the Pacific Northwest. We were asked to examine a large area: all of western Oregon south of the Columbia River to the northwest corner of California, extending to the Klamath and Trinity rivers of that state. In this work I run into both kinds of uncertainty.

We have encountered many problems of the first kind of uncertainty. Since the question we have been asked to answer is whether the cutting of forests has been a major cause of the declines in salmon populations, and since we are living almost 200 years after Lewis and Clark's expedition in the age of science, with highly sophisticated measuring devices including satellite remote sensing, used to view the condition of the land, and with sonar devices that can count fish, we expected that there would be basic information about the conditions of the forests and the number of salmon.

We wanted to know the conditions of the forests today and in the past so we could determine how much the forests had changed. We could then compare this information to the changes in the salmon populations. We divided the area into watersheds. (Any drop of rain that falls into one watershed flows out to the ocean in the same river, and this is the definition of a watershed.) At any given time, the vegetation in a watershed is in some set of conditions. There may be forests in one part of the watershed, cleared land elsewhere used for farming, other land cleared and developed into urban areas, and so forth. But the question, what is the condition of the land in the watershed? is like the question, which is the real Missouri River? All you need to answer it is a knowledge of the facts.

We asked the state government agencies for a map showing the condition of the forests in western Oregon, but no such map existed. So we were in a situation much like Lewis and Clark, searching for the real Missouri without a map. We were faced with uncertainty of the first kind.

During the first year of the study, the state Department of Forestry obtained a map of the vegetation of Oregon based on remote sensing from the Landsat satellite. Such a map has many possible sources of errors. The satellite does not measure or count trees directly, but only measures the reflection of light from the Earth's surface. This reflection is seen in chunks that are 80 meters on a side, and the smallest area that could be detected on this map was 320 acres. This area—half of a square mile—appears as a single dot represented by the intensity of light reflected in several parts of the light spectrum. Over the years, scientists have found that the ratio of certain infrared light to red light provides an indication of the amount of vegetation on the surface. But the correlations are crude.

The measurements from the satellite are converted to a picture that looks like a map. Scientists examined this map made for Oregon and compared the colors of certain spots with areas they knew about on the ground or had airplane photographs of. They interpreted the entire map from these check points. The map of the forests and other kinds of land conditions therefore had a lot of room for error, but it was the best we could do. The difference between the map made from satellite information and the real condition of the forests was a matter of uncertainty.

We also hoped to find a map made much earlier in the twentieth century so that we could see how the forests had changed, watershed by watershed. At first, no one knew of any such map. Then an old map was located. It had been made in 1914, commissioned by F. A. Elliott, the state forester. It cost $7,000, one-fifth of the state forester's entire budget for that year, and more than his own salary. But in 1951 it was thrown out; it was believed to be too big to store conveniently and to use. Fortunately, John McWade, a young night dispatcher for the Oregon Department of Forestry pulled the map from the trash. Later, a second copy was located in archives at Oregon State University. By luck, the map had been rescued. Here our work benefited from good fortune, the result of a chance event: somebody who knew the value of an old map happened by a Dumpster at just the right time. And here we were at the end of the twentieth century, working in a part of North America that Lewis and Clark had visited, and we were confronting the same fundamental problems of uncertainty and risk.

As a society, we do not have much problem with the idea of uncertainty in our information. We readily accept that measurements always have some degree of error, and that nobody is perfect and it is easy to make mistakes. But we do have trouble with the idea of risk in nature—that chance is an inherent and natural quality of nature. One of our problems is that we get the ideas of uncertainty and risk confused, in part because scientists present both in ways that look similar: a measurement that has uncertainty attached to it and a prediction that involves chance, both can be shown as an average value and a quantity that is the error connected to it.

In another study, I have been trying to find out how much carbon is stored in the major forests of the world. This is an important measurement because trees, like all green plants, can take carbon dioxide out of the air during photosynthesis. In forests, this carbon is stored in wood. A widely discussed way to reduce the buildup of carbon dioxide in the atmosphere, which is produced when we burn fossil fuels, is to plant forests and promote the growth of existing forests, so that more carbon dioxide is removed from the atmosphere. But to determine whether this is a practical thing to do, we have to know how much carbon forests can store. During the past 10 years I have had field crews travel to points chosen at random in much of North America. We have made measurements for the boreal forests of North America—the Christmas tree forests of the north, mostly in Canada—and the eastern deciduous forests—the forests of maple, oak, hickories, ash, and pine—that extend from Minnesota to Maine and from Newfoundland to Georgia. These two forests account for more than a half of all the forest land in North America—a large area to measure. Instead of trying to measure the whole area, we did the equivalent of a statistical polling of the forests. We selected points at random and sent field crews there to make measurements from which we could then calculate the amount of stored carbon. Because this is a statistical sampling, we obtain an estimate of an average amount and of the error associated with it. We present our results as: the boreal forests have 9.7 billion metric tons of carbon plus or minus about 2 billion. The estimated average is 9.7, but the actual value could be anything between 7.7 and 11.7. This is a specific statement of a measurement and its uncertainties. One of the ways our knowledge of nature has changed since the time of Lewis and Clark is that the field of statistics has developed, and we can state our errors quantitatively. This is of great help in the study of the environment.

RECOGNIZING AND ACCEPTING NATURAL CHANGE

Traveling up the Missouri, seeing the American West from a river's point of view, Lewis and Clark saw daily a nature that was continually undergoing change. This is a message that we both tend to forget and to remember. When confronted with it, as Lewis and Clark were when the banks caved in on them at the river's edge, we confront the reality. But on a calm day, when the current is steady and the air clear, we forget the storms of yesterday and think that nature, without our influence, is constant. With our power to bridge the river and dam its waters, we have come to believe that changes occur in the environment only because of what people do. But the situation is the other way around, as we can also see in the history of the Missouri.

The experiences of Lewis and Clark, along with the understanding of rivers by modern geologists, tell us that the natural Missouri changed at many time scales. Some changes occurred frequently. At any time the river was cutting away part of its channel in one place and depositing material elsewhere. Its flow also varied, sometimes rapidly—near its headwaters, overnight in response to a sudden storm—sometimes more slowly with the seasons or, even more slowly, with changes in climate over years, decades, and centuries.

Arriving at a relationship between ourselves and our environment takes work. The old way of dealing with environmental problems was to assume that, undisturbed by human activities, living resources were constant, and their environments were constant. We must change our thinking and come to accept the naturalness of change. But this is not easy. Change makes us uncomfortable because we become uncertain about our own situation, we feel insecure and mistrust our ability to predict what will happen in the future. We would prefer to know with absolute certainty whether a species is safe from extinction and whether there will be fish to catch in the river. We are reluctant to accept uncertainty in nature.

More than that, uncertainty as an idea confuses us. It even confuses professional environmental scientists. I heard one environmental scientist say in a speech at an annual professional meeting a few years ago that you couldn't predict anything about an ecological system that did not have an equilibrium condition, meaning that it remains constant when undisturbed. This was the same as claiming that one could only make predictions about the tamed Missouri, that the wild Missouri was chaos. This statement suggests that a fundamental misunderstanding of the role of chance and uncertainty in the environment occurs even among those whose professional work focuses on our living resources.

We can make use of the naturalness of change and randomness in solving environmental problems. Several years ago I was asked by the state of California to direct a study about water removal from Mono Lake, a famous lake that covered 40,000 acres in the high desert just to the east of the Sierra Nevada. Mono Lake was fed by streams from the mountains, but since the 1940s all the water that used to flow into the lake had been diverted to provide some of Los Angeles's water supply. By the 1980s, this water provided 17 percent of the total used by Los Angeles, and it was the best quality water the city obtained. The lake had no outlet, but in the high desert there was a rapid rate of evaporation. With no water supplying it, the lake was drying up.

The lake had covered 60,000 acres in the early 1940s when the water diversions began; it had lost two-thirds of its total surface area. It was used by more than one million birds and was a major nesting area for the California gull. The lake's waters were salty and alkaline, much like the Great Salt Lake in Utah, but with a different chemistry because volcanic gases bubbled up through the lake's waters and reacted with those waters. One of the results was strange but picturesque tufa towers, deposits of stonelike chemicals that rose above the waters. The lake's setting, below the high mountains in the clear desert air, had a certain beauty. Many people came to visit the lake, to appreciate its scenery, to see the birds, and look at the tufa towers. As the lake dried out, large sandy beaches were exposed. These contained arsenic and other heavy metals, and when the desert winds blew, the concentration of particles in the air exceeded EPA health standards. The Mono Lake Committee, a local environmental organization, lobbied for the bill that funded the study. Meanwhile, the Los Angeles Department of Water and Power claimed that the evaporation would eventually come into a balance with water supplied by rain and from subsurface sources and the lake's life would continue.

A key question posed by the debate over Mono Lake was the rate at which water evaporated. As the lake level falls, the topography of the lake's shore changes. Gulls nest on an island that protects them from coyotes. During a drought, the lake level had fallen enough to turn that island into a peninsula. Coyotes had been able to get out to the island and feed on gulls' eggs and chicks. Several years passed after the drought before the gulls returned to the island to nest. To predict what these effects might be, we needed a map of the lake bottom so that we could know its total volume and how its shape would change as the water level dropped. Although there had been a long and strong debate over these issues, no one had made a map of the lake's basin. But this problem of uncertainty was easy, because we just needed to know the topography of the lake. So we hired a firm that specialized in underwater maps and it produced a sonar-generated map of the lake, and our problem was solved.

The variability and randomness of the weather was another issue. Our report explained that there were three crucial lake levels, each providing a different set of benefits. After the study was completed, courts decided to choose the highest level. But how do you insure that the lake remains *above* that level when the climate always varies? This requires forecasting future climate. We are limited in our ability to make those forecasts, especially because we have collected weather records for only a number of decades.

From existing weather records, we calculated how much the lake level might drop if another drought occurred that was as bad as the worst one during the past 50 years. We found that the most severe drought would lower the level 12 to 14 feet. So to make sure that the lake never dropped below the lowest desired level, the lake level would have to be kept at 12 to 14 feet above that level during an average water year. It would then be allowed to fluctuate, dropping those 12 to 14 feet during a drought. After a drought, the lake would return to the higher level. Here, we were able to use our knowledge of random variations in the past weather to guide the future. Mono Lake is not so chaotic that it lacks any pattern. As it is with Mono Lake, so it is with many environmental issues. Rather than fear and avoid uncertainty and risk, we can build upon our understanding of them to help us conserve the environment and its living resources for the future.

CHAPTER FOUR

Thirty-Seven Grizzly Bears in the Wilderness

Knowing What's There, When, and How Many

Richard Mace, a wildlife biologist for the state of Montana, knows how tough it is to count grizzlies. Displaying a battered steel box with a jagged rip down one side, he explains that the box once held a tree-mounted camera . . . Apparently, Mr. Mace says, when the camera flashed, the grizzly slashed.

GRIZZLIES: *"COUNTING BIG BEARS: GRIZZLIES FIND WAYS TO AVOID THE CENSUS." WALL STREET JOURNAL, MAY 2, 1990*

About 5:00 p.m., on around May 11, 1805, Bratton, who had been walking on shore, rushed up to Lewis "so much out of breath that it was several minutes before he could tell what had happened." He had met and shot a grizzly bear, which then chased him about half a mile. The expedition was northeast of what is now the Pines Recreation Area in Valley County, Montana, near Fort Peck Lake. Lewis took seven men and trailed the bear about a mile by following its blood in the shrubs and willows near the shore. Finding it, they killed the bear with two shots through the skull. Upon cutting it open, they found that Bratton had shot the bear in the lungs, after which the bear had chased him a mile and a half.

"These bear being so hard to die rather intimidates us all," Lewis wrote. "The wonderful power of life which these animals possess," Lewis and Clark noted in the journals, "renders them dreadful; their very track in the mud or sand, which we have sometimes found 11 inches long and 7 1/4 wide, exclusive of the talons, is alarming."

Thus unsettled, six of the men came across another grizzly about three days later on May 14. Approaching "within 40 paces" four of them shot and wounded the bear, with two shots piercing its lungs. Although seriously wounded, "the furious animal sprang up and ran open-mouthed upon them." The two hunters, who had held their fire, then fired and each wounded the bear. One of the bullets broke his shoulder, which "retarded his motion for a moment; but before they could reload he was so near that they were obliged to run to the river, and before they reached it he had almost overtaken them. Two jumped into the canoe; the other four separated, and concealing themselves in the willows, fired as fast as each could reload. They struck him several times, but instead of weakening,:

> *Each shot seemed only to direct him toward the hunter; till at last he pursued two of them so closely that they threw aside their guns and pouches, and jumped down a perpendicular bank of 20 feet into the river. The bear sprang after them and was within a few feet of the hindmost, when one of the hunters on shore shot him in the head and finally killed him. They dragged him to the shore, and found that eight balls had passed through him in different directions.*

This incredible fortitude was from an old bear whose meat was too tough to eat.

"There is no chance of killing them by a single shot unless the ball goes through the brain," they noted in their journal, "and this is very difficult on account of two large muscles which cover the side of the forehead and the sharp projection of the center of the frontal bone, which is also thick."

The expedition encountered many kinds of wildlife, but the grizzlies were the most dangerous and frightening. Only occasional storms and their effects on the river and soils, and a few incidents with unfriendly tribes of Indians, were as threatening to the expedition. As a result, the members of the expedition were especially alert to the presence of grizzlies, and we can believe that their reports of these bears were quite accurate. This provides us with a unique insight into the abundance of one of the largest animals found in the American wilderness.

Today the grizzly bear is legally protected as an endangered species;

it was listed as a threatened species in the lower 48 states in 1975 under the U.S. Endangered Species Act. The U.S. Fish and Wildlife Service developed a grizzly bear recovery plan in January 1982.

Always dangerous to people, whose experiences often resemble those of Lewis and Clark, the grizzly poses some important and intriguing questions about the conservation of our biological resources. We have agreed, in our laws, to protect and conserve this animal. Having done so, and having succeeded, at least to a limited extent, in helping this species to increase in some places, we are forced to confront some important questions. What would it mean to be successful in conserving the bear? When would it be safe to remove the bear from the listings of endangered species? How many bears would be sufficient?

One answer to this question might be, when the bears reach the abundance that they had had before the exploitation of them and their habitat by people of European descent—the abundance at the time of the Lewis and Clark expedition. In regard to this question, we find surprising information about the abundance of the grizzly from the journals of the expedition.

LESSONS FROM THE GRIZZLY

Although confrontations with grizzlies were dangerous and frightening, the expedition met bears only occasionally, at intervals along their route. The first meeting with a bear was recorded on June 16, 1804, when the expedition was near where the present U.S. Highway 65 crosses the town of Waverly, Missouri. There they saw a "beautiful extensive prairie" where their hunters shot two bears, most likely black bears. On that day the men were bothered more by mosquitoes and ticks and by shifting sands in the Missouri River than they were by the bears. The next day Clark wrote that "the country abounds in bear, deer, and elk" and that the "lands are well timbered and rich for two miles to a beautiful prairie which rises into hills about eight or nine miles back." Black bear were then, as they are now, much less dangerous than grizzlies.

The Indians shared a great fear and respect for the grizzly. Lewis commented in his notes of April 13, 1805, "the Indians give a very formidable account of the strength and ferocity of this animal, which they never dare to attack but in parties of six, eight, or ten persons; and are even then frequently defeated with the loss of one or more of their party." Two Hidatsa Indians were killed by bear during the winter the expedition spent with the Mandans.

As I said, the first bear the expedition saw was a black bear, sighted the previous year in June 1804. Lewis and Clark did not mention another bear until the fall of 1804, when they were approaching the present location of Bismarck, North Dakota, not far from where they would spend the winter. Three French-Canadian traders told them that day that there were many white bears—meaning grizzly bears (so called because their coats are lighter than the black bear and, in certain lights, give off a kind of silvery tone) in the vicinity, along with mountain goats. The expedition continued on, and still did not see any grizzlies. Their first indication that the bears were nearby came on October 7, 1804, when Lewis and Clark saw tracks of a large grizzly near the mouth of the Sawawkawna River.

Their first encounter with a grizzly took place almost two weeks later on October 20, 1804, when they shot and wounded, but did not kill, a grizzly bear. The same day they saw tracks of others, which they observed were twice the size of human footprints. Soon after this first encounter, the expedition stopped its westward travel and built a camp where they spent the first winter with the Mandans. The bears, meanwhile, holed up for the winter.

The next spring, just as they were starting toward their passage through the mountains, Lewis and Clark saw "fresh bear tracks" on April 11, 1805, in a area that was "one fertile unbroken plain" as far as they could see, "without a solitary tree or shrub" except in the drainages, and where they saw a herd of antelopes and migrating birds—geese and swan—as well as prairie hens and bald eagles, on both sides of the Missouri River. The day before, they had come upon a strange bluff from which smoke and sulfur fumes were emitted; they were a few miles south of where the Little Missouri flows into the Missouri, an area now flooded by Garrison Reservoir in North Dakota. Some of the hills contained beds of coal which sometimes were ignited by prairie fires and then continued to burn; the sulfur smell came from burning sulfur contained in the coal. Again, the mosquitoes were more of a problem than the bear; both Lewis and Clark noted in their journals that the mosquitoes were "very troublesome."

It is interesting that Lewis and Clark found no grizzlies until they had passed beyond the countryside that had been traveled by other white men. Perhaps the original range of the grizzly extended east only to the western edge of the North Dakota plains, or perhaps hunters had eliminated them from the plains countryside farther to the east.

DANGEROUS ENCOUNTERS

On April 14, 1805, soon after the expedition left Fort Mandan, their first winter's camp, Lewis and Clark reached a point that they believed had never been seen by people of European descent and therefore for them they were in undiscovered country. On that day they saw two grizzlies. The countryside west of the Mandan village was rougher and less fertile, "extremely broken, without wood, and in some places seems as if it had slipped down in masses of several acres in surface," their journals recorded.

The next day, April 15, they saw a black bear and two grizzlies, along with deer, elk, goat, and buffalo, all on low ground near the river. They found tracks of bear on April 16, amid "great quantities of game," including herds of buffalo, elk, and antelopes.

The expedition was now on the upper Missouri between the points where the Yellowstone and Musselshell rivers flow into the Missouri, where the countryside is rolling, wide plains and where the river flows in a deeply cut, steep-sided channel. (Much of this countryside is now under water, beneath the Fort Peck Reservoir, and a great deal of the land surrounding this reservoir is ranched.) On April 28, when they reached what is now the eastern limit of Fort Peck Indian Reservation and a stream now called the "Little Muddy Creek," a tributary that reaches the Missouri River a few miles west of Culbertson, Montana, and about 25 miles west of the Montana–North Dakota line, they saw a countryside that was "much broken" with white and red bluffs along the river. They saw peculiar mineral deposits—salts that created a white cover "like frost," but they found the low-lying grounds along the river fertile and full of trees. On this day, they saw grizzlies in the company of abundant wildlife—deer, elk, buffalo, antelope, beaver—along with migrating geese, as had been the case in most of their previous sightings. The next day, April 29, Lewis and Clark wrote the first scientific record of the characteristics of the grizzly bear, noting again that they were "surrounded by deer, elk, buffalo, antelopes." The hills were becoming increasingly rough and high.

About a week later, on May 5, Clark and Drouillard, one of the

65

expedition's hunters and a man Lewis considered among his best, "killed this evening the largest brown bear [grizzly] we have seen." A week later, they met the bear in the incident described at the outset of this chapter. Then on May 15, when the expedition was near the present Devils Creek Recreation Area within the Charles M. Russell National Wildlife Refuge, another grizzly found a coat of one of the men on shore and tore it. Four days later, on May 19, they were near the location of the present Crooked Creek Recreation Area, where the Missouri River makes a bend from flowing southward to flowing northward. They killed a grizzly which, like the one met on the 11th, was able to run a long distance after he was wounded. "Though shot through the heart," they wrote, the bear "ran at his usual pace nearly a quarter of a mile before he fell." They killed another grizzly bear three days later, on May 22, and noted that all the bears they had seen in this part of the country were grizzlies. They saw five bears the next day, May 23, wounding one, and saw another bear on the 28th of May.

Then on June 2, two bears almost killed two of the men, one of whom ran and hid in thick bushes and was saved by his companion, who shot the bear and who had himself just narrowly escaped being killed by the bear a few moments before. Two days later, on June 4, they wounded another bear, and on June 6, another bear attacked one of the men near the camp. The man's gun was wet and would not fire, so he ran to a tree and climbed it, but the bear was so close behind him that he hit the bear with his foot as he scrambled up the tree. "The bear, not being able to climb, waited till he should be forced to come down; and as the rest of the party was separated from him by a perpendicular cliff of rocks, which they could not descend, it was not in their power to give him any assistance . . . at last the bear became frightened at their cries and firing, and released the man," the journals recorded.

Encounters with grizzlies continued in a similar fashion through July 1805. The bears were especially troublesome during the month the expedition spent camped and portaging equipment around the series of falls at the present location of Great Falls, Montana. Upstream from Great Falls, Montana, the countryside is abrupt, steep-sided wooded hills through which the river meanders.

They were now approaching the headwaters of the Missouri and were heading south, for the river travels northward from its origin until it makes a big bend as it passes through the rough plains north of Great Falls. Near its headwaters the river flows through beautiful countryside, with strangely shaped hills and mountains, some isolated on a rough plain, in countryside that today is still much wooded. They saw another grizzly on July 2, and then did not encounter one of the bears for three weeks until, on July 24 they saw, but could not approach or shoot, another bear. The next day they reached the Three Forks of the Missouri—the origin of the river, where the Jefferson, the Madison, and the Gallatin rivers come together to form the Missouri. Here they saw a large grizzly which ran from them.

They killed two more grizzlies on July 26, when the expedition was still near the headwaters of the Missouri River and the present site of the town of Three Forks, Montana. From the headwaters of the Missouri the expedition traveled up the Jefferson where they saw the last grizzly of the outward bound journey on July 31.

CONTEMPLATING GRIZZLY DISTRIBUTION

Having read the journal entries about encounters with grizzlies, I realized that these records have a lot to tell us about the distribution and abundance of the bears prior to European settlement of the American west. The bears were encountered mostly in the mountains and were not seen at all early in the trip in the tall grass prairies east of the present location of Bismarck, North Dakota, or later, west of the Rockies or on the Pacific Coast. The encounters tended to occur in clusters—Lewis and Clark reported seeing bears for a few days at a time, and then several weeks would pass without a sighting.

From this we get the sense that the bears were not distributed uniformly. They were generally confined to two regions of the trip—the upper Missouri and adjacent short grass prairies and the Rocky Mountain forests—the dry plains and the cold mountains. Even within these habitats their distribution was clumped, not uniform.

Although the encounters with grizzlies were dangerous for both the expedition and the bears, and often resulted in the death of the bears and the near death of one of the men of the expedition—and as a result the bears would loom large in the memory of anyone reading about the expedition—in fact the encounters with bears can be lumped into a small number of episodes, each lasting somewhere between several days and a week.

The bears were seen mainly when other wildlife was abundant, suggesting that the bears were following the other wildlife or all the wildlife were moving across the countryside more or less together. If there was a balance of nature including grizzly bears, it was not a smooth, homogeneous plain where the bears were distributed like picket fences, but a spotty patchwork within which the grizzly were rare animals tracking prey. There were not wall-to-wall grizzlies in the presettlement landscape of the American West. As I will explain later, such estimates are more than a naturalist's curiosity; a program to conserve these big, dangerous mammals has to take into account the habitats that are appropriate for them and the patchy distribution of them within that habitat, as well as their overall rarity.

We can group the expedition's encounters with the grizzly into about nine episodes, beginning with their first sighting of tracks on October 7, 1804, while they were still on the Great Plains, continuing with their first face-to-face meeting just before both the bears and the expedition overwintered, on October 20, 1804. The main encounters occurred during the spring of 1805 in Montana on the upper Missouri River, between the eastern border of Montana and Great Falls. No grizzlies were found east of Pierre, South Dakota, nor west of a north-south line passing through Missoula, Montana.

In total, the expedition encountered 37 grizzlies described as individuals. Speaking in general terms, these encounters occurred over a distance of approximately 1,000 miles, or an average of about four grizzlies per 100 miles traveled. I searched my bookshelf of natural history guides to see how this compared with maps of the geographic distribution of the species. To my surprise, I found that Lewis and Clark encountered grizzlies over an area considerably larger and more varied than that given for the east-west distribution in the Peterson Field Guide Series, *A Field Guide to the Mammals*, which states that the range is limited to high mountains of the West and the tundra in the far North. A range map shows the grizzlies occurring along a narrow line running down the boundary of Idaho and Montana and continuing southeasterly into Wyoming and Colorado. However, as I said earlier, Lewis and Clark saw the bears in the western plains and encountered them in dangerous situations from the eastern border of Montana to the Idaho-Montana boundary, a considerably wider distribution. The Lewis and Clark journals expand the original extent of the large mammals beyond what is portrayed in a standard modern field guide.

69

A little further search of the literature about grizzly bears yielded some additional curiosities. I found a chapter on "The Grizzly Bear" in *The Audubon Wildlife Report 1985*, a generally reliable source I had used many times. Under a section titled "Historical Perspective," the report states that the grizzly was "once present throughout most of the western United States and south into central Mexico" and moreover was "regularly encountered by the Lewis and Clark expedition along the Missouri River in Montana in 1805," a statement which, if taken literally, is untrue. The encounters with grizzlies when the expedition was in Montana were comparatively frequent and unquestionably dangerous and memorable, but in no way regular. A regular encounter or regular distribution would mean, to a naturalist, ecologist, or statistical sampler, that the bears were distributed like checkers on a board at the start of the game, in a geometric and readily predictable pattern. Predictable was hardly the word for the bears seen by the members of the expedition. These encounters occurred when the members were least ready for them, as in one of Lewis's encounters when his gun was unloaded. He wrote that he lamented his lack of forethought and promised himself never to allow such a situation to arise again. The bears were distributed like checkers in mid-game, but even more unpredictably.

The Audubon Report goes on to state that Lewis and Clark "encountered so many grizzlies at the site of present-day Great Falls, Montana, that they did not think it prudent to send a man alone on an errand of any kind." This paints a picture of the mountains crawling with grizzlies. But in reality, as I explained before, Lewis and Clark reported only 37 grizzlies during their entire outward journey.

That the Audubon Report gives a false impression about the bears might seem trivial. But because of the reputation of the Society and its report, it could influence approaches to the conservation of the bear. It suggests to experts that, if Lewis and Clark saw lots of bears, there must have been a lot and, if we are to restore the original abundance, there had better be a great many bears. This is not what you find in the journals.

I realized that we could use the information in the Lewis and Clark journals about the numbers of bears encountered and the distance the expedition traveled in the range of the grizzlies to get a rough estimate of the original abundance of this species, but only if we knew how far, on average, the expedition could see. If we assume that, on average, the members of the expedition could see about half a mile on each side of the river, then the men would have seen about one mile width in every mile traveled. This is not unreasonable because, in the region where they saw grizzlies, the river generally flowed in a channel below the level of the plain, and much of the land on the plain was not visible from a boat. A person standing on a flat level plain in a completely clear atmosphere could see about 12 miles in every direction, but this is rare. The possibilities range from zero visibility in fog and heavy rain to a maximum of 12 miles. If we accept an average of a half-mile visibility on each side of their path so that Lewis and Clark saw an average distance of one mile wide, and add to this that the expedition traveled approximately 1,000 miles during the time that they first saw grizzlies to the last sighting, then the average density of bears would be 37 per 1,000 square miles, which is 0.037 bears per square mile or 3.7 bears per 100 square miles (a square 10 by 10 miles).

This estimate of the density of the bears (the number per mile) is fragile. If the Louisiana Purchase had not been made and the expedition had been led by Frenchmen accustomed to the then recently developed measuring system of the meter, kilometer, gram, and kilogram, I might have guessed that Lewis and Clark could see about a kilometer rather than a mile from the river on average. A kilometer is about six-tenths of a mile. The density of bears would then be calculated as 0.057 bears per square mile or 5.7 bears per one hundred square miles. This bit of conversion from kilometers to miles warns us that we can get only a general idea of the abundance of the bears from a single trip, even though the records were kept very carefully about encounters. Of course, if Lewis and Clark had recorded the distance they were able to see bears each time they encountered one, we would have a more accurate measure. With the information that we have from the expedition, we could give a range of between 3.7 and 5.7 bears per 100 square mile.

How many grizzlies would that add up to in their habitat within what is now the United States of America? We can estimate this by taking the area in the region from Pierre, South Dakota, to Missoula, Montana, and multiplying by our density, 3.7 bears per 100 square miles. Montana alone covers 145,000 square miles. If Lewis and Clark's encounters were a truly representative sample, then the original number of grizzlies would have been about 5,600 in that state. If we add the western halves of North and South Dakota, which is about 73,000 square miles, then our estimate would be about 8,000 bears. If we include Wyoming and the mountain part of Colorado as well as eastern Idaho, we would be adding an area of 320,000 square miles in these mountain and western plain states, yielding a total of ($320,000 \times 0.037$) or about 12,000 bears. Since Lewis and Clark traveled mainly near the river, and since in this dry country wildlife would tend to congregate near water, my estimate would tend to be on the high side.

Interestingly, the Audubon Wildlife Report states that the "present verified range"—the range in 1985 when the report was published—is about 20,000 square miles in four states, and that the total population is estimated to be between 600 and 900 bears. This works out to between 3 and 4.5 bears per 100 square mile, essentially the same values that we obtained from the Lewis and Clark journals. A huge government report, "Grizzly Bear Compendium," gives a range from 1.6 to 5.1 bears per 100 square miles, also similar to the values we obtained from Lewis and Clark.

The presently estimated 20,000 square miles of grizzly habitat occurs mainly on government land in the four states—Idaho, Montana, Washington, and Wyoming. Only 5 percent is private land, and most is U.S. Forest Service land. Much of the rest is in four national parks: Glacier, Yellowstone, Grand Teton, and North Cascades. Habitat in and around Yellowstone National Park that appears to have grizzlies at present measures about 7,800 square miles.

I found another estimate by the Craighead brothers, who are two of America's experts on grizzly bears. They reported an average of 230 grizzlies between 1959 and 1967, which works out to an average density of 0.029 bears per square mile in Yellowstone National Park, close to my estimate of 0.037; a later estimate by them gave a range of 0.031 to 0.051. It is intriguing that my simple analysis of the Lewis and Clark observations gives a value for the density of grizzly bears that falls within the range of recent observations.

The area known to have grizzlies today, 20,000 square miles, is 6 percent of the area I estimated as the presettlement range of the bear, based on the journals of Lewis and Clark. How useful and accurate is an estimate of the original range of grizzlies based on the journals of Lewis and Clark? There are two ways to answer this question. The first is: ideally, to get a statistically valid sample, we would prefer a number of trips or a single trip planned to sample the bears at random locations in all kinds of habitats. The second answer is: if we have *no* other records, then those of Lewis and Clark are all that we have to go on and therefore they are valuable as a case history. As crude as our estimates are, the numbers obtained are useful in developing a plan to conserve grizzlies. It gives us a basis on which to determine how much more land as grizzly habitat we would need if we want to return the animal to its original distribution. And it gives us a better idea of how endangered this species is, because the vulnerability of a species increases as its habitat size decreases.

Viewing animals as one marches along a line resembles a common kind of ecological sampling method known as a line-transect. In this method one follows a specified path and records observations on that path, which is pretty much what Lewis and Clark did. However, the path is chosen so that the observations are not biased toward a particular kind of habitat or toward situations where bears might tend to frequent or tend to avoid. Because Lewis and Clark saw grizzly bears primarily while the expedition was on the Missouri River or hunting not far from the river, they were sampling a limited part of the bear's potential habitat and range—the river, its flood plain, and land within a day or two's walk from the river. To a statistician, this would be considered a biased sample, biased because Lewis and Clark did not sample the region at random, but only as they followed the easiest route.

A statistician might also point out that the zone Lewis and Clark traversed could be considered a sampling stratum, meaning a kind of area well-defined, about which we have information enough to tell us that it is distinctive from other areas. Because all animals require water and will come down to the streams and rivers, and because there may tend to be more berries, fruits, and of course fish for the grizzlies, one may be more likely to encounter a grizzly near the river than away from it. If this were the case, then Lewis and Clark's expedition would be biased in favor of finding bears, and their encounters would overestimate the original abundance. As long as our goal is to conserve the bears, this is an error in the right direction, because it would tend to make us conserve more, rather than fewer, bears. It is what one would call a conservative estimate—it errs in the direction of conserving the factor most important to us here.

APPLYING WHAT WE LEARN FROM THE GRIZZLIES TO CONSERVATION OF OTHER SPECIES

With the sole exception of information gathered in Yellowstone National Park, our knowledge about the abundance and density of grizzlies today is not much better than what someone could have surmised by a careful reading of Lewis and Clark's journals when the expedition brought them back to St. Louis in 1806.

If this is what we know about one of the most famous, most readily reported, legally threatened and therefore protected species, whose abundance and whereabouts are of considerable interest to outdoorsmen as well as government agencies, what could be our knowledge of other species? The answer is, in most cases, much worse.

The standard practice in estimating the original abundance of an endangered animal is to take the total area of potential former habitat (number of square miles or square kilometers), determine a likely density of the animals within that habitat (number of animals per square mile or kilometer), and multiply the two. In many cases, the estimate of density is based on observations where the animals are abundant, so the estimate of density is higher than a true average.

For example, recently a small oceanic bird, the marbled murrelet, was listed as threatened under the Endangered Species Act. This small brownish and white bird spends most of its adult life on the ocean, coming in to the land only to nest and breed. The bird nests along the coast of the Pacific Northwest of North America, from Alaska to northern California. Few nests of the murrelet have ever been found; by 1993 fewer than 30 nests had been found in the United States. Most were in trees and within the deep, old-growth forests, but two had been located in Alaska on barren island ground.

Estimates of the original abundance of the marbled murrelet have been made by determining the total area of old-growth forests within the bird's flying distance of the ocean and multiplying by the observed density of nests where these nests are known to occur. This approach makes several strong assumptions. It assumes that the birds were never limited by anything but nesting habitat so that there were always plenty of birds to nest if nest sites were available. Other limitations are possible. For example, it might be that the marbled murrelet numbers are limited by the availability of food in the ocean, or that periods of severe ocean storms kill many of the birds and lead to a long-term average abundance considerably below the maximum that could fill all possible nest sites. This method of calculating original abundance also assumes that the number before the influence of modern human beings and their technological civilization was always at a maximum. But just as the Missouri River meandered over its plain and changed its flow in response to rainfall in the mountains, so too one would expect that the abundance of any wild animal would vary over time with variations in climate and with biological factors, such as outbreaks of disease or variations in the abundance of food.

The method of calculating the original abundance of a species is important because of the present interpretation of the Endangered Species Act. Originally, a species could be listed as threatened or endangered if its numbers dropped to less than one-half of the estimated carrying capacity. The carrying capacity was typically taken to be the estimate of the presettlement abundance. In the case of the marbled murrelet, this would lead one to believe that the bird had been quite abundant in the Pacific Northwest. Because information is lacking one way or the other, one's belief in the abundance or rarity of that species becomes a matter of faith, not fact. The methods of estimating the presettlement abundance are based on several highly suspect assumptions.

An equivalent approach to estimating how many grizzly bears there should be would be to examine the times when Lewis and Clark encountered these animals, estimate the average density of bears per square mile, and then multiply that density by the assumed grizzly bear habitat, which might be assumed to be as large as all the Rocky Mountains (180,000 square miles) and the short-grass prairies (about 350,000 square miles), an area of about 530,000 square miles. Lewis and Clark's rate of encounter, 37 grizzlies per 1,000 square miles, leads to an estimate of the carrying capacity on 530,000 square miles of 19,610—let us say about 20,000 bears. Allowing for an overestimate because Lewis and Clark were traveling where the bears were likely to be, we might lower the average density to 2 per 1,000 square miles. This gives an estimate of about 10,000 bears in the 530,000 square miles. Other sources suggest that the presettlement range of the grizzly was actually much larger, covering most of the western half of the United States, all of the West Coast except northwestern Oregon and western Washington, and extending east to bisect North Dakota, angling into Iowa and Missouri and westward through the panhandle of Oklahoma and down into Texas to the Mexican border and beyond. This is an area about one and a half million square miles, which would imply a static carrying capacity of about 56,000 grizzlies.

The U.S. Fish and Wildlife Service has a recovery plan for the grizzly bear. Its goal raises a question about what is a minimum acceptable population rather than a maximum desirable population. The general idea of a recovery plan for a species of wildlife is to restore a population to some desired level, typically either to achieve some hypothetical presettlement, prehuman influence "natural" level, or to ensure that the population will be sufficiently large to be self-sustaining.

Returning the population to a presettlement level seems a safe thing to do, because the population had persisted for a long time under those conditions. But this idea was generally attached as well to a belief in the constancy of nature. Returning a population to its presettlement abundance was interpreted to mean that the population should be returned to a single size. As I explained in the example of the marbled murrelet, this old view of nature also carried with it the belief that each creature existed at its carrying capacity—at the maximum number that could be sustained by its environment. Such a belief, while consistent with the idea of a perfect balance of nature, contradicts the inherent changeableness of the environment, which Lewis and Clark came to know all too well in their travels on the Missouri. And scientists know now that populations of grizzlies and other animals and plants are, like the Missouri River, always changing. There is no single "natural" abundance. There is a range of abundances, all of which are "natural" in the sense that the population was at that level at some time during the past, prior to the effects of modern civilization. When we recognize this, then a plan to return the grizzlies to their original "abundance" becomes more complicated. We begin to wonder not what was *the* right number but what was the key to persistence. Was it some specific abundance that contained the key to the persistence of this species? Or was the variation in abundances part of the key to persistence?

To believe that there is a single magic number which is the only sustainable one is to believe that a species is fragile and that individuals within a population are not resourceful. This seemed hardly the case with the grizzlies that met Lewis and Clark. The grizzlies seemed fearless, strong, able to withstand a number of bullet wounds; they seemed quick to respond, resourceful. A population that persists and prevails over a long time must have the ability to respond to the changes that inevitably occur. We understand now that to be sustainable is different from continuing to exist at a single abundance; and that to exist at a single abundance may not be the best strategy for a species to persist.

While a single, maximum population size is neither the only "natural" condition nor a guarantee of sustainability, a very low abundance does cause concern about the long-term persistence of a species. If a species is becoming extinct, then, we think, it will get there by a continual, definite decline in its numbers until the number is one. But rarity and becoming extinct are not necessarily the same. There have been some spectacular recoveries of species whose population size was less than 20. There were only 14 known whooping cranes in the late 1930s; this species now numbers in the hundreds; there were about a dozen known elephant seals at the turn of the century; now there are more than 60,000. Numbers alone do not guarantee persistence, as we learn from the passenger pigeon, which was numerous enough to darken the skies when a flock flew over, but which was extinguished by hunting and other human actions that whooping cranes and elephant seals survived. This realization is leading to a new focus on what might be a viable population.

Some recent programs to restore endangered or threatened animals have begun to focus on this more realistic goal of a self-sustaining population. Apparently, this was the goal for the Fish and Wildlife Service's Grizzly Recovery Plan. Its objective was "to establish viable, self-sustaining populations in areas where the grizzly bear occurred in 1975," with a goal of 301 bears for Yellowstone, 560 for the Northern Continental Divide (in western Montana including some of the region where Lewis and Clark encountered the bears), and 70 for the Cabinet/Yack region (an area along the northernmost Idaho-Montana border), or a total of 931 bears for an area no bigger than 20,000 square miles, or a density at least of 0.046 bears per square mile—at the upper limit of what was believed to be the 1975 density, and within the range of densities I calculated as observed by Lewis and Clark (the range bounded at the lower end by an assumption that they could see on average a half a mile and at the upper end by an assumption that they could see half a kilometer).

When we believed that the presettlement population was at some magical maximum abundance and that it was by definition sustainable, the answer to the question, how shall we save a species from extinction? was easy. Let it alone and it will return to this number. But, given our new understanding, the goal of a self-sustaining population is no longer simple. The answer will be a range of abundances with some minimum that we would like to avoid. This range—and its minimum— will vary from species to species. And, as the whooping crane and the passenger pigeon tell us, other characteristics are essential to persistence. To accomplish the Fish and Wildlife's recovery plan for the grizzly bear, we must understand much more about the requirements of this species than a single number. We must understand what it needs from its habitat and the ecosystems within which it lives.

POPULATIONS BIG ENOUGH TO SUSTAIN THEMSELVES

Once we begin to focus on the goal of a self-sustaining population, rather than on some maximum abundance, we need to know what is the minimum population size that could be self-sustaining, so that we can set a floor below which we would not want the population to fall. This abundance has become known as the "minimum viable population." It is a population that is large enough to avoid specific kinds of hazards, due to genetic effects in a small population, due to local, inherent environmental variability, and due to natural catastrophes—rare events that occur over wide areas (such as storms and fires that might accidentally wipe out a local population). A minimum viable population means the smallest number of individuals that has a reasonable chance of persisting. In practice, the minimum viable population must be defined in terms of a specific chance of persisting (or a chance of avoiding extinction) for a specific time interval.

Based on genetic factors, it has been estimated that a population should not fall below 50 breeding adults even for a short time to avoid genetic problems and to keep the chance of extinction acceptably low. A population with 50 breeding adults will have many nonbreeding individuals, including newborn, young, adolescents, and old, postbreeding adults. Thus even for a short time several hundred individuals seem a minimum safe number. Also based on studies of genetics, it has been estimated that to maintain a population for a long time, 500 or more breeding individuals are preferable to avoid problems of low genetic variability. Here it is assumed that a population might drop briefly as low as 50 individuals without too great a risk of losing enough genetic variation to allow it to adapt to future environmental changes. But, if a population is kept this low for many generations, then a variety of genetic mechanisms may lead to a decline in genetic diversity that could make the population less able to respond to changes and more likely to become extinct. This is sometimes referred to as the 50/500 rule.

Causes of extinction are usually grouped into five risk categories: population, environmental, genetic, natural catastrophe, and human actions. Here, "risk" means the chance that a species or population will become extinct due to one of these causes. How great is this chance of extinction? Random variations in population rates—in birth and death rates—can cause a species in low abundance to become extinct. For example, blue whales swim over vast areas of ocean. Because the total population was once reduced by whaling to only several hundred individuals, there could be year-to-year variations in the success of individual blue whales in finding mates. If in one year most whales are unsuccessful in finding a mate, then births could be dangerously low. Such random variation in populations, typical among many species, can occur without any change in the environment. It is a risk especially to species that consist of only a single population in one habitat.

Changes in the environment that occur from day to day, month to month, and year to year can affect population size even though the changes are not severe enough to be considered environmental catastrophes. Environmental risk involves variation in the physical or biological environment, including variations in predator, prey, symbiotic, or competitor species. As an example, Paul and Anne Ehrlich described the local extinction of a population of butterflies in the Colorado mountains. These butterflies lay their eggs in the unopened buds of a single species of lupine (a member of the legume family), and the hatched caterpillars feed on the flowers. One year, however, a very late snow and freeze killed all the lupine buds, leaving the caterpillars without food and causing the local extinction of the butterflies. The plants survived and their roots produced new stems, leaves, and flowers the next year. Had this been the only population of that butterfly, the entire species would have gone extinct. In some cases, species are sufficiently rare and isolated that such normal variations can lead to their extinction. In other cases, species succumb to catastrophic variation in the environment.

A natural catastrophe is a sudden change in the environment not due to human action. Fires, major storms, earthquakes, floods, and meteorite impacts are natural catastrophes on the land; changes in currents and upwellings can be major catastrophes in the ocean. For example, the explosion of a volcano on the island of Krakatoa in Indonesia in 1883 was a catastrophe that caused the local extinction of most forms of life found there.

The difference between environmental risk and natural catastrophe is illustrated by the history of the extinction of the heath hen. Once a common bird of the eastern United States, it was reduced to low numbers by human-induced habitat change and hunting. By the last quarter of the nineteenth century, the heath hen existed only on the island of Martha's Vineyard, off Cape Cod, Massachusetts. In 1907, a part of the island was made into a preserve for this bird, whose numbers had been reduced to about 100. Predators of the heath hen were controlled. The population increased to 800 by 1916, when two things happened: a fire destroyed most of the nesting areas (a catastrophe), and the next winter an unusually heavy concentration of goshawks on the island (environmental risk) caused high mortality. The population fell to less than 200 and the bird became extinct by 1932, possibly due to population or genetic risks. As I suggested before, genetic risks are important to a small population. This is because only some of the possible inherited characteristics are found in any individual, and a small population may, by chance, have individuals with a narrow range of genetic characteristics, compared to the whole species. The species is more vulnerable to extinction because it lacks the variety once present, or because a mutation that leads to some kind of poor health becomes fixed in the population. Such genetic risks can be independent of environmental change.

Before they were removed from the wild, there were about 20 condors in California. It stands to reason that this small number was likely to have less genetic variability than the much larger population that existed several centuries ago. This increases their vulnerability. Suppose, for instance, the last 20 condors by chance had inherited characteristics that made them less able to withstand lack of water. Then, if left in the wild, the condors would have been more vulnerable to extinction during the recent drought years in California than a larger, more genetically variable population.

Suppose we apply these new ideas to the problem of restoration of the grizzly bears, as the U.S. Fish and Wildlife Service has planned to do. We find ourselves in an information dilemma. We confront the two kinds of uncertainty that I talked about in the third chapter, when Lewis and several of his men tried to find out if the Marias River was the real headwaters of the Missouri—we face lack of facts and we face the problem that populations are subject to chance variations. With the grizzly bears, we can reduce the first kind of uncertainty just by reading the journals of Lewis and Clark carefully. But because information is even more limited for most wildlife than it is for grizzlies, we cannot determine the facts or the risks with any accuracy. We must make value judgments; we hope that they are informed judgments. We have to establish a time period over which we hope that the animals will survive. This is usually referred to as a planning time period or planning time horizon. Shall we plan for 10 years, which is something we might hope to measure and therefore could put into a law? Shall we plan for 100 years, which covers several generations of bears, many, many generations of mosquitos, and perhaps less than one generation for some trees? Shall we plan for a thousand years, which suits our sense of the idea of persistence and reduction of the threat of extinction, but offers us no chance of direct observation beyond our own or our children's children's lifetimes?

Lacking information and unable to decide at this time on a planning period, scientists have tended to fall back on comparatively simple notions, the most prevalent of which is the 50/500 rule I described earlier. The recovery plan for the grizzlies project a population larger than this minimum.

WHAT THE GRIZZLIES TELL US

On June 28, 1805, the expedition was camped and in the midst of portaging around the Great Falls of Montana. Lewis noted in his journal that "the white bears have now become so troublesome to us that I do not think it prudent to send one man alone on an errand of any kind, particularly where he has to pass through the brush." The bears were bold enough to "come close around our camp every night, but have never yet ventured to attack us and our dog gives us timely notice of their visits, he keeps constantly patrolling all night." It was so dangerous, Lewis believed, that "I have made the men sleep with their arms by them." Reading this and the other accounts of the expedition's experiences with grizzlies, I was at first caught up in the excitement, and danger that the bears posed, and in the bravery with which the men responded. Lewis and Clark's encounters with grizzly bears were their most dangerous encounters with any animal and among the most dangerous of all their experiences. But the meaning of these encounters to us in our search for natural history is much deeper. The more I read of these accounts and compare them with my own experiences, my respect for Lewis and Clark grows, and the more valuable to us I realize are those dangerous nights they spent, as we try to discover our natural history, to reconstruct nature as it was prior to the advent of European settlement, and to sustain and restore parts of that nature. From their encounters with the grizzlies we learn about the limits of our present knowledge. We learn that, in spite of much emotion and desire directed toward the conservation of rare and endangered animals during the last 30 years, our knowledge remains terribly limited. We discover that we know little more about the range and density of the grizzly bears in the lower 48 states than what Lewis and Clark's journals tell us. We find that clear, objective, historical records can be a great help to us. And in the end, we know that we have a much longer journey ahead of us than Lewis and Clark if we are to be able to predict the results of our attempts to conserve endangered species.

CHAPTER FIVE

A Measured Journey

*When you can measure what you are speaking about and
express it in numbers, you know something about it, but
when you cannot measure it, when you cannot express it
in numbers, your knowledge is of a meagre and unsatis-
factory kind.*

WILLIAM THOMSON, LORD KELVIN, 1883

JEFFERSON'S SCIENTIFIC PLAN

Lewis and Clark's journey had the obvious
objectives of exploring lands just obtained
from France in the Louisiana Purchase under a treaty signed in Paris on
April 30, 1803, and discovery of the source of the Missouri River and
the best water route from there to the Pacific Ocean. Equally important

to those of us who confront and are concerned with great environmental changes, President Jefferson wanted to know about the natural history of the West. In his letters to Lewis, he made clear his desire that Lewis and Clark bring back a careful record of the state of the animals, plants, and environment in the unknown part of the continent. He told Lewis to record his observations of "the soil and face of the country; its growth and vegetable productions . . . the animals of the country generally . . . the remains and accounts of any which may be deemed rare or extinct." This he, Clark, and one of their sergeants, Ordway, did with remarkable faithfulness and accuracy. Through their notes we can obtain a unique picture of the frontier wilderness so important to America and its imagination; so important today to our perceptions about what we have done in the past to the environment and what we must do in the future to solve our environmental problems. "Perhaps no traveler's tale has ever been told with greater fidelity and minuteness, or has more nearly achieved absolute accuracy," Coues wrote in his introduction to his edition of the journals. "Our heroes proved also model journalists."

Jefferson had picked the leader of the expedition carefully. It is hard to imagine a person with a better background and experience to lead the expedition than Lewis. Born on August 18, 1774, near Charlottesville, Virginia, Lewis had learned hunting and gained a knowledge of plants and animals as a young man. As a captain in the army, he became Jefferson's private secretary, and requested permission to lead the expedition Jefferson wanted undertaken to explore the country from the Missouri River westward.

Although experienced in the woods and a careful observer of his surroundings, Lewis had had little formal education. In preparation for the scientific and natural history tasks of the expedition, Jefferson sent him to Philadelphia in 1803 to take crash courses in botany, zoology, geology, and in the use of scientific instruments.

A BIAS TOWARD SCIENTIFIC
INFORMATION

Every day Lewis and Clark measured or estimated the distances they had traveled, and they mapped the Missouri—meanders, oxbow cuts, fickleness, and all. This is a remarkable, unique feature of the expedition. It was a measured journey, a quantitative exploration. When Clark walked back across the bottom of an oxbow on August 12, 1804, he knew how many miles they had traveled each day by boat around the "bones" of the wishbone of a meander and he paced the distances he had to walk across its base to find the place they had started a day before.

Having surveyed in the woods of New Hampshire and having used compass, surveying tape, and map in the wilderness forests of Isle Royale National Park and the Boundary Waters Canoe Area of Minnesota, I know how difficult this kind of measuring can be. It is much easier to take a bulldozer, some jeeps, some microwave surveying devices, and drive a straight course for a road or canal across the countryside although it takes more advanced technology and leads to a much greater effect on the environment than it is to stumble over dead logs and jump from boggy hummock to hummock, keeping the line straight and the compass direction true, to map your way. Lewis and Clark's continual knowledge of where they were in quantitative terms is another unusual feature of their expedition.

As I mentioned earlier, as I write this book, I am also directing a study for the states of Oregon and California about salmon and their habitats. Lewis and Clark measured every foot of their travels and knew the exact distances they went each day, including the distance they went on the Columbia River, one of the most important salmon rivers in the United States. Lewis and Clark also calculated the total length of the river and wrote that number in their journals. As part of the study I have been directing, I needed to know the lengths of the 38 rivers in our project's area in Oregon and northern California. Ironically, the people we contacted at the Oregon Department of Fish and Wildlife and the Oregon Department of Water Resources told us that they did not keep this information and were not able to tell me the lengths of the rivers south of the Columbia, in spite of modern technology, modern science, modern transportation, and the great modern concern with salmon and their habitats.

SPRING   ON   PACK   ICE: COUNTING THE   BOWHEAD   WHALE

If our knowledge of the present status of the grizzly and of the length of rivers in Oregon illustrates what we should not be doing, is there an example of our doing something right? Our studies of the bowhead whale of the North Pacific is an outstanding example of what we have come to learn about present status and past abundance of a large mammal. Although separated by long distances and entirely different habitats, grizzlies and bowhead whales have several things in common: a habitat near the northern part of the Pacific Coast of North America; a history of being hunted by people of European descent since the beginning of the nineteenth century, and a presence today as threatened and endangered species (and therefore protected by U.S. law). In the 1970s, I became involved in a study of the history of the exploitation of the bowhead whale. John Bockstoce, an anthropologist studying the Eskimos, realized that he needed to understand Eskimo whaling to understand their culture, and then realized that he needed to understand Yankee whaling to understand what had happened to the bowhead. He asked me to join him in an attempt to use historical records to reconstruct the original abundance of this animal and to determine how many bowhead whales had been caught by Yankee whalers.

We used the log books kept by the first mate on whaling voyages. Each day, the first mate wrote down the location of his ship, the wind, cloud, sea and ice conditions, and he listed the number of whales caught. We were able to use this information much the way I used the records from the Lewis and Clark expedition about the grizzly bear. The records from ships' logs provided many independent observations, giving us a better statistical sample than the records from the journals from a single expedition. Not only were we able to make a somewhat more reliable estimate about how many whales there once were, we were also able to calculate the error associated with that estimate. This is an advantage that modern science has given us over Lewis and Clark: the development of statistical methods allows us to estimate the size of our uncertainty. This is very important. Today we teach beginning science students that a measure without an estimate of error lacks modern scientific validity; without that estimate, a measure is an interesting and often valuable case study, as it is with our estimate of the density of grizzly bears from the Lewis and Clark journals. The value lies in that it is a unique measure, and this makes up for the lack of our ability to provide an estimate of its error.

We estimated that there were about 20,000 bowheads, give or take

10,000, at the time that exploitation by Yankee whalers began. That exploitation of the bowhead whale began about 1840 and lasted until 1920. This information was used in helping to determine what number of bowheads represented a threatened or endangered population. But there is another intriguing story about the bowhead, one that is taking place today.

Every April since the early 1970s a small group of hardy scientists has trekked out onto the ice pack offshore of Alaska, found the highest point near a small channel of open water, and camped out, using the survival methods of the Eskimo. They carry with them acoustical and surveying equipment. The juxtaposition of these pieces of high technology and the Arctic cold is what makes possible an accurate count of the bowhead whales.

Why would anyone care enough to go through that suffering in the cold on the ice in the Arctic spring to count a rare and presently unused mammal? The long story has two pieces. The more recent piece has to do with conservation of the bowhead; the earlier piece with its exploitation. The bowhead became the center of an intense controversy over conservation in the 1970s. Like the other great whales, it was protected by U.S. law under the Marine Mammal Protection Act and it was also subject to negotiated agreements for its protection by the International Whaling Commission (IWC).

The bowhead, like all baleen whales, feeds on ocean plankton—the small animals and algae that float in the ocean waters near the surface. These whales feed by opening their mouths as they swim. Their modified baleen teeth, which resemble huge combs, filter the small organisms, which the whale then wipes off with its tongue. Arctic waters are productive in plankton and the bowhead characteristically travels and feeds near the shore, where it is comparatively accessible to the Eskimo.

In the spring, as the ice pack breaks up, the bowhead swims near shore from its wintering grounds to the area north of the Bering Sea where it spends the summer, primarily in the Beaufort Sea.

If the water is less than 100 feet deep, the pack ice is often grounded and builds up along the shore, but sea currents and winds push it offshore and create an opening through which the whales can pass. It is, however, a narrow opening, so that all the whales have to travel within a narrow channel not far offshore. So counting the large animals is comparatively easy. The Eskimo understood this near-shore migration and made use of it by around 1000 A.D.

In 1972 the IWC requested information about the size of the bowhead whale population, and by 1976 scientists started to learn how to count the population along the shore. Sighting and counting whales in the cold from a lonely rise on the ice is a difficult task. How do you avoid counting a whale twice if it turns around and circles back to feed? How many of the whales pass through the channel but are not counted?

Various methods were tried to correct for these two errors, one of omission and one of commission. The first method involved two groups of observers, located about one kilometer apart, and communicating by radio. When the southern group saw a whale, they would radio the observation to the northern group, which would then look for it. The percentage of whales counted by the first group and missed by the second gave a measure of the error associated with counting the whales, and allowed a statistical estimate of how badly the method undercounted the population. By observing a whale at two locations, it was sometimes possible to determine if a whale had reversed direction. Using this method, some estimate could be made of double-counting.

When the method was first tried, comparatively few whales were seen: 327 in 1977 between April 25 and June 2. This led to a complete moratorium on the harvest of the whale, but then a special meeting of the IWC was held, and a small Eskimo catch was permitted for subsistence and cultural needs.

In 1978 only 280 were counted. But in that year a new method was tried, one that made use of the sounds whales make. Hydrophones were used to listen to the whales. Bowheads were making 4,000 calls per hour and these transmitted well. In 1980, more than 6,000 bowheads were heard during nine days of acoustic monitoring. This is 20 times the number of whales seen. Direct visual sighting turned out to be a poor method.

By 1982 the acoustical methods had become more sophisticated. Sonobuoys detect acoustical pressures and the frequency-modulated sounds of the whales made it possible, with a set of these buoys, to triangulate and locate each whale.

Using these methods, the scientists obtained a 10-year observation, which suggested the whale population was growing. The growth rate was approximately 3 percent a year, but the statistical error of this estimate was broad, and it was possible that the growth rate ranged anywhere from 0.1 percent to 6.2 percent per year. From this, the scientists concluded that while the bowhead population was increasing, we didn't know at what rate it was growing. They also estimated that there were approximately 7,500 whales, but that the statistical error allowed the abundance to lie somewhere between 6,400 and 9,200.

If there were 9,200 whales increasing at 3 percent per year, then the net addition was 270 whales—about equal to the total number thought to be there when the counts were first made! If there were 6,400 whales and the increase was 0.1 percent, then the net addition each year would be 6 whales. This is quite a range, and it would be difficult for one to set a management goal from it.

However, one could continue to track the population over time and continue to make the same calculations, treating this whole thing as an experiment. Over time, one could adjust the catch so that the population would increase or remain more or less constant. The methods presently in use to count the bowhead are among the best done for all endangered species everywhere. It is an example of what we should be doing.

MAPPING AN ENVIRONMENTAL FUTURE

With the exception of such cases as the present counting of the bowhead, we rarely approach the conservation of our environment with the same methodical intensity, the consistent recording of quantities, found in Lewis and Clark's journals. Oh yes, we have digital devices readily at hand: pocket calculators, hand-held field computers, geopositioning satellites, remote sensing maps, and huge computer databases that go by the elaborate rubric of geographic information systems. I have used all of them. But in spite of all the gadgetry, we generally fail to measure what we need to. One of the shocking gaps in our ability to deal with our environment is our failure to have what is referred to as "base line information" and "monitoring," which is to say that we don't know, in quantitative terms, where we have been or where we are going.

The U.S. Geological Survey (USGS), which mapped our countryside and provided excellent maps for all of us to use, is cutting back on these maps. As I was preparing for my trip to Iowa and Nebraska to see some of the campsites of the Lewis and Clark expedition and to visit that part of the countryside through which they had traveled, I went to the local map store to buy some of the larger scale U.S. Geological Survey maps that I had found useful elsewhere in retracing parts of the expedition. Because maps of a nation seem so fundamental, so much a part of the "infrastructure" essential to getting many things done in our society—from finding mines to building roads, let alone protecting the environment—I thought USGS maps would only become more plentiful and more accurate over time. With our satellite observations and geopositioning satellites and microwave surveying devices, I assumed there would be better and better maps. But when I asked for my favorite kind of map, known as "1:1 million," I was told that they were no longer in production. Many were out of print, and only a few were still available. It is becoming harder, rather than easier, to know the lay of the land and the location of off-road places in our country. Our methods of measurement are incredibly better than those of Lewis and Clark. But President Jefferson charged them with the tasks of mapping their route, measuring the distances they traveled, and observing and recording the natural history of the American West. As a nation we seem enthusiastic about the environment, and many people seek recreation in remote areas. The technology for measuring and mapping gets better and more accessible. A few days before writing this, I received an advertisement in the mail for a global positioning satellite device that would tell me exactly where I was. But the question: where was everything in nature, the mountains, the rivers? seems to have become less of a national interest. Maintaining records of what we have measured and mapped continues to elude us.

MAPPING FOR MODERN ENVIRONMENTAL ISSUES

I have run across the problem of lack of essential information time and time again in my research, but I had never expected it to happen with maps. And many other kinds of information have not been available that would have helped environmental problems. Much of my professional work in the last 10 years has focused on trying to map some basic features of our environment. One project I directed was designed to determine the amount of organic matter and carbon stored in the vast forests of North America. These measures were necessary for many reasons relating to global environmental problems. In particular, there has been much discussion in recent years about the possibility of a great global climate change caused by the burning of fossil fuels.

One of the products of the combustion of fossil fuels is carbon dioxide. Carbon dioxide is one of the "greenhouse gases" that are transparent to visible light from the sun, but absorb infrared radiation from the Earth's surface. Carbon dioxide acts like glass in a greenhouse, which has the same characteristics, allowing sunlight to heat the Earth's surface and then trapping the heat energy so that it cannot escape. Increasing the concentration of carbon dioxide in the air could warm the climate rapidly, leading to many potentially undesirable effects. Experts had begun to suggest that we could reduce the rate of this change and reduce the undesirable effects of global warming if we could plant trees and increase the growth of forests. Trees, like all green plants, take up carbon dioxide in the process of photosynthesis, separating carbon from oxygen and producing sugar, the first step in forming organic compounds on which all of us depend. Experts began to talk about "carbon offset" programs, in which a nation that burned fossil fuel could pay to plant or maintain an amount of forest land that would take up an equivalent amount of carbon dioxide that the nation had burned. But there was one problem with this idea: no one had a good idea of the amount of carbon actually stored in forests. There were many guesses about the amount—professional best estimates, in which experts had extrapolated from individual studies of forests here and there, multiplying by the total land area believed to be in forests. These estimates tended to be based on studies of old-growth forests, because those were the kinds of forests that had attracted the most attention. Estimates of how much carbon could be stored worldwide based on those measures were likely to overestimate the potential storage capability of forests, in the same way that Clark might have misjudged the actual distance from St. Louis to the Pacific Ocean by including the length of all the meanders, rather than the straight distance to be calculated from his maps.

AN EDUCATED GUESS

For years, scientists have been willing to accept educated guesses about how much carbon was actually stored in our forests and might be stored in the future, rather than to seek exact measures. When I realized that we did not know how much timber there was and how much carbon there was in the major forests of our nation, I went to government agencies and tried to interest them in a major program to make these measurements. The techniques necessary were not much more sophisticated than those used by Lewis and Clark on their trip westward. But I couldn't interest a single government agency in the project. Finally, the Andrew W. Mellon Foundation saw the importance of these basic facts and provided support for a study of the boreal forest of North America —funding the first statistically valid estimate of the total amount of timber and total stored carbon in the timber in this huge forested area. There seems to me to be a peculiar decline in our government from Jefferson's fundamental concern with the basic elements of science, from Jefferson's curiosity and desire to know and measure the American West to our apparent disregard of the need to know where we are and where we have been, where nature is and where nature has been, in quantitative terms. We think we live in the information age and in the environmental age, but somehow we have prevented the two from meeting and mixing.

I began the carbon storage study funded by the Andrew W. Mellon Foundation with an analysis of the boreal forests of North America and followed this by a study of the forests of eastern North America, which included the types of forests that Lewis and Clark saw early in the trip along the Missouri in what is now Missouri, Iowa, and Nebraska. Lloyd Simpson, a forester with much field experience, began to work with me. We hired teams of young college students and graduate students. We designed a scientific sampling scheme, which involved picking points at random over the entire region of each study, and then sending a team to each selected point. We designed a computer method to pick points at random, but the idea was the same as throwing darts at a map of North America and then going to where each dart hit the map. This resulted in a plan of scientific exploration that sent the teams to some of the wildest areas still remaining on our continent.

One of the points fell in Canada near Wood Buffalo National Park, the summer feeding and nesting grounds of the few remaining whooping cranes. The exact point was not far from an obscure lake that the team could only reach by float plane, given the time that we had available to do the study. On the way to the lake, one of the field team members chatted with the pilot. He asked him what the lake they were heading for was like. "I've never been there," the pilot said. There was a silence, and he added, thoughtfully, "Come to think of it, nobody has ever been there." In my own way, I had sent a team of people into a wilderness. It was a smaller scale by far than Jefferson's orders to Lewis and Clark, but it was of the same spirit, and my experience in seeking to know the basic facts about life in our environment gave me a special empathy for the Lewis and Clark expedition. Jefferson and I had another thing in common. In both his case and mine, most of the government did not appreciate the reason for scientific measurement and exploration of the kind we thought important. In our day, we seem willing to go with guess and by golly. It is as if Clark were to throw away his compass and chronometer.

I have set out to discover nature as it was changed by Western technological civilization, but I have discovered along the way a funny thing about our own times. We live in a time when we think that everything can be measured, and therefore it probably has been measured. But the more we are able to measure what we know about the environment, the more cavalier we seem to be in our care of it. We also seem to believe that measurement and the appreciation of the beauty of nature are contradictory activities, one nullifying the other. This was not the attitude of Lewis, and in my experience, the activities required to make measurements about nature have always shown me new ways to look at nature and to see its beauty.

When I explained the need for such a methodical approach to environmental issues to a reporter who was interviewing me, the response of the inquirer was, "You seem to have a bias toward scientific information." It was enough to make me want to find that saloon that had been moved from Kansas to Missouri, where one could measure the fact that it was now legally possible to buy a drink.

Buffalo and Winter on the Plains

Technology Meets Wilderness

On the high plains above the Niobrara River . . . the
profusion of animal life caught their attention,
rather than the terrain.

GARY E. MOULTON

"Last night we were alarmed by a large buffalo bull," Captain Lewis wrote on May 29, 1805. The expedition was camped at the mouth of the Judith River near the present Judith Landing Recreation Area in Montana. They were near the western end of the range of the buffalo and would see the animals only a few more times on the outward journey. Today this area is part of the Upper Missouri National Wild and Scenic River region, beautiful country through which the Missouri has incised itself, cutting a sharp path through steep cliffs of colors varying from white to yellow. Above the river are rolling plains and occasional hills, with the Rocky Mountains in the distance. Traveling on modern roads that avoid the river, one could pass through this countryside without knowing the Missouri was nearby.

The lone buffalo swam across the Missouri, climbed over the expedition's large pirogue boat, "ran up the bank in full speed directly toward the fires, and was within 18 inches of the heads of some of the men who lay sleeping," Captain Lewis wrote, then climbed over one of the canoes before the guard of the night "could alarm him or make him change his course." The animal ran down between four fires and within a few inches of the heads of a second row of the men, "and would have broken into our lodge if the barking of the dog had not stopped him. He suddenly turned to the right, and was out of sight in a moment, leaving us all in confusion."

That buffalo was no doubt frightened by the sleeping men and by their possessions—boats and tents. His behavior, although dangerous to the expedition, was very different from that of the grizzlies, who attacked the men even when unprovoked. This buffalo was trying to find a way out, away from the men.

Most of the expedition's encounters with buffalo were less dangerous to the men than this, but they were much more dangerous to the buffalo. As one of the primary sources of food, buffalo were important to the expedition and were sought wherever possible. Hunters sent out by the captains from the river camps searched down these animals for miles. It is unlikely that there were many occasions when buffalo were nearby and the expedition did not know about them. As a result, we can use the encounters of the expedition with buffalo to gain some knowledge about the distribution and abundance of these great creatures of the plains.

The expedition saw its first buffalo on June 6, 1804, when the men were just west of Columbia, Missouri (somewhat south of where Interstate 70 crosses the Missouri River today). Buffalo were sighted for the second time on June 28, when the expedition reached the Kansas River (at the present location of Kansas City). Once across the Kansas River, Lewis and Clark found that buffalo herds moved "with great method and regularity"—by now the expedition had passed the settled countryside of the Missouri and had journeyed into the plains and buffalo country.

The men of the expedition did not shoot a buffalo until August 23, more than two months after the first sighting. By that time, they were in South Dakota, about 400 miles upriver from their first encounter (near the present towns of Yankton and Vermillion, South Dakota). They came to "cliffs of yellow and blue earth" along the south side of the Missouri. Camping near the cliffs, they saw to the north "an extensive and delightful prairie," the journals record, "which we called Buffalo prairie, from our having here killed the first buffalo." The river flows along the edge of the cliffs, meandering in a wide flood plain, five to ten miles in width, and this flood plain is set within a larger plain intersected by wooded hills.

They seemed to be in the midst of a large herd of buffalo. Two days later, on August 25, Lewis and Clark traveled overland to an Indian spirit mound nine miles from where the Whitestone River flows into the Missouri. "From the top of this mound," which they estimated rose about 70 feet above the valley, "we beheld the most beautiful land-

scape; numerous herds of buffalo were seen feeding in various directions."

Several weeks went by before they found any more buffalo. On
September 5, they visited an Indian village on Ponca Creek in northeastern Nebraska, where the Nebraska-South Dakota line trends north-
west-southeast, near the modern town of Verdel and present-day Ponca
State Park. Here the Missouri remains unchanneled and unleveed, meandering through wooded hills, cutting away the banks along the low
bluffs of the park. The cliff edges are pock-marked with swallow nests.
Cottonwoods, willows, and ash line the shore. Sandbars and snags of
old logs make travel on the river hazardous. Under the deep shade of
the trees in the forests on the bluffs is a rich, dark humus soil. The
bluffs, which Lewis and Clark described, are generally light in color, but
are composed of banded, horizontal rocks that shade into dark, almost
coal-like deposits.

The Indians had left their village to hunt buffalo, and the expedition
found nobody there, but a buffalo wandered into the deserted village
and was shot by the man of the party named George Gibson. The next
day, September 6, they passed bluffs of bluish and reddish stone along
the south shore of the Missouri, known today as Ponca Bluffs of the
Niobrara geological formation. Lewis and Clark saw "great numbers of
buffalo" in a region of abundant wildlife, where they also saw pronghorn, elk, deer, turkey, geese, beaver, and caught a large catfish at their
evening camp.

On September 8, Lewis and Clark reached a house where a trader
named Trudeau had lived in the winter of 1796–97; they were still in
country visited and described by French-Canadian traders. They saw
buffalo that day and the next and the next. "Great number of buffalo
and elk on the hillsides feeding," Clark wrote, but deer were scarce.

They had reached an area in South Dakota we can no longer see, as it was flooded by Fort Randall Reservoir. Almost a week went by without buffalo and then the expedition joined the herds again, encountering buffalo on September 16, and seeing the animals almost daily for the next week, on September 17, 18, 19, 20, 22, and 23. This suggests that they were traveling in company with one of the large herds.

More than three weeks passed before they reported buffalo again, on October 17, when they were just south of the present town of Cannon Ball, South Dakota, and near the end of their first year's westward travel. "The leaves are falling fast" the journals record. They saw buffalo for the next three days, noting on the 19th that they "counted 52 herds of buffalo."

WINTER WITH THE MANDANS

On October 21, they reached the Mandan and Hidatsa villages where they would spend the winter, near the site of modern Bismarck, North Dakota, a city noteworthy today for having the lowest temperature recorded in the lower 48 of the United States for many winter days. About two miles from where they camped that night, they saw a beautiful plain "covered with herds of buffalo." They shot one for food that day and another on the next day, October 22. The hunters reported seeing about 200 animals, all males.

Lewis and Clark knew of the Mandan villages before the start of their journey as a place of peaceful Indians, where they might spend the winter. Careful as ever, they knew it would be impractical to proceed farther that year because the mountains were impossible to cross at this time of year.

Winter had approached the expedition with a deliberateness recorded firmly in the pages of their journals. Observant of everything and determined in their attempts to record what they saw, Lewis and Clark wrote of the change in the seasons. On the first of October the leaves of ash and poplar and most of the shrubs had begun to turn yellow and "decline." There was a slight "white" frost on the fifth of October, and they saw brant and geese "passing to south"; frost the next night and teal, gulls, and mallards. On the 13th the cottonwoods were yellow and their leaves falling; on the 14th the leaves of all the ash, elm, and all other trees except cottonwood had fallen; on the 17th snow geese passed overhead, white birds with black wings. Antelopes passed on their fall migration. On the 19th there was a hard frost, freezing the clay near the water as well as water in containers. A half inch of snow fell on the 22nd. By the 25th all the leaves on the trees had fallen, including the cottonwoods, but the snow did not stay on the ground. Violent winds struck on the 28th and 29th, and in this way the winter came.

They located a site for a winter camp on October 26, 1804, began to build wooden huts on November 2, and stayed until April 7, 1805. They named their camp "Fort Mandan." The site, near the river, was later washed away by a Missouri River flood. No more sightings of buffalo were reported until December; the expedition members spent the time building cabins, cutting firewood, and preparing for the winter.

On the 6th of November Clark was awakened by the sergeant of the guard to see the northern lights, which appeared as streaks of light, floating columns. The next morning the clouds to the north were black and the wind blew hard all day. They built huts of cottonwood, "this being the only timber we have," Clark wrote on November 6. Sergeant

Gass described the huts they built as "in two rows, containing four rooms each, and joined at one end forming an angle." The floor was of split planks, covered with clay and grass. The roofs reached about 18 feet above the ground. Two storerooms were built in the angle formed by the other huts. They were still in "discovered" country, land that had become known to white men and men of mixed parentage, mainly French-Canadian traders, trappers, and hunters, the usual raggle-taggle of the curious, the rough, the ill-fit, and the outcasts of civilization. While the expedition was building the huts, the Mandans were out hunting buffalo, sometimes sharing the catch with Lewis and Clark and their men. On November 13th, they moved into their huts and began their winter stay in earnest. The next day Clark wrote that the ice was "running very thick" as the river rose and some snow fell. On the 16th "a very white frost" covered "all the trees" with ice, and all the men moved into huts, finished or not.

With the huts finished enough to protect them from the worst of the weather, the men could then turn to hunting, and on the 19th of November the hunters returned with "32 deer, 12 elk and a buffalo," the first mention in the journals of buffalo since mid October, more likely because Lewis and Clark had been occupied with preparation for the winter rather than because of the absence of buffalo in the area.

The weather improved toward the end of November. November 23 was a "fair warm day" as were the next two, then the weather turned again and became very cold and windy. On the 30th of November the Mandan chief told Lewis and Clark that some of his hunters had been attacked and killed by Sioux. "We thought it well to show a disposition to aid and assist them against their enemies," Clark wrote. Lewis and Clark took 23 men, armed and on horseback, to the chief and promised to defend the Mandans, but the chief suggested that they wait until

107

spring because the snow was too deep for the horses and it was too cold. Winter was closing in on them and their crude huts were barely completed, but they took up arms and went out with their horses to help their hosts against enemies. So began their first winter on the plains.

They measured temperatures at noon each day. The weather varied drastically. There were three occasions when the thermometer recorded temperatures of 40 below zero Fahrenheit. Early in January 1805, the temperature fell to 40 below and soon after climbed above freezing. Food became scarce for people and horses. Lewis wrote in his journal on February 12, 1805, that the Indians were forced to feed their horses on cottonwood bark.

HUNTING BUFFALO

In December, when the cold weather was upon the land, the Mandan village was visited by a large buffalo herd that remained in the vicinity of the camp for 10 days. On December 7, 1804, the chief of the Mandans told Lewis and Clark that there was a "large drove of buffalo" nearby and "his people were waiting for us to join them in a chase." Lewis took 15 men and joined the Indians, who were already killing buffalo from horseback. Lewis and his men shot 14, "five of which we got to the fort by the assistance of a horse," and the men brought what else they could on their backs. It was necessary to bring the buffalo meat back to camp immediately. Buffalo left out over night were eaten by wolves, "which are in great numbers," wrote Clark, and "always in the buffalo." Also, the Mandans considered a dead buffalo unmarked by an arrow or other sign to belong to whoever found it.

The next day, December 8, Clark went out with 15 men, killing eight buffalo, two of which they shot seven miles from the village. The temperature was 44 degrees below freezing and several of the men suffered frostbite and two slipped and injured their hips. "I feel a little fatigued," Clark wrote, "having run after the buffalo all day in snow," which was 6 to 10 inches deep.

On December 9, Lewis went out hunting with 18 men. They stayed out until the next morning, sleeping "in the snow on a cold point with one small blanket," during what Lewis called "a cold disagreeable night." By this time the ice had hardened on the river so that buffalo crossed without breaking through. Lewis and his men killed 9 buffalo, but many were "so meager that they [were] not fit for use." On the 12th, pronghorn were seen but the weather was "so cold that we do not think it prudent to turn out to hunt." Never one for idleness, Clark measured the width of the river by walking across on the ice; he found it to be 500 yards wide. On December 14 and 15, Clark went on a hunting party and noted, there was "much snow" and it was 52 degrees below freezing. Buffalo continued to be seen on December 18, but again the weather was too cold for hunting. Then the buffalo disappeared and were not seen until the beginning of the new year.

Lewis and Clark next reported buffalo on January 6, 1805, when Clark was out hunting them with 16 men. They killed 8 and hunted again on the next day, January 7. They saw buffalo on the 8th, and hunted again on the 9th, when 10 were killed. Then, once again, the buffalo disappeared from the area of the village.

On February 4, Lewis wrote that "no buffalo have made their appearance in our neighborhood for some weeks" and their "stock of meat" was nearly exhausted. Clark decided to take a group of men and go down river to hunt. They put their baggage on small wooden sleighs which they pulled themselves and brought three pack horses to carry the meat.

On their first day out, February 4, they found nothing to hunt and had nothing to eat. On the next day, Clark broke through the ice, soaking his feet and legs. On that day they killed a deer and 2 buffalo, but the buffalo were in too poor a condition to eat. They saw buffalo on February 8, but found them too lean to be worth taking. On the trip they killed 16 elk and 40 deer, which provided the bulk of their meat for the next month; only three buffalo were killed. Clark returned to the winter camp on the night of February 12. He and his men had walked 30 miles on the ice and through the woodlands, in some places struggling through snow up to their knees. They saw no more live buffalo that winter. Staying in one place, along the frozen river, they had seen buffalo about once a month.

On March 6, 1805, the Mandans set fire to the prairie. Clark attributed the lighting of the fire as a way that the Indians produced an early crop of grass to attract the buffalo. The last mention of buffalo while the expedition was at Fort Mandan occurred on March 29. "Few Indians visit us today," Clark wrote. "They are waiting to catch the floating buffalo which break through the ice in crossing, those people are fond of those animals tainted and catch great numbers every spring." Such drowning of buffalo that fell through river ice in the winter was common and reported by other early explorers. In 1795, explorer John McDonnell counted more than 7,360 carcasses on one part of the Saskatchewan River.

The expedition renewed its westward journey on April 7, and they continued to find buffalo only occasionally and then in patches. On April 13, Lewis wrote that they saw buffalo and elk at a distance but killed none. "We found a number of carcasses of the buffalo lying along shore, which had been drowned by falling through the ice in winter and lodged on shore by the high water when the river broke up about the first of this month," he wrote. The next day they shot a buffalo and an

110

elk, "both so poor as to be almost unfit for use." They saw great numbers of buffalo during the next few days, until April 17, but do not mention killing any of them. They were now on the part of the Missouri that is flooded today by Garrison Reservoir.

On April 21, they found themselves again among "immense quantities of buffalo, elk, deer, antelopes, geese, and some swans and ducks, out of which we procured three deer and four buffalo calves, the latter we found very delicious," wrote Lewis, "I think it equal to any veal I ever tasted." They were now at the location of Little Muddy River in Williams County, North Dakota, camping across the river and some distance from Williston. These herds continued to remain near to the river and the expedition through April 23, when another buffalo calf was taken, and on through April 26, when they were at the confluence of the Yellowstone and Missouri rivers. On that day Clark saw buffalo cows and calves on a sand bar and had his men kill the fattest cow and several calves. The countryside at the confluence of the rivers, through which both the men and the buffalo were passing, was a plain, extending "in every direction" with trees only along the rivers, where there was "indifferent timber," Clark wrote, consisting of typical floodplain species: cottonwood, elm and ash, as well as shrubs such as willow.

Clark was especially impressed with the land near to where the two rivers joined. About a mile above the confluence he saw "a beautiful low level plain" which was "bordered by an extensive woodland for many miles up the Yellowstone River," and would make "a beautiful commanding situation for a fort." Forts were later built across the river but near to this location. On the 27th of April they crossed into what is now Montana, and made camp about a mile below Nohly in Richland County. On April 29, they continued to be "surrounded with deer, elk, buffalo, antelopes, and their companions the wolves." They killed a buffalo on May 1, another on May 2, saw "vast quantities" of buffalo on the 3rd and the 4th. The buffalo continued to be so common that on May 8 they wrote that "we are surrounded by buffalo, elk, common and black-tailed deer, beaver, antelopes, and wolves"; a similar observation was made the next day, May 9.

A week passed and on May 16, when they were at a location now under Fort Peck Reservoir in Montana, they shot 2 buffalo. The next day Lewis wrote that the buffalo were "not so abundant as they were some days past." However, they took one buffalo on May 21, when they had reached the Musselshell River. Buffalo were becoming scarce, they wrote in their entries for May 23 and 25, while on the 29th the buffalo ran through their camp, as mentioned.

As they entered the beautiful white cliffs of the upper Missouri at the end of the month, they saw a few buffalo on May 31. White and brightly colored and contrasting layers of cliffs rose along the river, in some places several hundred feet above the water, and were "so soft as to yield readily the impression of water," they wrote in their journals. They were again in the company of buffalo, seeing the animals in the plains distant from the river on June 1, and taking two buffalo the next day, June 2. They saw buffalo at the confluence of the Marias River and the Missouri. Clark and his group killed two buffalo on June 6 and again on June 7.

On June 9, Lewis and Clark decided to leave heavy goods, including their large boat, in a cache near the downstream end of the Great Falls on the Missouri and to attempt the ascent and pass through the mountains with less equipment. Busy with this work, they did not mention buffalo for several days, so we do not know if any were in that vicinity at the time.

On June 13, having camped about five miles south of the location of the modern town of Fort Benton, Montana, they passed through rolling countryside which Lewis described as "a most beautiful and level plain of great extent" reaching 50 or 60 miles, within which "were infinitely more buffalo than I had ever before witnessed at a view." Still busy attempting to determine the course of the Missouri, they did not mention buffalo again until June 17, when Clark wrote of "innumerable numbers of buffalo" and of some buffalo drowned in the rapid currents of the river near what is known today as Crooked Falls in Cascade County, Montana, north of Malmstrom Air Force Base. On that day 2 buffalo were taken for food and for their skins.

The expedition then reached the "great Cataract" of the river—the series of falls known as the Great Falls of the Missouri—on June 18. Here they saw buffalo swimming across the river above the falls, some of which were "drawn into the rapids and with difficulty made shore half drowned." One was shot for food. Clark again observed "immense herds" in "every direction." They saw the herds of buffalo again the next day, June 19. They were near Giant Springs, the largest fresh water spring in North America, where about 134 thousand gallons of fresh water are released each minute from deep, limestone caverns. The springs are now surrounded by cement walkways and foot bridges and protected by a quiet park at the northwest end of Great Falls, Montana. During the month that they spent portaging around the Great Falls, Lewis and Clark were often within view of large numbers of buffalo, but these appeared and then moved off, only to return repeatedly.

The expedition then camped at the Great Falls and began their long portage, which took from June 21 to July 14. Buffalo continued to be abundant near the falls. On June 21, Lewis noted that "immense quantities of buffalo" were coming to the river to drink "as usual." On June 30, Clark wrote that he thought they could see 10,000 buffalo in a single view.

On July 3, the expedition had completed the portage around the Great Falls and celebrated, drinking the last of the liquor and dining on bacon, beans, dumplings, and buffalo. Lewis wrote that "the buffalo seem to have withdrawn themselves from the neighborhood," but the animals were "still abundant about the falls." On that day, one buffalo and two pronghorn were killed.

They saw a large herd near the camp on July 5, and 3 were taken after a chase for food and skins, which they intended to use to cover their baggage. The "buffalo again appeared in great numbers about our camp and seem to be moving down the river," Lewis wrote. About their behavior, he wrote on that day that "it is somewhat remarkable that although you may see ten or a dozen herds of buffalo distinctly scattered and many miles distant, yet if they are undisturbed by pursuit, they will all be traveling in one direction."

Men sent to hunt buffalo on July 7 returned with three skins, reporting that the buffalo "had gone further down the river" and away from the route of the expedition. Again on the 8th three buffalo were shot. The hunters told Clark that the "immense herds" had "almost entirely disappeared" and were believed to have gone down river. The expedition was passing out of buffalo country.

Again on July 15 they reported many herds of buffalo, just as they were beginning to travel after the portage around the falls. They had reached the Smith River near the present town of Ulm, Montana, which today is a small settlement with a few grain elevators, about 11 miles up river from Great Falls. After this they did leave the buffalo country and saw no more of these animals for the rest of their outbound journey. The sightings of buffalo by the Lewis and Clark expedition thus ended when they were not far up river from the Great Falls on the Missouri, about to begin their climb through the mountains, and within the transition between mountain forests and the open plains that were the habitat of the buffalo. This seems to mark the western limit of the species for Lewis and Clark.

WHAT WE LEARN ABOUT THE BUFFALO FROM LEWIS AND CLARK

From the encounters of the expedition with buffalo, we come to understand that the herds were not a continuous, uniform, homogenous population filling the plains, but occurred sporadically, in bunches, often very large bunches. The buffalo were an important food source for the expedition and, as we see from the journals, were sought out wherever possible, even in the dangerous middle of winter when frostbite threatened. It is unlikely that days would have passed when the immense herds were seen and not noted by Lewis, Clark, or one of their sergeants. Their encounters with these animals were surprisingly few, given their need and desire to find them, although one might say that this was affected by the expedition's dependence on rivers for transportation in the prairie country that was the habitat of the buffalo.

Although everyone who writes about the buffalo refers to immense herds, the animals seemed to have been organized into smaller units of 5 to 50 animals that may have functioned as family units, much as one finds in herds of elephants in Africa, but with large numbers of these groups seeking the same resources and therefore appearing together on the landscape.

American mythology paints the plains filled with buffalo, and indeed the evidence available suggests that there were herds of almost unbelievable numbers. But what we learn from Lewis and Clark's accounts of the buffalo is somewhat different. When they came upon

115

buffalo, they found great numbers, but these encounters were relatively few, tending to group into periods of a week or two during which the expedition remained in sight of or in hunting distance of one of the herds, and the two, men and buffalo, accompanied each other for only a short while. This was true even during the five winter months they spent with the Mandans in North Dakota, when buffalo meat was badly needed and they hunted for them whenever the weather allowed. There were only 60 days during the outward journey that the expedition reported any live buffalo. These reports occurred mainly in sets of consecutive days that fall into 17 separate episodes from June 6, 1804, to July 15, 1805, a period of 404 days. They saw buffalo on only 15 percent of the days they were in buffalo country.

Although buffalo were still abundant and still roamed free over many thousands of miles when Lewis and Clark passed their way, the geographic range of the buffalo had been considerably reduced even by that time, compared to the range when the first European settlements were established in North America. Their first sighting took place once they were west of Columbia, Missouri—past the settlements, where buffalo had been eliminated earlier. This was the characteristic pattern: buffalo were hunted to local extinction or driven out as farms with fences and grazing lands with European cattle were established. The plow and the buffalo were considered incompatible.

A "DARK BLANKET" OF BUFFALO

There are two immensely impressive facts about the buffalo: the great abundance of these animals before exploitation, and the speed with which these animals were brought to the edge of extinction. These two features of their history were encapsulated by Mari Sandoz, the Nebraska native and one of America's great twentieth-century prairie writers, in her book *The Buffalo Hunters*.

The buffalo continued to be abundant on the Great Plains for decades after Lewis and Clark. All the early writers tell of immense herds of buffalo in such terms, but rarely do they count the buffalo to give us an estimate of their abundance. An exception was General Isaac I. Stevens who, on July 10, 1853, was surveying for the transcontinental railway in North Dakota. He and his men climbed a high hill and saw "for a great distance ahead every square mile" having "a herd of buffalo upon it." He wrote that "their number was variously estimated by the members of the party—some as high as half a million. I do not think it any exaggeration to set it down at 200,000."

One of the better attempts to estimate the number of buffalo in a herd was by Colonel R. I. Dodge, who took a wagon from Fort Zarah to Fort Larded on the Arkansas River in May 1871, a distance of 34 miles. For at least 25 of those miles he found himself in a "dark blanket" of buffalo. Dodge estimated that there were 480,000 in the mass of animals he saw in one day. At one point he and his men traveled to the top of a hill, where he estimated that he could see six to ten miles, and from that high point there appeared to be a single solid mass of buffalo extending over 25 miles. At 10 animals per acre, not a particularly high density, there would have been between 2.7 and 8 million animals.

Just before and just after the Civil War "there were always buffalo somewhere" along the tracks of Kansas Pacific Railroad. In the fall of 1868, "a train traveled 120 miles between Ellsworth and Sheridan through a continuous, browsing herd, packed so thick that the engineer had to stop several times, mostly because the buffaloes would scarcely get off the tracks for the whistle and the belching smoke." That spring a train had been delayed for eight hours while a single herd passed "in one steady, unending stream." We can use such experiences to set bounds on the possible number of animals seen. At the largest extreme, we can assume that the train bisected a circular herd with a diameter of 120 miles. Such a herd would cover 11,310 square miles or more than 7 million acres. Suppose people exaggerated the density of the buffalo, and there were only 10 per acre—a moderate density of a herd. This single herd would have numbered 70 million animals!

Some might say that this estimate is probably too high, because the herd would more likely form a broad, meandering, migrating line, rather than a circle. However, the observations by General Stevens and Colonel Dodge suggest that buffalo would spread out over a wide area and did not tend to form a single, narrow line. Suppose that line more or less followed the railroad track and only gave an appearance of covering the entire countryside. Even so, the herd must have been wide enough to appear to occupy much of the country on either side of the train; otherwise the crew might have tried to scare away a very narrow herd. Let's suppose the herd occupied a distance a half mile on either side of the train, so that the train passed through a square mile of buffalo for each mile traveled. This would have given the appearance of "innumerable" animals, but in patches, more along the lines that Lewis and Clark reported. A half-mile is also a reasonable distance for people to see buffalo and believe they are surrounded by them to a vast distance. In this case, the herd would have covered 120 square miles or 76,800 acres. At 10 animals per acre, the moderate density we used before, there would have been 768,000 animals—about three-quarters of a million animals in a single herd. This represents the lowest extreme of our estimate.

There were many herds, and even if the numbers of a single herd were at the low end of our estimate, the total number of buffalo must have been in the tens of millions. Many writers estimate the total abundance at about 40 to 50 million. In 1867 the guesses of the number of buffalo between the Platte River and the Concho River in Texas ranged from as high as 50 million to as low as 15 million. But as should be clear from what I have discussed in the previous chapter, the methods for estimating numbers were not much better than the back-of-the-envelope calculation I have just made here.

Although the range of our estimates is great, the impression remains the same—there were huge numbers of buffalo in the American West even as late as 1868—numbering in the tens of millions and probably 50 million or more. Ominously, that same year the Kansas Pacific Railroad advertised a "Grand Railway Excursion and Buffalo Hunt." Some say that many hunters believed that the buffalo could never be brought to extinction, because there were so many of them. This belief was common about all living resources of America throughout the nineteenth century. The same was said about the great forests of white pine in Michigan, in the Paul Bunyan country. It was part of the American myth of incredible, seemingly infinite resources of the new continent.

AMERICA'S HISTORY OF EXPLOITATION OF ITS LIVING RESOURCES

The history of the buffalo and the effects of people of European descent on this species epitomize the general history of the relationship between environment and Western civilization in North America. This

119

history can be divided roughly into five periods. The first, the period of discovery, began with the arrival of Europeans. During this period, the geographic ranges of many species were reduced, but the impact on entire species, although large in certain cases, was small overall in comparison to the events that followed.

The second period, of intense exploitation, began at different times for different resources, but generally began between the end of the War of 1812 and the end of the Civil War; it extended until the First World War. During this period, natural biological resources of the continent were extracted as if they were mineral resources—unrenewable and not expected to be otherwise.

A third period, of awakening conservation, began at the end of World War I and lasted until the 1960s. Exploitation continued, but was accompanied by the first attempts at professional management of forests, fisheries, and wildlife, and the beginnings of a national conservation movement—a political and social movement that had its intellectual antecedents in the nineteenth century. During this period, the goal of management was single-purposed—to maximize the production of a single resource for harvest, as if wild, living resources were a farm crop or could be treated as one.

A fourth period, environmentalism, began in the 1960s. Public awareness of environmental degradation and the decline of wild, living resources grew, spread, and became established, and there was a rapid development of environmentalism as a political and social movement accompanied by the passage of landmark legislation to protect and conserve the environment—such as the Clean Water Act of 1970, the Marine Mammal Protection Act of 1972, and the Endangered Species Act of 1973.

A fifth, unnamed period may be beginning now, with our nascent

120

attempts to humanize the previously strident environmentalism and to find a better balance between the perceived need to use natural resources and the perceived destruction of those resources. The American buffalo illustrates each historic stage.

Lewis and Clark passed through buffalo country during what I have called the first period of the relationship between people of European descent and the environment of North America—the period of discovery. The buffalo, like all the other natural resources of the New World that were found to have some utilitarian benefit, were discovered, observed as curiosities, shot as the occasion arose for food or hide or simply to remove them where they seemed to be obstacles to the establishment of a European way of life. During this period, the rate of destruction of the buffalo was much slower than it would be later on, but even so the species was eliminated from a large part of its geographic range. The number of buffalo hides that could be processed was limited by the abilities of the Indians who did most of this work.

Cabeza de Vaca, the famous Spanish castaway who spent eight years with the Indians in the 1530s and later recounted his experiences when he returned to Spain, saw buffalo in southern Texas in the 1530s. In 1612, explorer Samuel Argoll sailed on the Chesapeake Bay, and saw "a great store of cattle" which were "heavy, slow, and not so wild as other beasts in the wilderness." This description suggests he had seen buffalo. In 1701 there was an attempt to domesticate buffalo in a new settlement on the James River in Virginia. Near Roanoke, Virginia, buffalo were common at a salt lick until the mid-eighteenth century. One herd was reported in southwestern Georgia in 1686. Buffalo were killed off in Georgia by 1780, in South Carolina by 1775. By the time of the Louisiana Purchase in 1803, buffalo no longer were found in the states of the United States of America, having been eliminated east of the

Mississippi. But some evidence suggests that the buffalo had only recently reached the East Coast when Europeans began to settle and explore that area.

These records and others suggest that before the arrival of Europeans, buffalo may have occupied one-third of North America, reaching their northern limit in the boreal forests of Canada, their southwestern limits in the chaparral of southwestern Texas. Buffalo were found in Canada as far north as Great Slave Lake in the Northwest Territories, to latitude 60 degrees north, just north of the present Wood Buffalo National Park, which lies in northern Alberta and the boundary of the Northwest Territories. Fossils of bison, some as old as 40,000 B.C., have been found from New Jersey to California.

The second environmental period, the period of intense exploitation, began for the buffalo in 1864 when buffalo robes and tanned hides began to be shipped from St. Louis eastward. New technologies made it possible to increase the use of buffalo. Modern rifles made it easy to kill them. Trains made transport of hunters and hides easier. A new tanning process, developed in Germany, allowed the treatment of many more hides, and the finished hides provided a better, more desirable grade of leather. The European market opened for these improved hides. Railroads made possible massive transportation of many hides, creating a huge market.

With the increased value of the hides, many people began to hunt buffalo. "The rush of new hunters to the Kansas plains resembled the stampede to a new gold strike," Haines wrote in his book *The Buffalo*. The animals were seen as a commodity, like gold, to be removed as quickly as possible for individual profit. Even railway construction crews spent their winters, when it was not possible to work on the railroads, hunting buffalo. An economic crash of 1873, which had a number of environmental ramifications, made for hard times for the homesteaders in Kansas, Nebraska, North and South Dakota, and many began to hunt buffalo. Although many saw buffalo as a way to riches, ironically few of the buffalo hunters got rich.

The Civil War had its effect on the buffalo. During the war, buffalo hides were used by the military, increasing the market. After the war, army veterans, skilled in shooting rifles, headed west, where they used these skills against the buffalo. A major increase in exploitation of many of America's biological resources occurred just after the Civil War. As new lands opened up in the West, displaced Southerners found their way westward, and our nation shifted away from war to the development of transcontinental railways and the settlement of the West. Wild Bill Hickok became one of the major buffalo hunters, along with Buffalo Bill Cody. In 1869 Hickok was asked to guide a party of ladies and gentlemen from Massachusetts to hunt buffalo.

The homesteaders and railroad men did not know the best way to hunt or to handle the hides. They were not efficient in skinning the hides or in handling them afterwards. In the high years of 1872 and 1873, so many hides were taken that prices dropped to as little as 25 cents. As would happen many times around the world, people with a marginal livelihood encountering a rapidly expanding market for a biological resource contributed considerably to its demise.

Records of the number of buffalo killed were neither organized nor all that well kept, but enough are available to give us some idea of the number taken. In 1870 about two million buffaloes were killed. In 1872, one company in Dodge City handled 200,000 hides. Estimates based on the sum of reports from such companies and guesses at how many more would have been taken by small operators and not reported, suggest that about 1,500,000 hides were shipped in 1872 and again in

1873. In these years, buffalo hunting was the main economic activity in Kansas. The Indians were also killing large numbers of buffalo for their own use and for trade. Estimates range to three and a half million buffalo killed a year during the 1850s.

The killing of the buffalo was also done as part of the fight against the Indians, to eliminate them by cutting off their food supply. In 1865, General Mitchell, in response to Indian attacks of the fall of 1864, set fires to drive away the Indians and the buffalo, killing vast numbers of animals. Colonel R. I. Dodge was quoted in 1867 to have said, "Kill every buffalo you can. Every buffalo dead is an Indian gone."

We tend to think that environmentalism is only a late-twentieth-century social and political movement, but to the contrary, Mari Sandoz writes that after the Civil War there were "angry protestations in every legislature" over the slaughter of the buffalo. Much earlier, in 1776, a book—*The Natural History of Florida*—had condemned "the wanton destruction of 'this excellent beast.' " In the 1870s, laws were passed to outlaw professional buffalo "hide men"—men who made their living shooting buffalo for their hide only—in Montana, Idaho, and Wyoming. Congress made some attempts to limit the hide hunters.

When the U.S. Biological Survey sent George Grinnell to survey the herds along the Platte River, he estimated that there were only 500,000 buffalo there, and that at the present rate of killing the animals would not last long.

As late as the spring of 1883 a herd of an estimated 75,000 crossed the Yellowstone River near Miles City, Montana, but fewer than 5,000 reached the border. By the end of that year—only 15 years after the Kansas Pacific train was delayed for eight hours by a huge herd of buffalo—only a thousand or so buffalo could be found, 256 in captivity and about 835 roaming the plains. A short time later, there were only 50 buffalo wild on the plains.

The incredibly rapid demise of these animals demonstrates the power of nineteenth-century technology when put to a destructive purpose, and illustrates the general effects of the second major period in the relationship between Western civilization's people and the environmental resources of North America.

Other big game animals of North America have undergone similar declines. The estimates of the presettlement abundance of elk are on the order of 10 million; the Audubon Society estimates the present abundance at about 500,000. The period of exploitation continued to the beginning of World War I. During that period most of the original forests of the East and Great Lakes States were cut, the great whales were exploited by Yankee whalers from New Bedford, and the elephant seal and the sea otter were hunted for their fur until they too, like the buffalo, were thought to be extinct or so near extinction that the remaining should be left for museums.

Many people before me have told the story of the demise of America's living resources during the nineteenth and early part of the twentieth century. It is not my purpose to merely add to the lament. Rather, it is to assert clearly that this kind of destruction in America was the conscious and deliberate result of people who were opening up the land, who saw the land and its forms of life primarily as commodities or obstructions to be removed once and for all, and only rarely as what we refer to today as "resources"—things to use and also to maintain. We, who inherit this history of destruction, if not by direct ancestry, then by participation in a society whose ancestry and history it is, also inherit a major and difficult question: what can we do now and in the future so that such destruction does not continue, and so that we can, wherever possible, recover and restore these resources for the civilization of the next millennia?

Today, this same process is at work in the destruction of rain forests.

In Costa Rica, for example, there are about 275 logging operations. All but a handful are very small—a man and his truck and a few helpers—who barely survive on what they can obtain, and sell at the lowest price. Their situation is much like the poor homesteaders in Kansas in the 1870s; such economic situations drive the prices down so low that those who seek to harvest the resource and also sustain it cannot afford to do so.

It is also clear that once a biological resource such as the buffalo is brought down to very low numbers, people may continue to scavenge them. Even at the end, when the buffalo were believed to be doomed to extinction, hunters went out to try to shoot the last ones as trophies. Knowledge of this exploitive legacy is behind every modern environmental conflict, and the resolution of these conflicts must take this history into account.

The history of the buffalo is especially important for those who are in the businesses of utilizing biological resources today. The strong reaction of environmental groups to any new utilization or to any increased one, or even to maintaining a past level of harvest, may perplex those whose livelihood depends on the resource and are unaware of the larger historical context, because they see that resource as a single factor with its own importance, independent of all others. As with the buffalo, high harvest rates, even though experienced over a comparatively short time, become familiar and may be accepted as normal by those who live off these resources. In contrast, those conservationists with an historical perspective view such current harvests as continuations of the errors of exploitation that dominated America's use of wild, living resources in the past. This leads to a "fortress mentality"—where the fight against use of a wild, living resource is seen as a last stand against a long history of exploitation and destruction worldwide. Those who defend the environment are defending it against its past and for its future, not merely for its present condition. From this point of view, the present possible decline of salmon in the Pacific Northwest of North America becomes a part of a long history worldwide of overfishing and habitat destruction. The continual elimination of salmon from rivers had become part of European civilization, from the European coast of the Atlantic, to the Atlantic coast of North America. So too, from this point of view, do the present cutting of forests in the Pacific Northwest and in tropical rain forests in Asia, Africa, and Latin America become the latest episodes in a 4,000-year-old history of the clearing of forests, a history that has been integral to the spread of civilization.

A *momentum* of resource exploitation provides the background to present conflicts. The solution to any one problem raises the central dilemma of the relationship between civilized, technological human beings and their living resources. From this larger perspective, we realize that our task is not simply to correct each small, local, recent problem, but to find a completely different way of doing things, one that moves away from 4,000 years of history. We learn from Lewis and Clark's encounters with buffalo, and with the encounters of those who came before and after, that even immensely abundant living resources, seemingly beyond all our ability to count them, are vulnerable to human technology. This is the lesson of the huge patches of buffalo that moved slowly across the landscape, feeding the expedition that used Lewis's newly designed rifle, in many instances the first encounter of this wild resource with modern technology.

CHAPTER SEVEN

Wolves, People, and Biological Diversity

Yes, I'n tell you about wolves. My partner and me, we went up in the Sawtooths and got two elk and was headun home when we looked around and seen eleven wolves after us. We cut a elk loose and they et that. In another mile we give them the other elk and they et that. Then we left our horses and run for it, and they came up and et the horses. I said to my partner that I would rest and shoot a wolf and then run while he was restun and then he could shoot one. So we did. I shot one and the wolves pounced on it while I was runnin; and then my partner, he shot one. Well, we kept that up till we had shot ten of them. Then my partner yelled, "God a-mighty, Jim, look!" I looked behind me and there right on our tails was the biggest wolf anybody ever laid eyes on. He was as big as a house. And then I remembered he'd have to be that big, seeing as how he'd et two elk, two horses and ten wolves.

LEWIS AND CLARK AS NATURALISTS

Lewis and Clark contributed considerably to knowledge of the biological diversity of North America. As I mentioned earlier, one of Jefferson's charges to the expedition was to obtain and send back botanical and zoological specimens for scientific collections. To ensure that the expedition would be a scientific one as well as one that sought an overland route to the Pacific, Jefferson had sent Lewis to Philadelphia before the beginning of the trip. There Lewis learned from the experts of the day how to make botanical and zoological collections, how to write scientific descriptions, and how to prepare specimens for storage and transportation. Both he and Clark were outdoorsmen, familiar with wildlife and with the preparation of skins. Both were excellent naturalists, with curiosity about their surroundings and abilities to see what was new and different. To fulfill Jefferson's charge to them, they usually shot or otherwise caught an individual of each species of wildlife, and measured and described the specimen. They collected sample plants and pressed them; their plant collection still exists at the Philadelphia Academy of Natural Sciences. They saw and were the first to describe many species of animals and plants unknown to science. Their observations are therefore helpful to us in considering one of the environmental issues that receives the greatest attention in the media today—conservation of endangered species, and, more generally, conservation of biological diversity.

Lewis and Clark's first zoological specimen was a badger, previously unknown to western science, which they obtained on July 30, 1804. It was so unlike anything they had seen that it took comparisons with a number of mammals for them to complete their description. Clark wrote that Joseph Field killed an animal that fed mainly on prairie dogs, and to this purpose burrowed in the ground. He described the animal as having a shape and size "like that of a beaver, his head, mouth &c. is like a dog with its ears cut off, his tail and hair like that of a ground hog, something longer and lighter, his internals like a hog's." He wrote that the hair was like that of a bear, with a "white streak from its nose to its shoulders."

Among their biological credits is the naming of and the first written description of the mule deer, entered into their journals on May 10, 1805. They also provided the first written descriptions of the bobcat and western gray squirrel. They were the first to record a number of new species of animals and plants which have since become extinct. On June 26, 1804, Clark wrote in his journal that he saw many "Parrot Queets," apparently the Carolina parakeet, now extinct; this was the first observation of that species west of the Mississippi.

They found the rattlesnake, garter snake, the horned lizard, and various snails. West of the Rockies Lewis and Clark encountered 33 species of land mammals, as well as the "leathern-winged bat," 30 species of land birds, and 26 species of aquatic birds. Of marine life, they listed the sea otter, seals, porpoises, and whales; skate, flounder, several kinds of salmon, anchovy, clams, periwinkles, cockle (a thin clam), and jellyfish, as well as some kinds of freshwater shellfish.

130

In spite of their interest and responsibility to report to President Jefferson about the animals and plants, and despite the keenness of their observations, Lewis and Clark were more than two months into their journey before they saw a gray or timber wolf. It was on July 21, 1804, when they had reached the mouth of the Platte River and were in the midst of the tall grass prairie, and away from the settled lands of what would become the state of Missouri. That evening they saw and heard calls of the "big wolf," the term they used to distinguish the timber wolf from the coyote, which they called the "small" or "prairie wolf." From St. Louis to the Platte, the wolf seemed to have vanished. Feared and hated by settlers and traders, wolves no doubt were often shot by them. Modern scientific studies show that wolves are shy of people and would have fled settled areas anyway. In fact, there is no known case in North America of an unprovoked wolf attacking a human being and no recorded human death caused by a wolf.

We could consider the justifications for conservation of endangered species in terms of many of the species first described by Lewis and Clark, but it is most instructive to pick the wolf, because it has been such a powerful negative symbol for many people. If we can justify the conservation of wolves, then it should be much easier to justify the conservation of the warm and cuddly, and the elegant and beautiful, eagles and whooping cranes; and even easier to justify the conservation of those that we want to harvest and have commercial value, like salmon and caribou.

Although wolves have been a symbol of power among some cultures, the desire to conserve wolves, and strong actions to push for their conservation, are relatively new in western civilization. People have hated wolves throughout most of Western history. Ancient Greek and Roman writers, including Aristotle and Plutarch, mention the evil and dangerous nature of the wolf. In Dante's *Inferno*, the wolf represents human greed. The wolf also represents a powerful symbol of the character of wild nature. In its wariness of people, the wolf epitomizes our predominant contemporary image of nature: nature as separate from human beings and human beings as divorced from nature. Where we are, there are no wolves; where the wolf lives, there is wilderness.

Occasionally the wolf represents a symbol of good, as in the story of the female wolf who was supposed to have fed Romulus and Remus, who then founded Rome. And not all cultures share the western civilization dislike of wolves. Some American Indian tribes had wolf clans, considering the wolf to be a fetish and a "brother."

Because of the ancient symbolic meaning to people, wolves, perhaps more than any other large animal of the American West, force us to ask why should we save endangered species, why we should expend large sums and restrict land use, hunting, fishing, and other activities on behalf of certain species.

In contrast to the evil image of the wolf, the big predatory cats generally evoke admiration, with lions appearing on many European crests and "lion-hearted" meaning a good quality. I don't remember seeing the term "wolf-hearted" in any literature of Western civilization, but if it does appear somewhere, one would not expect it to be a compliment.

Bounties for killing wolves existed in Europe before the European settlement of the New World. In North America, bounties for killing wolves predate the founding of the United States. The first bounty law was passed in 1630 by Massachusetts; in 1632 a similar law was passed in Virginia. Hatred of wolves continued to be common among early European settlers of the American West. The destruction of wolves in the United States took place in part as a result of the spread of cattle ranching, because ranchers believed that wolves were dangerous to livestock. Federal predator-control laws, encouraging the killing of wolves and providing bounties for their carcasses, were first passed in 1915, when it was a common belief that wolves and mountain lions had only destructive effects on wildlife. Most populations of wolves in the United States were destroyed rapidly as a result. Most of the wolves were gone by 1925, only ten years after passage of the first federal predator control law. As recently as 1970, 30 states still provided bounties for killing wolves, including some states in which there were no wolves left to kill.

Attitudes toward the wolf began to change after World War II. Aldo Leopold wrote eloquently about the possible ecological importance of wolves in his classic book *A Sand County Almanac*, first published in 1949. Programs to protect the wolf from extinction began in the United States in the 1960s, accompanying the widespread changes in attitudes toward the environment and the beginning of the modern environmental social and political movement. In 1965, Michigan passed a law to protect wolves, which at that time were known only to survive in that state on Isle Royale National Park and to number somewhere between 20 and 40 animals. In 1967, Wisconsin passed a similar law, although there were no wolves in that state to protect. The 1973 U.S. Federal Endangered Species Act provided much more substantial protection for wolves, as it did for all species listed as endangered and threatened. As a consequence of the Endangered Species Act, the U.S. Fish and Wildlife Service established recovery teams in the 1970s for the conservation of wolves.

The amount of effort spent today to conserve the wolf would probably surprise most early settlers of North America, who feared and hated these predators and made up tall tales about them, like the story of the two men supposedly chased by wolves quoted at the beginning of this chapter.

Following their standard objective reporting style, Lewis and Clark

133

record their encounters with wolves in typically neutral notes about sightings, abundances, and actions of the wolves. As the folk tale quoted at the beginning of the chapter suggests, this was quite unusual in recorded anecdotes. More typical is the account of Snowshoe Thompson, who lived in the western mountains in the second half of the nineteenth century. The only time he was ever frightened during his travels through the western mountains, he wrote, was when he met a pack of wolves in Hope Valley in 1857. "In my childhood in Norway, I had heard so many stories about the ferocity of wolves that I feared them more than any other wild animal." He came upon a pack of wolves feeding on a carcass. As he approached them, the wolves came toward him "in single file" and sat down in a line to watch him. This gave him "cold chills." When he reached them, they began to howl. "I thought it meant my death. The awful cry ran across the silent valley, was echoed by the hills, and re-echoed far away among the surrounding country." He expected the pack to attack him, but they only sat and watched him. He attributed his survival to his own presence of mind, but a modern wildlife expert on wolves might attribute the events to wolf pack behavior—a well-organized pack, alert, curious, watched the man pass and sent up a warning call. Snowshoe Thompson's account mixes childhood stories and strong emotional reactions in his tale of his meeting with North American wolves. Lewis and Clark's journal entries, in contrast, are cool and collected, focused on what they observed and not what they might have been told in myth and folktale. This is why their journals are so valuable to us as we seek the real character of nature before it was changed by European civilization, and why they are so useful to consider in the issue of the conservation of endangered species and biological diversity.

Lewis and Clark's encounters with wolves were infrequent; after their first sighting they saw them only two more times once they had crossed the Platte River and before they reached the land of the Mandan Indians near what is now Bismarck, North Dakota, in late October 1804, where they spent their first winter. Rarely did they see wolves in any abundance. The members of the expedition saw the timber wolf occasionally throughout that first winter and into the next year, until they reached the Columbia River in eastern Washington in the summer of 1805; after that they saw them no more until they returned to the plains.

In their second encounter, Lewis and Clark saw wolves where there were few other animals, a unique occurrence. This happened on August 21, 1804, when they saw wolves on sand beaches along the Missouri River near the mouth of the Big Sioux River, three miles upstream from Floyd's River, named by Lewis and Clark in honor of Sergeant Floyd, who died just south of this location and just a few miles south of the modern city of Sioux City, Iowa. Perhaps the wolves had come down to the water to drink.

The third encounter of the expedition with wolves, which took place on September 15, about a month after the previous one, was more typical. One of the sergeants went by land to follow the White River, a tributary of the Missouri, upstream. About 12 miles upstream he saw "great quantities of buffalo, as well as deer and villages of prairie dogs, near which were wolves." This was the first indication to the expedition that wolves typically followed the buffalo.

Three days later they saw large wolves "very numerous" with buffalo, elk, antelopes, along with eastern deer "in great abundance," mule deer, porcupines, rabbits, and "barking-squirrels," their term for prairie dogs. They assumed, but did not see, that the wolves fed on these small rodents as well as on the larger animals.

Several weeks passed before they saw wolves again. On October 6, 1804, men from the expedition sent out to hunt, sighted two wolves near where they had shot an elk and where they saw many water birds —geese, swans, brants, gulls, plovers, and various kinds of ducks. Two weeks later, on October 19, the expedition arrived at a lake and saw along the shore "52 herds of buffalo and three of elk at a single view" and some wolves. The abundant wildlife continued the next day, including elk, deer, goats, buffalo. By this time, Lewis and Clark had begun to get the general picture. "Wolves follow their [prey's] movements and feed upon those which die by accident or which are too poor to keep pace with the herd," the journals record. Afterwards, the journals repeatedly refer to wolves as the "usual attendants" of the big game. In this way, the wolf was different in its activities from the grizzly, which the expedition often encountered away from other animals or, if near them, usually along water courses used by many animals.

After the expedition settled in late October 1804 for its first winter, fewer opportunities arose to observe wolves. The cold weather and the scarcity of food focused the efforts of the expedition on survival more than observation, and on indoor rather than outdoor activities. As I explained in the chapter about buffalo, during this winter the members of the expedition went out primarily to hunt for food. After October 19, 1804, they did not see wolves again until December 7, 1804, when they were living in their cabins near the Mandan Villages. On that day Captain Clark joined a group of Mandans hunting buffalo. "Whatever is left out at night," he wrote of the buffalo killed, "falls to the share of the wolves, who are the constant and numerous attendants of the buffalo." They saw wolves in January 1805 and once again in February, and then reported no more wolves during the winter with the Mandans.

The next spring, soon after they left their first wintering quarters, the members of the expedition began to see wolves again. On April 29, 1805, when they were passing the mouth of the Yellowstone River and near the mouth of Big Muddy Creek, they found themselves "surrounded with deer, elk, buffalo, antelopes, and their companions the wolves, which have become more numerous and make great ravages among them." Again, a week later, on May 5, their journals record that "Buffalo, elk, and goats or antelopes feeding in every direction" and "a great number of wolves." The next day they reached the mouth of the Milk River, a tributary of the Missouri and the river that flows through the ancient, preglacial valley formerly occupied by the Missouri itself. "The upland is perfectly naked" they wrote, and "as usual, we are surrounded by buffalo, elk, common and black-tailed deer, beaver, antelopes, and wolves." They saw well-fed wolves near buffalo carcasses on May 29, in what is now the Upper Missouri Wild and Scenic River area.

It was several weeks before they saw wolves again, on June 3, when they had camped and were trying to determine which of two rivers was the true Missouri, the experiences I talked about in chapter 3. Here they "had a very extensive prospect of the surrounding country. On every side it was spread into one vast plain, covered with verdure, in which innumerable herds of buffalo were roaming, attended by their enemies, the wolves." On June 12, Lewis traveled through "a handsome, open, bottom [ground] with cottonwood" and in a three-mile walk climbed a ridge and saw below him the plains and the Rocky Mountains beyond, and on the plains "immense herds of buffalo," antelopes, mule-deer, and "some wolves." Similar observations of vast quantities of buffalo with wolves following were recorded on June 17. Three weeks later, on July 5, they killed two wolves when they were near a large herd of buffalo. Their last observation of wolves occurred on July 7, when once again the wolves were following the buffalo herds.

NATURE'S MACHINERY AND THE CONSERVATION OF WOLVES

Now that we know the experiences of the expedition with the timber wolf, it is useful to step back and ask again why we should conserve the wolf. This question raises the general and widely discussed issue of biological diversity, an issue that appears more and more frequently in newspapers and on television. In its broadest context, the issue concerns the conservation of all forms of life on the Earth, and not only the conservation of the diversity of species, but also the conservation of genetic diversity and diversity of habitats.

There are four kinds of answers to the question why should we help save wolves from extinction, known as utilitarian, ecological, moral, and aesthetic. The utilitarian answer means that a species has some direct benefit to people. Many plants and animals were directly important to the expedition and to the Indians. When they lacked other sources of protein, Lewis and Clark ate dog meat, which they obtained from the Indians. For most of the trip, however, buffalo, deer, elk, and pronghorn were essential foods, and salmon was important once the expedition crossed the Continental Divide. These animals had a direct utilitarian value: survival.

Lewis and Clark were alert to the utilitarian benefits of the animals and plants of the West. The beaver, of course, was well known and was heavily exploited in North America, its fur popular in America and Europe. One of the purposes of the expedition was to determine the potential for fur trade with the Indians of the West, and therefore Lewis and Clark carefully recorded the distribution and abundance of this animal, as well as its lodges, dams, and tree cutting. Their observations are so good that they tell us that the beaver was once plentiful on streams which, as one writer has put it, "have not know them for so many years that it is hard to believe they were ever present."

Not only were the big game a principal food for the expedition and the Indians, but there were also important medicinal plants. On May 27, 1804, Lewis collected a plant known in Kentucky as yellow root which he said was a remedy for sore eyes—a disease which he described as causing high fevers and headache as well as violent inflammation of the eyes. Lewis described how to prepare the plant for use: you wash the roots and let them dry in the shade, then break them into pieces about one half inch long and put them in a bottle two-thirds full of the root. The bottle is filled with water (preferably rain water) and left to stand, with occasional shaking, for six hours. The water is then applied to the eyes. And as I mentioned in the first chapter, the medicines that Lewis brought on the trip were either simple minerals or came from plants.

Even the grizzlies, which were so dangerous to the expedition, had a use—their hides were used by the expedition. In contrast to the grizzlies, the wolves, the other big mammalian predator commonly seen by the expedition, were neither of use nor a threat. If there were then or is now a reason to conserve wolves, it would seem to lie beyond some direct, practical benefit of the wolves to people. But since the wolves always followed the herds and, like human beings, hunted and ate the big grazers and browsers, the wolves might have some effect on buffalo, deer, elk, and pronghorns indirectly useful to us or important to nature. Wolves not only followed herds of bison, deer, and antelope, they also concentrated where there were kills of these animals, either due to some accident, a natural catastrophe, or hunting by people. Clearly, the wolves depended on their prey, but perhaps, because both prey and predator had persisted for a long time before the arrival of people of European descent, there was some dependence of the buffalo, elk, and deer on the wolf. Perhaps there was a connection through a system larger than any of these species alone. This suggests a second answer to why one would want to save wolves: a mechanistic one—that the wolves play some essential or important role in nature's machinery. This answer has to do with the effects of wolves on other animals, which might lead to a cascade of effects on other forms of life and even to effects on aspects of the environment. Scientists refer to such cascading effects as an effect on an ecological community or on an ecosystem.

While doing some of the initial work on this book, I found two newspaper reports published a day apart, one revealing that the belief in the powerful effect of wolves on their prey was alive and well in the daily news, the other revealing our contradictory feelings about wolves. The *Santa Barbara News Press*, dated July 2, 1993, reported that the U.S. Fish and Wildlife Service planned to reintroduce wolves into Yellowstone National Park, where they had been locally extinct for 60 years, as part of a plan to help conserve this endangered species. The next day, July 3, the *New York Times* reported that Alaska's Game Board announced that wolves could now be legally shot in that state from the ground, but that it would be illegal to track or kill them from the air. This decision was a compromise between the goal of conservationists to stop all hunting of wolves and the goal of hunters to shoot wolves from airplanes.

The rationale given by the Alaskan Game Board for allowing

wolves to be killed had to do with the effects of wolves on caribou, not with the wolves themselves. Once important food for northern Indians and Eskimos, caribou had become a popular sport-hunting target. Hunting of caribou had been stopped in 1991 because of concern with decline in their abundance. But in spite of the hunting ban, the herds had not recovered. Only 4,500 caribou remained out of 11,000 estimated to be present in 1989. Hunters claimed that wolves were eating too many caribou and claimed that wolves had to be killed to save the caribou herd. The hunters and the Alaskan Game Board argued that wolves were capable of having a large impact on the abundance of their prey. Interestingly, the number of wolves had also dropped precipitously during the same period, a fact they apparently ignored. Hunted at the rate of about 1,000 a year from airplanes and on the ground, the Alaskan wolf population had dropped from an estimated 10,700 in 1989 to between 5,000 and 7,000. The original plan had been to continue to allow hunting of wolves from airplanes, but a tourist boycott had been instituted in response to the state's plan to shoot wolves from the air. Hence the compromise Game Board decision.

The finding of the Alaskan Game Board was consistent with the concepts dominant and published in the science of ecology during much of the twentieth century. For a long time, this science accepted a theory that was supposed to explain the connection between predator and prey, and give an essential role to each. According to this theory (known as the Lotka-Volterra theory of predator-prey interactions), the prey species would increase uncontrollably—exponentially—without its predator. The prey population, let's say the deer, would grow so large that it would overeat its food supply and its population would diminish rapidly, perhaps leading to the local extinction of the species. Then, of course, the predator, say the wolves, would become extinct without prey to eat. According to this theory, the prey and predator together produced populations that followed exquisitely symmetric patterns. Either both populations would achieve a constant abundance and would remain at these abundances indefinitely, or the two would oscillate forever, exactly out of phase, like two guitar strings tuned to the same note and the second plucked exactly at the moment when the first reached its peak of vibration.

Living in a mechanical and electronic age, we seek such explanations and are comforted to find them. For the past two hundred years our civilization has experienced the power and success of the machine and, more recently, its electronic extension. Our lives are filled daily with the comfort of well-running machines; the steady humming of a well-tuned automobile taking us down the road; the steady, deep hum of jet engines outside the airplane that carries us from coast to coast; and at home, the steady rumble of the many electric motors that make our lives pleasant—the condenser in the refrigerator, the pump in the central heating system, the cooling fans in micro-computers. We accept the necessity that gear must mesh with gear; that piston must fit within cylinder; that there is a required purpose for the things under the hood of our cars, that each performs some function required for the whole.

By analogy, we hope to find that the wolves are required by the system within which they live, and by the prey on which they feed. Our lives are filled with such mechanisms, and we tend to believe that such mechanistic explanations are the real ones and the ones we must always find to make a persuasive argument. According to the Lotka-Volterra equations, the predator is a fine-tuned control mechanism to regulate, in a very precise sense, the abundance of the prey. The hypothetical predator is much like the prey's thermostat. If the prey population starts to overheat and gets too large, the predator population

142

increases too, responding to the need, and the greater number of predator kill more prey, thus bringing the population back to its balance point. If the opposite happens and the prey population drops below its balance point, then the predator adjusts. With less to eat, the predator has fewer offspring, and the abundance of predator declines, the predation declines, and the prey are able to increase back toward the balance point.

A long-term study of the timber wolf at Isle Royale National Park, and its principal prey there, the moose, sheds some light on this idea of control of the numbers of a prey by its predator. My first encounters with wolves occurred in the early 1970s on that island. For several decades Isle Royale was the major preserve for wolves east of the Mississippi in the United States. In the early 1970s there were about 40 wolves on the island. Their principal food was moose, but the wolves fed also on beaver and smaller mammals.

The wolves of Isle Royale are among the best studied large predators in North America; they were the subject of years of observation about pack behavior, begun and led for many years by Durwood Allen, a professor at Northwestern University. He and his students observed the wolves in the winter from a small, low-flying airplane. As long as no one shot at the wolves from the air, the wolves became accustomed to the machine and ignored it. Wolves are relatively easy to see from the air against the snow cover on the island, although much of the island was and is forested.

I had gone to Isle Royale with my colleague from Yale University, Peter Jordan, a wildlife expert who had worked there for many years, to study what factors might limit the numbers of moose—whether it could be wolves or might be some other characteristic of that wilderness. Moose are browsers—they eat the leaves and twigs of woody plants. Only occasionally—mainly in the spring—do they eat grass or herbs. During the summer they feed on flowering plants that grow in wetlands and in lakes and ponds, some with floating leaves, like pond lilies, some completely submerged, like potamageton, some with their roots in the mud below the water and their leaves and flowers emerging along the shore, like sedges and irises. Lacking upper front teeth, a moose pulls leaves from a tree or shrub, leaving behind the leaf stem. The stem takes about a week to dry up and fall off the tree or shrub. The moose leaves a week's record of its feeding habits. We had people working with us walk a line and count the number of stems without leaves. From this we measured how much of each tree and shrub species the moose on the island took. We collected samples of leaves and twigs of the woody plants, as well as dried feces of moose, and put all these samples in a Chevrolet carryall, which we drove back to New Haven, Connecticut. No doubt this would seem an odd professional scientific activity to most people. The shortest route from northern Michigan to southern Connecticut was through Canada, and on the first trip back we came to the Canadian boundary where a large sign said: "You must declare any unusual objects." We pulled the car off to the side and went into the office, where we showed the custom official a letter from the Isle Royale National Park ranger, stating that we were carrying scientific samples that consisted of leaves and twigs of woody plants and droppings of moose. The customs officer insisted on inspecting most of the bags to make sure this wasn't a ruse to smuggle in some illegal substance.

By walking lines chosen to fit in with a statistically valid sampling method, we could estimate the total take of vegetation by the moose during an entire year. Back at Yale, other colleagues measured the amount of essential chemical elements in these leaves and twigs, so that we knew how much calcium, magnesium, nitrogen, sodium, and other elements the moose were able to obtain. We analyzed moose tissue, urine, feces, hair, and hide so that we could estimate how much of each element a moose of each age lost each year. I developed a computer model of the moose population on the island, based on the many years of study of the numbers of these animals, the numbers dying, and the number born each year. From this model we could determine the amount of nutrients of each kind needed by the number born, and to replace all the elements lost by the entire live population. Comparing available chemical elements in the food to the amount of each needed by the population, we found that the moose were limited primarily by the amount of sodium that they could obtain. Flowering plants have no need for sodium and contain little. However, for some unknown reason, the water plants concentrate this element. Most of their sodium was supplied by the water plants the moose fed on during the summer. This seemed to explain why it was important for the moose to wade in the water.

Our study at Isle Royale suggested that wolves played a minor mechanistic role, if any, in controlling the population of the moose. Moose populations were *affected* by wolf predation—when there were many wolves, there were fewer moose. But the wolves did not *control* the abundance of moose in any exact way. Moose and wolf populations varied greatly during the 1970s and afterwards, but not in a way that would support a scientific argument that the wolves were a fine-tuned control of moose abundance, nor were these variations consistent with the old Lotka-Volterra theory that had the predator and prey varying in completely regular, but out-of-phase oscillations. The moose were limited ultimately not by the wolves but by simple table salt. Recent studies of other big game predators suggest that, while these animals may have some effect on the numbers of the animals on which they feed, they do not exert a strict control that brings the populations of prey into some kind of balance with their environment. I and others who have searched the available scientific literature have never found a case where a large mammalian predator actually functions as a precise controlling mechanism for its prey.

Although salt is something we take for granted today, it was a valuable trade commodity among primitive peoples. Lewis and Clark invested considerable energy to obtain salt once they reached the Pacific Ocean. During most of their second winter, which they spent near the mouth of the Columbia River, much effort was invested in making salt from sea water. They had their men walk several miles from their camp to the shore, where they maintained fires to boil sea water.

Modern engineering devices that are used to control machines—like an autopilot on an airplane—give us some insight into why a wolf might not be able to exert a precise control over its prey. For an autopilot to keep an airplane flying smoothly, without wandering continually around the intended course, it must be able to respond faster than the forces affecting the plane. A poorly designed autopilot might do the job in calm weather, but not in a storm or gusty winds. If the response time of the autopilot is slower or about the same as the rate of change in winds and other forces, the autopilot will get behind in its task; it may make the plane move left and right, up and down most of the time, or worse, it might even apply a correcting force at the wrong time, so the plane starts to get out of control. So it is with the wolf as a control device for moose. The generation time of a wolf is not all that different from that of a buffalo, elk, or deer. Although in a good year when prey are abundant, a wolf pack will have more pups survive and the population will grow, the response is not fast compared to the growth rate of the prey. The wolf population responds too slowly to control its prey precisely. It reminds me of the way my mother used to drive a car. She would speed up until the car was going a little too fast, then remove her foot from the accelerator and let the car slow down until it was going too slow; the car would continually be jolted fast and slow, fast and slow. In such a case the control response from eye to foot is a little too slow and there is a continual overcompensation. If all worked as in the theory, then there could be even, regular oscillations.

Although a pack of wolves may not be able to keep its prey at some single, exact number, it is possible for the wolves to have some regulating effect on the prey, dampening the rises and falls of the prey. The wolves may be able to kill enough moose so that a rapidly expanding moose population does not reach as large a number as would happen without the wolves. Starving moose, without a predator, might do more damage to their habitat than weakened moose killed quickly by wolves. If this happens, then the moose would do less damage to their habitat; when the moose population crashed from lack of food or other resources, then it might not decline to as low a number as it would have without the wolves. We don't know, however, if this works to any great extent in nature.

Because wolves affect, but do not exert complete control over, their prey, the ecological justification does not seem to provide an answer by itself to the question why should we save wolves. Perhaps the effect of wolves on the moose could, with further study, be shown to have greater importance, but that does not help us make our decisions today. We can take the position of what is known in courts as that of a "reasonable-person." What would a reasonable person do, with evidence that wolves might play some role, but not enough evidence to resolve how much? A reasonable person, faced with the unknown effects of wolves, would choose to conserve this species until it could be better determined whether or not it played some essential role in nature. This is a legitimate point, but it is weakened by the fact that so little resources are ever focused on any attempt to answer the question: do wolves play some essential role within the ecosystem of which they are a part?

A BROADER PERSPECTIVE

To understand what might be an essential ecological role of a species, we have to look at a broader picture, at the biological diversity of the Earth as a whole. About a million and a half species have been named, and speculations as to the total number vary from three to thirty million and beyond. Is it necessary to have all these species if life is to continue on the Earth?

In thinking about this question, I am reminded about all the parts in the small, single engine airplanes that I have flown. Think just about the instruments in the cockpit. Are all of them necessary?

The answer depends on what you are doing. For a short while, I took some training in aerobatics. My purpose was not the aerobatics themselves, but to learn how to fly very light planes with a tail wheel, known as "tail-draggers," that could be landed on the rough grass on the Serengeti Plains. The best known of these is probably the Piper Cub. When I sought to learn to fly this kind of plane, the only instructor I could find taught aerobatics in a plane called the Citabria. Since aerobatics are done only in clear weather, and since the pilot has to react fast to what he sees, few instruments are needed and the fewer— the less distraction to the pilot—the better. Most of the time, I flew

148

more standard airplanes equipped for instrument flying. For these, there were a number of navigational instruments. The first direction-finding instrument developed for airplanes was called the ADF (for automatic direction finder). It was simply a movable radio antenna. Turning a dial on the instrument panel rotated an antenna. You could tune it to an AM radio station or to a special AM signal just for aircraft. The dial on the instrument panel told you what direction to fly so you would go toward the source of the signal. It was not very accurate, but it did work. This was supplemented by much more precise ILS (for instrument landing system) devices. An ILS dial has two needles, one mounted horizontally and one vertically. When both are centered, the plane is on a direct approach to the runway and at the correct rate of descent. If the horizontal needle moved up, the plane was too low and would land before it reached the runway. If the vertical needle pointed to the right, the plane was to the left of the runway. This has been the standard device for many years, but when I learned to fly under instrument conditions, the ADF was still in airplanes and a pilot was required to know how to use it, on the grounds that, if the more precise devices failed, the ADF could serve as a backup. Today, however, the ADF is being phased out. Is it or was it necessary? The answer depends on one's point of view about redundancy, but also is affected by tradition. Pilot instructors who had grown up with the ADF wanted their students to know how to use it. Even with something as carefully designed and purposefully designed as an airplane, there is some ambiguity about how much redundancy of function is necessary.

Then there is the question of stand-by and back-up devices. On modern aircraft there is a gyroscopic compass that gives precision information about direction, and another gyroscopic device, the attitude indicator, that tells you whether the plane is flying straight and level, diving, climbing, or banking, and at what angles. These are essential to safe flying under instrument conditions—flying through clouds and rain. The gyroscopes in these instruments are driven by a small air pump. The standard equipment on single engine planes is to have just one air pump, but if that pump fails in the middle of an instrument landing, the situation can be dangerous. It seemed to me that a back-up pump would be valuable and, if I ever were able to buy my own plane, that would be one of the first additions I would make. For me, this second pump was an important safety factor, but most other pilots seemed satisfied with just one.

There is an issue of redundancy with the engine as well. Engines of small single engine airplanes are much like those in automobiles except that they have two separate ignition systems. Since ignition is essential and the failure of a sparkplug is a common cause of engine trouble, this redundancy is considered necessary in an airplane, but not in an automobile. The required redundancy for the same kind of engine differs with its use.

In an airplane, then, there are necessary and in-use parts, and redundant parts—spare parts that are on-line or off-line. There are also accessories that make flying more pleasant, such as well-designed earphones and microphones for hands-off radio communication, rather than a hand-held microphone and a loudspeaker; there is a heater and sometimes an air conditioner. Some would argue that these are not merely conveniences, but necessities for the safest kinds of flight.

If determining what is necessary and what is merely convenient is this difficult for a small airplane with perhaps a few hundred to a few thousand parts, then what can we say about life on the Earth? At least people have made airplanes and they have specific purposes, so we know both the design and the purpose. Ecological justifications for the conservation of species seem to require that all species are necessary in one of the ways I have described for an airplane—either on-line and in use or as redundant, back-up equipment for safety—in the case of life on the Earth, the safety is in terms of the persistence of life within some specific area, or all life on the Earth.

One of the difficulties we face in evaluating the importance of species is that we did not make the Earth and its life, we merely find ourselves players in the game, trying to discover the rules before we lose. This is quite different from an engineered system such as the space shuttle: human-made, the purpose of its components are known. But since we don't know the function of every species, it would be foolish to throw away something that might be an essential part just because we didn't know what it does.

One way to approach this difficult problem is to ask what is the minimum set of species that is needed to persist for a long time on the Earth. Lacking very much understanding of how ecosystems work, we have a hard time answering this question from present ecological theory, or from laboratory experiments. But we can get insight from recent scientific discoveries about the most ancient life on the Earth. Studies of ancient fossils show that for two billion years life on the Earth consisted only of bacteria. This period in the history of Earth is longer than the entire period since, which extends for about one and a half billion years. Some kinds of bacteria carry out photosynthesis and make their own food. Other bacteria fix nitrogen from the air, and put it into simple compounds that all living things can use. Bacteria carry out many kinds of chemical reactions; in fact, all the kinds necessary for bacterial life to persist. From this we know that a functional life on Earth can persist for a very long time with a much smaller diversity of life than at present. At present, there are about 4,000 species of bacteria named. There may have been many more in the heydays of bacterial life on the Earth, but even so, the overall diversity of life was much less than it is today. Multi-cellular, multi-organ life forms with a sophisticated cell structure—organisms called eukaryotes—which include all plants, animals, and fungi—are not necessary if one's goal is only to have some kind of life persist on the Earth, without regard to the kind of life. Simply said, bacteria could get on quite well without us, without the grasses and flowers of the prairies, without the bison and grizzly and without the wolves.

An Earth with only bacteria would produce a very different, unfamiliar landscape. The landscape through which Lewis and Clark traveled would be barren not only of animals and plants but would be without soil, and without some of the more curious minerals that they saw in the bluffs and hills that are the products of life that evolved after the long era of bacteria only. In that bacteria-only world, the only life one might have noticed would have been the kind similar to that which you can still see in the hot springs of Yellowstone National Park, a place Lewis and Clark did not visit themselves, but passed relatively nearby. A visitor to that bacteria-only American West might have seen greenish, orangish, and yellowish stains in the waters, especially the saltier ones such as occur when waters are pushed up from the deep earth. Free-flowing rivers like the Missouri would have been pretty much devoid of any life. This world is not what we want. The minimalist explanation of the least-life requirements to sustain life on the Earth is not enough. It does not conserve what people really want. The mechanistic justification for conservation of wolves is helpful, but not sufficient by itself. We need something more. As we learn more about how ecological systems work, we will find more and more evidence about the ecological importance of various species. In the long run, the ecological justification will become more and more helpful to those who want to conserve endangered species.

The third reason put forward for the conservation of endangered species is an aesthetic one; the fourth is moral. These are best discussed together. Wolves are social animals, living in packs that can be as small as four or five or as large as twenty. There is a rigorous social structure, with a lead male and female, which scientists refer to as the "alpha" male and female. The alpha pair has pups which are cared for by other adults as well as by the parents. If food is plentiful, some other wolves with lower status may also have pups. The alpha male affirms his dominance through his posture and, when challenged, in fights. The personality of the lead male seems to be able to influence the behavior of the entire pack. A study of wolves at Isle Royale over more than 20 years revealed some interesting aspects of this feature of a wolf pack. As I said before, most of the study has been done in the winter from low-flying airplanes, because the wolves can be readily seen from the air.

For a while all the wolves on Isle Royale were in one pack, which had a distinctive lead male, with fur that was becoming white. As long as this male was dominant, the pack seemed to be successful in hunting moose and able to maintain integrity, and the pups showed many signs of play behavior. This lead male aged and became lame. Then this male disappeared. His remains were found later by scientists searching on the ground. They discovered that he had been killed by other wolves, apparently succumbing to challenges by younger males. After the death of this wolf, the male that replaced him lacked the same strong dominance. Play behavior decreased. The pack divided into two, with one half occupying the eastern portion of the island, the other dominating the western part. Care of the young, great sociability, and the importance of individual leadership are qualities that people tend to admire, and therefore one might expect people to have more appreciation of wolves. Perhaps such stories can help bring people to appreciate this endangered species.

Wolves avoid people on the ground, and it is extremely rare to see them when one is on foot on the island during the summer. My colleague Peter Jordan has worked on and off on the island since the 1960s and has seen only one wolf during the summer when he was out working in the forests over a 15-year period. A graduate student whose thesis concerned the wolves of Isle Royale worked there two summers and did not see a single wolf when he was on the ground in the summer. He made progress by indirect observations of their habits during the summer and direct observations from airplanes in the winter.

But what I remember most about the wolves of Isle Royale is their calls at dusk and during the night. In early summer the island was full of nesting white-throated sparrows whose call is a rising or falling third of an octave, as if these birds are singing part of a musical chord. The sparrows differ slightly among themselves in the key they sing and whether their calls rise or fall, so that when there are many of the males calling one hears a series of musical chords in a major key fluted through the forest. One night I was awakened by the cheerful sounds of these chordlike tones which, in my half-awake state, made me think I was hearing a recording of a peculiar but happy symphony. As I lay awake, I then heard a pack of wolves begin to call. They called as a group, with their howls rising and falling. Several wolves howled together, with their tones covering minor thirds, an eerie and wild sound. At the first sound of the wolves, the sparrows ceased their calls. It was as if a new musical movement had begun, a shift from cheerful to melancholy. Few other sounds bring out the primitive wildness of the woods as do these haunting calls, played against one another. For me, that waking moment was one of my deepest contacts with the sense of wilderness, an experience I will always appreciate and never forget. I count myself as a supporter of the conservation of wolves, on the basis of our mutual relationships communicated by their calls in the nights, calls that are the essence of wilderness and therefore of a character of nature. They evoke both an aesthetic and moral sense for the conservation of this species. For me, these are powerful justifications to save the wolves. And my guess is that, down deep, it is this aesthetic and moral attitude that underlies the desires of most people who work to save endangered species.

But most discussions, even those that mention the four justifications, tend to put most emphasis on the utilitarian and the ecological, as if no one would take the aesthetic and moral seriously. Recently I listened to an excellent talk about the conservation of biological diversity in tropical rain forests. After the speaker quickly listed the four categories of justification I have talked about here, he then spent all of his lecture on the possible medicines that might be found—he relied completely on the utilitarian benefit. A recent publication by the Wilderness Society explaining the importance of biological diversity began with a story about how bacteria in Yellowstone National Park Hot Springs have recently provided an enzyme that makes it efficient to produce a new medicine.

But the change in Alaskan wolf-hunting policy because of a tourist boycott demonstrates the power of aesthetic and moral justifications.

The money and time invested in vacations to national parks demonstrate the powerfulness of aesthetics in our lives, as does the amount of money spent on entertainment of many kinds.

None of the four reasons given for the conservation of endangered species is sufficient by itself for all situations. As I said earlier, although the four reasons are often listed, most of the talks and writings I know of emphasize the utilitarian above all the others. When this justification cannot be relied on, there is a tendency to emphasize next the ecological—the mechanistic justification. All of this discussion forces us to the conclusion that a strong basis for the conservation of wolves is prudency, aesthetics, and morality. These are not the weak sisters of the utilitarian and ecological justifications; in fact, it seems easier, given present knowledge, to argue for aesthetic and moral justifications than for ecological ones for many species. My own experiences as a scientist studying wilderness brought a sense of spiritual connection to nature when the wolves called in the night. This did not replace or take away from the scientific curiosity about the potential ecological role of wolves in the northern ecosystem. All four kinds of explanations function together in support of the conservation of species. An attempt to justify the conservation of wolves on utilitarian or ecological grounds, when behind it all we really want to keep them here for aesthetic and moral reasons, does not work. It is worth repeating that each of these justifications has its place, but that all four are necessary if we are to understand the human desire to conserve the great diversity of life around us, along with the utility and prudence that lies with the conservation of species.

In my experience, we get ourselves into trouble when we have one motivation and attempt to justify it with another. An example of this has to do with Pacific yew, one of the trees that Lewis and Clark would have seen during their second fall and winter near the Pacific Coast when they were in the geographic range of this species. As I said earlier in this chapter, the possibility that new medicines might be obtained from plants and animals is often the primary argument put forward to justify the conservation of biological diversity. But recently a new drug, Taxol, was discovered in the Pacific yew to be a powerful treatment for breast cancer. The chemical was obtained from the bark of the Pacific Yew, an uncommon tree of the Pacific Northwest coastal forests. Once this medicine was discovered, the desire to save the lives of women with breast cancer led to cutting many of these trees down. Immediately, some environmental groups raised a cry of alarm, saying that this was a practice that would lead to the extinction of this species. If the chemical is truly useful, and it is, then a pharmaceutical company would have a vested interest in developing a sustainable supply, either by inventing ways to make the chemical artificially, or by developing sustainable forestry practices for this species. But the cry of alarm over the actual use of the Pacific yew suggests that there were other motives behind the utilitarian one, and these motives are aesthetic and moral. I believe it would have been better to bring all four justifications out in the open and explain them, in combination. This would lead to a rational approach to growing, using, and conserving the Pacific yew.

At the end of the twentieth century, after two centuries of the mechanical age, we find great comfort in mechanistic explanations. Perhaps at some level we believe that these are the only true ones. But a mechanistic explanation also can reinforce the belief in the separation between people and the rest of nature: if the mechanistic explanation is correct, then the machinery of nature functions without us.

There is a great need for us to find a place not only for wolves and for endangered species in nature, but for ourselves. We need to understand and accept our own roles in nature and our need to be connected with nature. Taking this as a clearly understood premise, we can then consider what is necessary to meet our needs as well as those of wolves and other endangered species. We can look more clearly at scientific information and determine when and under what conditions mechanistic explanations do have a basis in fact and knowledge. In doing so, we would be observing nature in much the same manner as Lewis and Clark.

CHAPTER EIGHT

Through the Mountains

People Within Nature, Nature Within People

Our journey westward was but a long series of encounters. Your Majesty, encounters have become my meditation. The moment one accosts a stranger or is accosted by him is above all in this life the moment of drama. The eyes of Indians who crossed my trail have searched me to the very depths to estimate my power. It is true the world over.

CABEZA DE VACA, *COMMENTING ABOUT HIS EIGHT YEARS AS A WANDERER IN NORTH AMERICA, BEGINNING IN NOVEMBER 1528*

I began this book with the search by Lewis and Clark for a road through the wilderness in Lolo Pass of the mountains of Montana. Since that chapter, I have discussed a variety of aspects of nature in the American West before European settlement, as one way to come to an understanding of the character of nature and how we have changed it. One of the themes of this book is the intimate connection between human beings and nature. In the last chapter, I discussed how important human aesthetics and human ethics are in the defense of the conservation of endangered species. In many of the experiences of the expedition that I have recounted, the presence of people or the experiences of others than those on the expedition have been an important factor. But the profoundness of the dependence of the expedition on Native Americans has not yet been a specific focus. In this chapter, the topic is the importance of Native Americans to the success of the expedition, as well as the role of Native Americans in shaping the landscape and therefore in affecting nature.

On July 27, 1805, the Lewis and Clark expedition reached Three Forks, the point at which the Gallatin, Jefferson, and Madison rivers converge to form the headwaters of the Missouri River. They were confronted with the greatest challenge and greatest threat of their outward bound journey: the passage over the Rocky Mountains. They approached Three Forks by canoe, but the men spent much time wading so that they could push and pull their canoes upstream in the shallow waters; it was clear that soon canoes would be useless. Horses were needed to transport the expedition and the materials through the mountains, but Lewis and Clark had not been able to bring horses with them on the narrow, upper Missouri, and had left them behind on the

160

plains. Now they were searching for Indians of the mountains, with whom they could trade for horses.

On that Saturday, Lewis wrote in his journal, "We begin to feel considerable anxiety with respect to the Snake Indians. If we do not find them or some other nation who have horses, I fear the successful issue of our voyage will be very doubtful or at all events much more difficult in its accomplishment."

Lewis made every effort to search out and approach Indians in a way that would be accepted as friendly. But the mountain Indians were at war with neighboring tribes down river, and they fled at the first sight of strangers. Earlier, on Tuesday, July 23, 1805, he had raised small flags on the canoes, hoping that Shoshone Indians would see them and understand that the party was not a group of Indians, and therefore not the enemy.

In reaching the headwaters of the Missouri, they had also reached the homeland of their Indian guide Sacagawea. Sacagawea was a Lemhi Shoshone who was born about 1788, taken prisoner about 1800, and married by Charbonneau, a French-Canadian fur trader, in about 1804. Lewis and Clark had first met Charbonneau and Sacagawea at the Mandan villages, where the expedition had spent the previous winter. Both Charbonneau and Sacagawea accompanied them on the rest of the trip, serving as interpreters. On February 11, 1805, during the expedition's winter with the Mandans, Sacagawea gave birth to a boy, to be later named Jean Baptiste Charbonneau and later to be cared for by Clark, who took the boy to St. Louis and later sent him to Europe to be educated.

On Monday, July 22, 1805, Sacagawea told Lewis and Clark that she recognized the country and that they were near her relatives, information which "cheered the spirits of the party." Then, the next Sunday, July 28, she told Lewis that the expedition was camped exactly on the spot where she and her relatives had camped five years before. Here they had been attacked by Hidatsas. Her group retreated up the Jefferson River, but was pursued by the Hidatsas who captured them, killed four men, four women, and some boys, and made prisoners of the rest, including herself. Afterwards she had been brought eastward where she had come to live with the Hidatsas in North Dakota and become the wife of Charbonneau.

Lewis and Clark continued to search the mountains for Indians, without success, for almost two weeks. On August 1, Lewis left camp with three men to search for Indians, taking his Sergeant Gass, his best hunter Drouillard, and Charbonneau. They traveled by foot over rough mountains and into treeless, hot valleys for a distance Lewis estimated to be 11 miles, without success. Meanwhile Clark traveled up the Jefferson River, finding it crooked and full of islands. Still trying to travel by canoe, his men found the Jefferson so rapid as to require great effort to move upstream. Clark found tracks of an Indian on August 3, but these suggested that the Indian had seen them and run away.

On Monday, August 5, Lewis and Drouillard found an "old Indian road," a day on which Lewis estimated he walked 25 miles. By that day, Clark noted that the men were "much fatigued from their excessive labors in hauling the Canoes over the rapids." On the next day, Tuesday, August 6, one of the canoes overturned, wetting baggage including the medicine box, and as a result one rifle was lost. Clearly, they could not proceed much further without horses. On Thursday, August 8, Sacagawea told Lewis that she recognized a peak which her people used as their summering grounds and which they called Beaverhead Rock. (This peak, located in Madison County along Montana Highway 41, about 12 miles southwest of the town of Twin Bridges, remains known today by the same name.)

Lewis finally saw an Indian on horseback on Sunday, August 11, while traveling with his hunter, Drouillard, and Shields. Lewis believed he was a Shoshone because of his dress and his "elegant" horse, which he rode without a saddle. With his usual keen sense of diplomacy and care, Lewis attempted to approach the Indian in the gentlest and friendliest manner. He made a standard signal of friendship by holding a blanket at two corners and "then throwing [it] up into the air higher than the head" and then bringing it down to the earth as if to spread it. This was repeated three times. However, the two men with him did not have the same finesse and did not halt, but continued to approach the Indian, even though Lewis attempted to signal them to stop. This caused the Indian to move away, even though Lewis called repeatedly the word "Tab-ba-bone," which he thought meant white man. Failing to make contact with this Indian, Lewis wrote that he felt "mortification and disappointment" and was "chagrined" by the behavior of his men with whom he spoke about their failure. Continuing his careful planning, Lewis next attached some moccasins, some strings of beads, some paint, and a looking glass to a pole which he inserted in the ground in hopes of attracting Indians.

CONTACT WITH THE SHOSHONES

It was not until after Lewis had reached the absolute upper limit of the drainage of the Missouri, crossed the Continental Divide, and wrote that he "first tasted the water of the great Columbia River" that he was able to make contact with the Indians. Crossing the Continental Divide, which the expedition did on August 12, was "one of those great objects of which my mind has been unalterably fixed for many years," Lewis wrote in his journal.

On the next day, Tuesday, August 13, Lewis followed an Indian road. He was now on Lemhi Pass on the Lemhi River, and had crossed from what is now Montana into what is now Idaho. About four miles farther, he saw one man and two women. Once again he attempted to approach them with an unfurled flag, but first the women fled and the man soon followed. About a mile farther, he came upon two girls and a woman, whom Lewis and his men surprised and approached so closely that the women apparently believed there was no escape and sat on the ground "holding down their heads as if reconciled to die." Lewis took the older woman by the hand to show her his skin. Then he gave her some beads, a looking glass, and other small gifts. He painted the woman's face and the faces of the two girls with vermillion, which Lewis believed was an Indian emblem of peace. Then, using sign language, he asked them to bring them to their camp. This they began to do.

In about two miles they were met by 60 mounted and armed men, who embraced Lewis and his men according to their customs. Lewis spoke with the chief, whose name, he recorded, was Ca-me-ah-wait. He and his companions remained with this group for several days, but the Indians vacillated between friendliness, fear, and hostility. Lewis came to believe that the Indians thought Lewis was in league with their enemies and was leading them into an ambush. Finally, on Friday, August 16, Lewis gave his gun to the chief and told him that "if his enemies were in those bushes . . . he could defend himself with that gun," adding that he was "not afraid to die" and that he "might make what use of the gun he thought proper or in other words that he might shoot me."

Lewis was waiting for the rest of the expedition to catch up with them, and was concerned that the group of Indians might leave and "secrete themselves in the mountains where it would be impossible to find them." But the expedition did join them on Saturday, August 17, and Sacagawea discovered that Chief Ca-me-ah-wait was her brother. By amazing coincidence, the very first Indians, Shoshones, with whom they were able to make contact in the Rockies turned out to be Sacagawea's own family.

On Sunday, August 18, Lewis traded a uniform coat, a pair of leggings, three knives, some handkerchiefs, and other materials that he estimated were worth $20 for three "very good horses." So the two things the expedition needed most desperately, horses and friendly guides, had been obtained. Good fortune, Lewis's astuteness and diplomacy, his and Clark's strength and courage, the hard work and cooperation of the men, and the assistance of Sacagawea, all contributed to this important development. So it was that the greatest wilderness expedition ever undertaken in North America by people of European descent ultimately depended on courage, intelligence, technology, and the cooperation of the peoples of that land. As it would be on the return, the way west over the mountains was accomplished successfully because Lewis and Clark were traveling in the country known, lived in, and traveled through by Native Americans. The integration of people *and* nature was the foundation of their success.

Here, at a location now under Clark Canyon Reservoir, but then below the forks of the Beaverhead River, the expedition made camp with Sacagawea's relatives, and here they remained until August 24. From the point that the expedition left the Missouri River to the point at which they put boats into the Clearwater River, a tributary of the Columbia, they traveled 340 miles, "200 miles of which is a good road, 140 miles over a tremendous mountain, steep and broken."

During the journey over the Bitterroots, game became scarce and the expedition began to eat their pack horses. They had hoped to find an easy portage between the Missouri and the Columbia, so that a Northwest Passage would become a reality. Instead they found a harsh and challenging mountain crossing.

Although Lewis and Clark depended on the Indians for the success of their expedition, the statements that they made to Sacagawea's relatives gave quite a different tone. Lewis spoke to the Indians and told them that they were dependent on "the will of our government for every species of merchandise as well for their defence and comfort" and he told them of the strength of the United States government. He said that the purpose of their travel was to "find out a more direct way to bring merchandise to them." For this reason, it was mutually advantageous that the Indians help Lewis and Clark, so that eventually the Indians could receive Western merchandise and that "they should render us such aids as they had it in their power to furnish in order to hasten our voyage," including their horses and guides to take them over the mountains. Lewis was of the impression that "every article about us appeared to excite astonishment in their minds" from the way the men looked, to the canoes, the guns, and even Lewis's dog.

WILDERNESS AND TECHNOLOGY

On January 14, 1805, while wintering with the Mandans, Clark wrote that one of their hunters, who had been sent out for several days, returned to say that another member of the expedition, Whitehouse, was so badly frostbitten that he could not walk home. In spite of the cold, Lewis reported on the same day that there was an eclipse of the moon, which he observed with the small refracting telescope that was part of his sextant, having "no other glass to assist me in this observation." He was able to "define the edge of the moon's image." He wrote that clouds interrupted his observations, making the observation of the "commencement of total darkness" inaccurate. "The last two observations, the end of total darkness and the end of the eclipse, were more satisfactory," he wrote. These observations Lewis used to locate the longitude of their winter fort, which he calculated to be 99° 26′ 45″; the true position being 101° 14′ 24″.

While we think of "man and nature" as a primitive experience— men pitting themselves against nature without the aid of civilization— in fact technologies played a key role in the success of the expedition, especially the compass, the gun, blacksmithing, knowledge of surveying, how to make wheels, wagons, ax handles and, of course, how to write. The gun played a key role, as we have seen in other chapters, saving several of the men from grizzly bears; hunting with guns provided the staple food, meat. During the long portage up the Great Falls on the Missouri, the expedition made a primitive carriage with wheels to transport their heavy materials, using cottonwood growing along the river. At least one of the members of the expedition knew blacksmithing, and during the first winter he did blacksmithing for the Mandans in exchange for corn. He repaired many objects along the way.

This was a scientific, as well as an exploratory, expedition. To determine their position, Lewis took with him a quadrant, a compass, plotting instruments, surveying equipment—poles and chains—artificial horizons, and a theodolite, along with maps and charts; thermometers and hydrometers for weather observations, and a microscope to examine specimens. He carried a copy of Linneaus's book of botanical study.

The importance of such equipment was emphasized on June 29, 1805, when the expedition lost their large compass. Exploring the area along the Great Falls of the Missouri River that day, Clark, Charbonneau, Sacagawea, and York, the only black man on the expedition, were caught in an intense storm. They took shelter under rocks along the slopes by the river, putting guns and compass under what Clark referred to as "a shelving rock on the upper side of the creek," which appeared safe to him. However, the rain came hard and turned to hail "more violent than ever I saw before," Clark wrote. "The rain fell like one volley of water falling from the heavens and gave us time only to get out of the way of a torrent of water which was pouring down the hill." Everything was eroding away along the slope. Clark grabbed his gun with his left hand and helped Sacagawea, who was holding her child, up the slope. The compass was lost. The hail was so intense that other members of the expedition who were out on the plains were "much bruised" and "some nearly killed," while "one was knocked down three times," and they returned to camp with bloody heads. Clark wrote that the loss of the compass was serious "as we have no other large one." The next day, two men returned to the falls and found the compass "covered in mud and sand near the mouth of the river." Not only did the compass help the expedition find its way, but the compass, the sextant, and other measuring instruments were used to map the path of the expedition, to chart the rivers and important landmarks, and to measure the distance traveled every day.

One of the factors that made the expedition successful was the careful design and selection of this equipment. Much as modern backpackers use the best available light-weight equipment, so Lewis and Clark used and depended on their technology. Their skills, wisdom, diplomacy, and technology, along with the assistance of the Native Americans, made it possible for the small party to pass through several thousand miles without resupply and communication with their own civilization.

PEOPLE AND LAND

It often seems that the common impression about the American West is that, before the arrival of people of European descent, Native Americans had essentially no effect on the land, the wildlife, or the ecosystems, except that they harvested trivial amounts that did not affect the "natural" abundances of plants and animals. But Native Americans had three powerful technologies: fire, the ability to work wood into useful objects, and the bow and arrow. To claim that people with these technologies did not or could not create major changes in natural ecosystems can be taken as Western civilization's ignorance, chauvinism, and old prejudice against primitivism—the noble but dumb savage. There is ample evidence that Native Americans greatly changed the character of the landscape with fire, and that they may have had major effects on the abundances of some wildlife species through their hunting.

Lewis and Clark observed fires in the prairies and forests on many occasions. Some may have been lightning caused, but others were started by Indians. For example, on July 20, 1804, the journals note that a group of the men that day saw "plains to the south rich, but much parched with frequent fires, and with no timber, except the scattering of trees about the sources of the runs, which are numerous and fine."

Later, on August 15th, they saw smoke in the distance, and took this to be a sign of Indians, and sent some men to investigate. They returned to report that a small group of Sioux had recently passed and had left some trees burning, and that the wind "blew the smoke from that point directly over our camp." As I will discuss in a later chapter,

169

there is much more evidence that the Indians used fire as a powerful tool to alter landscapes.

Similarly, the Indians had, at least in some instances, powerful effects on wildlife. On May 29, 1805, the expedition reached the mouth of the Judith River (where that river enters the Missouri in Montana) and passed "remains of many mangled carcasses of buffalo which had been driven over a precipice of 120 feet by the Indians and perished," Lewis wrote. "The water appeared to have washed away a part of this immense slaughter and still there remained the fragments of at least a hundred carcasses," creating "a most horrid stench." He continued that "in this manner the Indians of the Missouri destroy vast herds of buffalo at a stroke."

Lewis described the intricate and clever hunting methods of the Plains Indians. A young man who is one of the fastest is disguised in a buffalo skull, wearing the head and horns as a cap. He then positions himself between a herd of buffalo and a precipice. Other Indians surround the herd and reveal themselves to the buffalo at the same time. The disguised Indian then runs before the buffalo as they stampede and leads them to the precipice. The disguised Indian hides in a crevice in the cliff located previously. "The part of the decoy I am informed is extremely dangerous," Lewis wrote, "if they are not very fleet runners the buffalo tread them under foot and crush them to death, and sometimes drive them over the precipice."

TWO STORIES: THE NEZ PERCE
AND LEWIS AND CLARK'S

Although Lewis's speech to the Shoshones suggested that his government had great power over the Indians, which in due course it would,

170

that power was only a potential one. Lewis was attended by fewer than 40 companions, and in the eyes of at least some of the Mountain Indians, the expedition appeared much less powerful than Lewis's posturing would suggest. This is revealed in a remarkable book, *Do Them No Harm!*, by Zoa L. Swayne, who lives in Orofino, Idaho, within the boundaries of the Nez Perce Indians' reservation. For more than 50 years, she gathered information about an encounter between the Nez Perce and the Lewis and Clark expedition, which took place between September 20 and October 10, 1805, and again in 1806 on the return. The expedition camped with the Nez Perce and built canoes to take them down the Clearwater, then to other rivers, and finally to the Columbia River. She heard stories from Nez Perce descendants, stories that had been handed down through generations about the encounter between these Indians and the first white and black men they had ever seen. She found other accounts from Nez Perce descendants in old newspaper articles and in manuscripts. In her book, she quotes from the journals of Lewis and Clark and then gives the Nez Perce stories of the same incidents. The events are the same, but the interpretations quite different.

The encounters began, according to Clark, when on September 20, 1805, they were in the Weippe Prairie, Clearwater County, Idaho, where the Indians collected edible bulbs of a lily called camas. He saw "beautiful country for three miles" with many Indian lodges. One mile from the lodges he saw three Indian boys, who ran from him and hid. He handed his rifle to one of his men and got off his horse and "found [2 of the boys and] gave them small pieces of ribbon and sent them forward to the village." Then one of the men of the village "came out to meet me with great caution and conducted me to a large, spacious lodge."

The story handed down from generation to generation of Nez

171

Perce, as recounted by Zoa Swayne, is that it was a hot day and most of the able-bodied men were on a war party. Only a few scouts remained in the village as lookouts for enemies, along with older men, the women, and children. Three boys of about six or seven took their small bows and arrows and went out to a trail to the mountains where they came upon ground squirrels and began to shoot at them. They became so involved in this activity that they did not notice the approach of Clark and his men until they heard the sound of the horses. They hid behind tall grass, thinking that the strangers had not seen them. They saw men whose faces looked like buffalo hide because they had beards. The man in front handed a strange-looking stick to the one behind him. Then he "opened a pack on his horse and, with a shiny knife, cut off three strips of red material about as long as a water snake. With these fluttering in his hands, he headed straight for the grass where the boys thought they were hidden." He handed a fluttering red strip to one of the boys and with sign language asked him to go to his village and tell people to come. The correspondence between the details of the folk stories of the Nez Perce and the notes by Clark tells us that the events were accurately remembered over the generations.

The next day, Saturday, September 21, Clark wrote that the people "were glad to see us and gave us dried salmon." Clark and his men camped at the village. He asked the chief about the path of the river, smoked a pipe with him, and gave him a handkerchief and a silver cord. That Sunday, September 22, Clark and his men joined Lewis and the rest of the party at a camp at a second village. "The plains appeared covered with spectators viewing the white men and the articles which we had," Clark wrote, but his men were weak from lack of food and from the effects of eating roots to which they were not accustomed. Some Indians stole a knife, compass, and other articles from one of the men.

According to the Nez Perce stories, there was an old woman named Wat-ku-ese in the first village who was the only one who had seen white men before, and those men had cured her of an illness. She was pleased to see the seven men of Clark's advance party. Then she heard that there were more white men coming and that all of them would camp at the next village. According to the stories,

> Wat-ku-ese could not sleep . . . These [white] men faced great danger. With all the warriors gone on the warpath, her people would feel threatened by the numbers. The seven who first appeared were objects of curiosity; but great numbers of men were a threat. Wat-ku-ese knew that swift death could come to every stranger in the silence of the night. A man, armed only with a kopluts [skull-cracker], could slip among sleeping people and deal a death blow without a struggle . . .

Wat-ku-ese knew these white men were friends, but that her people would not know this. She decided she had to get to their camp as soon as she could. She rode her horse to their camp, becoming exhausted in the heat of the day, exhausting her horse and having to walk a part of the way.

As she feared, the Nez Perce were beginning to fear the expedition. They wondered why a Shoshone Indian, Sacagawea, had been brought with them, since these Indians were their enemy. They were frightened by the black man. They began to talk about the possibility of killing the members of the expedition while they were asleep, fearing that otherwise the white men would kill them. But Wat-ku-ese arrived, exhausted and faint, and fell asleep in a tepee. After a time she came out and called to the men whom she had heard plotting to kill the white men. These are good men, she called to them. "Men like these were

good to me. Do not kill them. Do them no harm! Do them no harm!"
And with those words she died.

There is no record in the journals of Lewis and Clark that they
were in such danger, although they had some minor troubles with the
Indians. Can we accept this story as true? The similarity of Lewis's
encounter with the young boys as told by Nez Perce stories and as
recorded in the journals of Lewis and Clark suggests an accuracy in the
stories passed down. If the rest are as accurate, then from these stories
we learn how much the expedition depended on the friendliness of the
Indians, as well as on the paths and roads they created, the food they
bartered for with them when they were near starving in the mountains,
and the horses they traded them for.

So it was, on their return the next summer, Lewis and Clark knew
that there were Indian roads and Indian guides, that there were deep
snows in the summits of the mountains, and they knew it was the
Indians and their established ways that would get them through.

The expedition encountered many groups of Indians, from the
Otos, whom they met early in their trip on their way up the Missouri,
to the Clatsop Indians of the mouth of the Columbia River. Unlike the
writings of many of their white predecessors and successors, the journals of Lewis, Clark, and Gass describe these encounters—sometimes
cordial and mutually beneficial, infrequently hostile and dangerous—
with great individuality and specificity. In one incident, a tribe was so
friendly and honest that one of the Indians tracked the expedition for
three days to give them a hatchet they had left by accident at the camp
they had set up by that Indian's village. In other incidents, during their
travel down the Columbia, the tribe they camped near attempted to
steal everything in sight, and Lewis and Clark were obliged to have
guards alert all night with their guns ready. But the truth of the matter

is that the journey through the Rocky Mountains ultimately depended on the assistance of the Indians who not only guided the travelers but also traded with them to provide food and horses for transportation, showed them where to hunt, fish, and gather edible vegetation, and how to build canoes and shelters.

In an imaginary American West without its Native American inhabitants, either the Lewis and Clark journey would have failed in the mountains, or it would have taken many more people and a much longer time to accomplish. It would have been more of an invasion than an expedition, with marches to fixed camps that would have had to have been supplied and resupplied by packmen traveling back and forth over previously discovered terrain, much as a mountain-climbing expedition succeeds in conquering Mount Everest today, but on a grander scale, much as an army conquers a country.

Long parts of the journey were made without direct outside help from the Indians. From the time that the expedition left their first wintering grounds with the Mandans, they did not see a single Indian until "Captain Lewis sighted a "lone horseman" as they neared the mountains on August 11, 1805, at a time when the continuation of their journey hung on the need for a friendly encounter with Indians who would make some kind of trade for horses." Once they left the Mandan villages, Lewis and Clark entered countryside never before visited by people of European descent. They were the first whites seen by most of the Shoshone Indians they met in the mountains. Without taking anything away from the bravery, courage, initiative, and strength of character of the members of the expedition, qualities the members exemplified over and over again, in the end the expedition succeeded as a small band of people in less than a three-year journey, because of the help of the friendly tribes they met along the way.

CHAPTER NINE

Down the Columbia

Salmon and the Nature of Change

Thousand years, all this here water
just a going to waste . . .
You just watch this river, and pretty soon, ever'body's
a-gonna be changin' their tune.
The big Grand Coulee and the Bonneville Dam run a
thousand factories for Uncle Sam . . .
makin 'everything from sewing machines to fertilizer
. . . atomic bedrooms . . . plastic!
Ever'things gonna be plastic.

WOODY GUTHRIE, *"COLUMBIA TALKING BLUES,"*
© *USED BY PERMISSION.. WRITTEN WHEN HE WAS*
AN EMPLOYEE OF THE BONNEVILLE POWER
ADMINISTRATION

In the West, whiskey is for drinking, but water is for fighting over.

MARK TWAIN

ANCHOVIES, SALMON, AND SINGLE-FACTOR THINKING

For many years I have followed the way that professional fisheries' biologists have recommended managing the world's great fisheries. This management has been a great curiosity, because it has been purposeful, well-meaning, but generally a failure, producing crashes in populations of the fish under management. One of the most recent and spectacular has been the decline in fish on the Grand Banks off of Newfoundland, where the fish populations have dropped so low that fishing for many species has been stopped. But the largest fishery in the world in terms of tons of fish caught commercially was the anchovies fishery off of Peru. There, in 1970, 7.3 million metric tons were caught. Only two years later, the catch dropped to 1.8 million metric tons—15 percent of the earlier amount. The 1970 catch was spectacular in size, but the decline within two years was equally impressive. So great was the decline in anchovies that it is only in recent years that these fish seem to be increasing to anything like their former abundance.

The Peruvian anchovies live in a region subject to changes in ocean currents, called El Niño, which have become quite famous in recent years. Under normal conditions, prevailing winds blow off the coast,

177

and these drive surface ocean waters away from the land. Currents rise to replace the water that has been pushed westward. These upwelling currents bring nutrients to the surface that stimulate the growth of algae, which in turn stimulates the growth of the food of anchovies and the anchovies themselves. But every once in a while—about every seven years—the winds fail, the upwelling stops—El Niño is occurring —and the fish populations drop. But the management of the anchovies, like almost all the world's fisheries then and now, did not take such environmental variation into account. The fisheries managers assumed the environment was constant, except for the amount of human harvest. Harvest levels were set based on "normal" years. This led to overfishing during years of poor upwellings, and the combination of variations in ocean currents and human policies led to the crash of the anchovies.

As I have mentioned several times before, as I write this book I am directing a study of the salmon of western Oregon and northern California. Living for the first six months of the study in Portland, Oregon, I was able to travel along the Columbia River and see many of the places mentioned by Lewis and Clark in their journals. Along with five other scientists who made up a panel that helped me direct the study, I traveled up many of the larger and smaller rivers and streams of western Oregon to look at the condition of salmon habitats. We saw streams in pristine areas, streams along farms, streams in Medford, Oregon, where a few salmon still managed to spawn amid the litter of shopping carts and pieces of old cars.

In December 1993, we followed a small stream inland from Newport, Oregon, to where coho (a species of salmon) were spawning. It was a clear, brisk day with some scattering of snow on the shaded ground. In a stream about twice as wide as a city sidewalk, salmon weighing 20 pounds and more struggled uphill, their back fins above

178

the water. On one side of the stream was a paved road; on the other, occasional houses and one large clearcut in a forest where a buffer zone had been left along the stream to protect the salmon habitat. We watched the last stage in the trip of one of the most complicated life cycles of any animal in the world. Born in small streams, coho feed on small freshwater animals until they are big enough to attempt the migration downstream and then into the ocean. There, they feed and grow for several years, returning three or four years later as adults. They encounter as many different factors in their lives as any animal. Living for thousands of years in country whose only human inhabitants were Native Americans, the migrating fish we watched did not seem stopped by their proximity to macadam or houses or clearings. But overall, there has been a decline in the number of areas where these salmon spawn, and the citizens of the Pacific Northwest have become concerned about these declines. Were these salmon going to suffer the same fate from environmental variation and mismanagement as the Peruvian anchovies? It was my job to find out.

Watching the coho struggle upstream, I couldn't help but make the comparison between their long, adventurous expedition, repeated by thousands every year, and the expedition of Lewis and Clark. Both are extraordinary and fascinating. Lewis and Clark understood the complexity of the countryside through which they were traveling, and the many different factors that affected the life around them. In this way, their observations of nature in the American West remain quite different from the general approach to management of fisheries that occurs worldwide. And, when Lewis and Clark crossed the Continental Divide in 1805, the two wanderers, salmon and the small band of men and one woman and her child, came together. This chapter is about what happened when Lewis and Clark met up with the salmon and what has happened to the fish since. It is most of all a story about

179

thinking from a single-factor approach, and what can go wrong when you do this about a nature that is anything but single factor in its causes and effects.

L E W I S ' S   F I R S T   T A S T E   O F
P A C I F I C   S A L M O N

Lewis had a rare culinary experience the day in August 1805 I mentioned earlier when he and some of his men traveled along an Indian road in the Lemhi Pass (an area that remains wild today) and met Chief Ca-me-ah-wait. Ca-me-ah-wait's people lived along the Lemhi River, a tributary of the Salmon River, which in turn is a tributary of the Snake River, in turn a tributary of the Columbia River. The chief took Lewis into his "bower" and "gave him a small morsel of boiled antelope and a piece of fresh salmon roasted." This was not only "the first salmon he had seen," but it also made Lewis "perfectly satisfied" that he was now on the waters of the Pacific.

The men of the expedition were the first people of European descent to cross the Continental Divide into Idaho and the first to be seen by this group of Shoshones. "All the women and children of the camp had gathered around the lodge to indulge in a view of the first white men they had ever seen," Lewis wrote. The tribe lived near to the spawning areas of salmon, where the adult salmon could be easily caught. Lewis walked to the Lemhi River and saw that its bed was of "loose stones and gravel," a significant observation, for those gravel beds are essential for the spawning of salmon; the mining of gravel and alteration of land along the streams that affect the stream's supply of gravel are among the many factors attributed to the decline of salmon in the Pacific Northwest.

Salmon and their close relatives, ocean-going trout, were a main element of the diet of the Indians of the Pacific Northwest, even for these Shoshones who lived far inland in the mountains along the Lemhi and other tributaries of the Salmon River. From the upper reaches of the Columbia in what is now the state of Washington, to the mouth of that great river at the Pacific Ocean and along thousands of miles of tributaries, the Indians depended on salmon abundance.

This dependence became clear to Lewis on August 19, 1805, when the expedition was camped on the Horse Prairie Creek, still in the mountains, on their way overland to the Salmon and then the Snake River, which they would reach two days later. They were with another group of Shoshones, called the Chippeways. "From the middle of May to the first of September these people reside on the waters of the Columbia," Lewis wrote, ". . . during this season the salmon furnish the principal part of their subsistence," along with fruits.

Obtaining salmon took much time and effort for the Indians, Lewis observed later, on Thursday, October 10, 1805, when the expedition was along the Snake River near the Idaho-Washington border and the site of modern Lewiston, Idaho. On that day he wrote that "the Chipunnish have very few amusements, for their life is painful and laborious . . . During the summer and autumn they are busily occupied in fishing for salmon."

Afterward, "as the fish either perishes or returns about the first of September," he continued, "they are compelled at this season in search of subsistence to resort to the Missouri, in the valleys of which, there is more game [than] even within the mountains." These Native Americans not only fished on tributaries of the Columbia, but traveled widely, moving across the Continental Divide to hunt in the plains to the east. For them, both the buffalo and the salmon were sustenance. Their repeated travels had created a trail, and they had techniques to catch both kinds of game.

The expedition was not in as advantageous a situation. In these wild mountains, with their goal of reaching the Pacific rather than settling and living on the land, they had to take food as they could find it. On the next Friday, August 23, Lewis wrote that "the season is now far advanced," and "the Indians tell us we shall shortly have snow. The salmon have so far declined that the natives themselves are hastening from the country; not an animal of any kind, larger than a pheasant or a squirrel, and of even these a few only, will then be seen in this part of the mountains; after which we shall be obliged to rely on our own stock of provisions, which will not support us more than ten days."

Having traveled through the mountains of Montana and Idaho, the expedition built canoes and made its way down the Clearwater River, then down the Snake, and on the 16th of October, 1805, reached, at last, the mouth of the Snake and found the Columbia River. Because Lewis and Clark had arrived in the mountains near the end of one of the salmon runs, they did not see the great abundance of these fish until they reached the Columbia; here they were far enough downstream so that spawning was still in progress. Their arrival at the Columbia meant that they had found a kind of Northwest Passage, difficult as it was, and that their final goal, the Pacific Ocean, was to be achieved comparatively easily, or so it seemed at the time, by travel down the river—no more struggling upriver as they had on the Missouri, no more struggling over the mountains as they had through Montana and Idaho.

The incredible abundance of the ocean-going, river-breeding fish was observed by Clark on October 17, the day after the expedition had reached the Columbia. Local Indians gathered on the banks to look at the strange, bearded men. Then 18 canoes of the Native Americans accompanied Clark and his men up the river. Clark saw salmon everywhere, swimming in the water, lying dead along the shore, and drying on scaffolds built by the Indians. The numbers were "almost inconceivable," he wrote. "The water is so clear that they can readily be seen at the depth of 15 or 20 feet; but at this season they float in such quantities down the stream, and are drifted ashore, that the Indians have only to collect, split, and dry them on the scaffolds." The great abundance of salmon continued for days afterward. On Tuesday, October 22, the expedition reached the Great Falls of the Columbia. There, on a small island, "there were such quantities of fish that we counted 20 stacks of dried and pounded salmon," the journals record. But as we shall see, even this biological resource, capable of traveling hundreds of miles up rivers and streams to spawn, had a limit to its productiveness.

The fish that Lewis and Clark saw once they had reached the western divide and began to follow the Lochsa, Clearwater, Snake, and Columbia rivers to the Pacific Ocean, included seven species: five species of salmon—chinook, coho, chum, sockeye, and pink salmon—and two species of ocean-going trout—steelhead and sea-run cutthroat. These are known today as anadromous fish, meaning that they spawn, hatch and rear in freshwaters, travel to the ocean where they grow and put on most of their weight, and then return to the fresh water rivers to lay eggs. These seven species are closely related, belonging to the same genus.

The importance of salmon and the effort devoted to this food source was made clear in the journals. The Indians on the Yakima River caught and dried salmon on scaffolds built of wood. Eastern Washington is dry because it is in the rain shadow of the Cascades. (The rain shadow is discussed in the next chapter.) There was little wood in the vicinity, and the Indians on the Yakima had to transport wood needed to process the salmon a long distance. Elsewhere, Clark saw that the Indians dried salmon to preserve the fish by burying them in the ground in straw.

From these accounts and others in the journals of the expedition, we learn that Pacific salmon and ocean-going trout were an essential part of the diet of Indians who lived over a large area, from the remote mountain tributaries of the Salmon and Snake rivers in the mountains of Idaho, some 300 airline miles from the ocean, to the tribes that lived along the Salmon and Snake, to the tribes that inhabited the shores of the Columbia all the way to the river's mouth, where the expedition would spend the winter of 1805–06. Thousands of miles of streams were involved.

There were many difficult passages for the fish on their way up-stream. The most difficult passage on the Columbia itself occurs at The Dalles, where a geological fault crosses the river and the hard basalt rock, laid down in the Miocene (about 20–25 million years ago), resists erosion. The expedition traveled down the Columbia River rapidly, reaching these cascades on October 24, 1805, only a week after the expedition had arrived at the mouth of the Snake River and had first seen the Columbia. On that day, Clark went with a group of men to view the rapids and decide how to get their canoes past them. He saw that at first the water fell 20 feet "perpendicular" and then passed a "tremendous black rock" that seemed to "choke up the river." Then for a mile the river traveled through a narrow channel, in some places not more than 45 yards wide. He found that the "water was agitated in a most shocking manner," boiling, swelling and forming whirlpools. He decided that portaging the canoes over the rocks along the shore would be impossible, but that "by good steering" they could canoe safely. As a result, he "determined to pass through this place notwithstanding the horrid appearance of this agitated gut." They succeeded in passing safely through "to the astonishment of all the Indians," Clark noted. In spite of these obstacles to upstream migrations, salmon were apparently quite abundant; Clark counted 107 storages of "dried pounded fish" that he estimated contained 10,000 pounds of fish. Below the rapids, the river widened and became "a beautiful gentle stream of about a half a mile wide." Lewis and Clark had passed the last major geological obstacle between themselves and the view of the ocean. They had now to face the winter storms of the Pacific Northwest.

PEAK CATCHES AND ENDANGERED SPECIES

In the early 1990s, sockeye and chinook salmon of the Snake River were listed as protected under the Endangered Species Act. Sockeye obtained the more extreme listing as an endangered species, while chinook obtained the less severe listing as threatened. Such listings mean that these fish can no longer be taken without special federal permits and that nothing can be done, including alterations of their habitat, that might increase any threat of extinction or of reduction of these populations. The plight of the salmon had become so bad by October 1993 that a team of scientists, asked to prepare a restoration plan for the Snake River salmon, suggested that young salmon be taken by barge down the rivers as a way to get them past the dams that limit their passage. They also suggested that a two- or three-year experiment be conducted to increase the release of water from the Lower Granite

Dam on the Snake River during the time of downstream migration of the fish to see whether this would lead to an increase in the abundance of the fish. But this experiment would reduce production of hydroelectric power, water for irrigation and for barge traffic. Norm Dicks, a U.S. congressman from the state of Washington, said that all the recommendations from the panel could cost as much as one billion dollars over 10 years.

What happened to these fish during the almost two centuries since Lewis and Clark saw them? In the chapter about the buffalo, I explained that the history of exploitation by people of European descent can be divided into five periods: a period of discovery which, for salmon on the Columbia River System, can be said to begin with Lewis and Clark. This period lasted for a half a century after the expedition. The second—intense exploitation—began for the salmon with the development of the Oregon trail, when people from the East began to migrate to the Pacific Northwest and settle there, and expanded rapidly right after the Civil War. The third period, of awakening conservation and the first attempts at professional, rational, scientific-based management of wild, living resources, began approximately at the end of World War I and continued until the 1960s. This was the period in which management had a single purpose—to maximize the production of a single resource for harvest. A fourth period of environmentalism began in the 1960s, with great growth in public awareness of environmental issues and with the decline of many wild, living resources. Although landmark legislation was passed in this period, the management of fisheries continued to follow the single-factor, maximization of harvest strategy that dominated the third period. We may be witnessing a fifth, yet unnamed period, a period to which I hope this book may be a contribution.

Right after the Civil War, the catch of salmon and ocean-going trout on the Columbia increased exponentially, as new kinds of fish-catching devices were invented and applied. There were mechanical traps, driven by water power—the movement of the Columbia's waters downstream—that took the fish into a device resembling a Ferris wheel and dumped them into holding tanks. There were line fisherman and net fishermen. Some describe fishing on the Columbia during the salmon runs as a series of mechanical trapping devices spread in a continuous line across the river.

Records of the catch on the Columbia have been kept since 1866, when a mere 15,000 chinook were caught by settlers on the river. As word spread about the incredible numbers of salmon and as new harvesting machines were invented, the catch more than doubled each year for the first few years. The second year, 1867, the catch more than quadrupled, to 66,000; that nearly doubled to 102,000 the next year, and more than tripled the next year to 367,000. In four years, from 1866 to 1870, the commercial catch of chinook had increased 20-fold. As with many natural resources, the incredible initial, exploited abundance was so great that it seemed a resource to grab without care for the future. It was another classic example of exploitation of America's wild living resources, and it took place concurrently with the exploitation and demise of the buffalo discussed earlier.

Even this wonderful resource had its limits, and the salmon have a limited capacity for production. The pattern of the harvest was like that of the rapid increase in buffalo hunting after the Civil War, peaking in a surprisingly short time, and then declining. The one major difference in these examples was that killing of the buffalo was done to destroy the food supply of the Plains Indians as well as for commerce, while the harvest of salmon was simply for commercial value and for sport fishing. (Although, of course, this had an effect on Native Americans.)

Perhaps even more interesting—the time it took to reach that peak catch was similar to that for the buffalo: about two decades. At first, only chinook were taken in great numbers as a commercial catch. But the catch of chinook peaked in the early 1880s, declining after 1884. As the most desirable species declined, the next most desirable was taken, and so on through the list of the species. And as each species became a major commercial item, records were kept of its harvest. In 1889, the year that we first have records for commercial harvest of sockeye, 348,000 of these were caught on the Columbia River; the same year 236,000 steelhead were taken. Coho salmon and even chum salmon, so called because they were too small to use whole and were packed in chunks or "chums" and were at first considered too small to be worthy of harvest, were added in the early 1890s. The total catch of chinook, coho, sockeye, chum, and steelhead reached 3.3 million fish in 1896. The catch rose above 3 million again in 1911 and in 1915, reaching its greatest size, 3.6 million, in 1918. Harvests continued to range between 2.5 and 3 million until 1934. But a harvest of two and a half to three million salmon was too much for the populations of these fish on the Columbia, and the new dams also began to take their toll. In 1934, the catch dropped to 1.4 million. The last commercial catch that surpassed one million on the Columbia occurred in 1948, except for one anomalous year, 1986, when there was a huge one-year increase in the catch of coho. By 1990, the total catch of all species had declined to 257,000, smaller than all the catches after 1869—smaller than the catch four years after the commercial exploitation began.

The total number of salmon and ocean-going trout swimming up the Columbia is believed to have numbered between 10 and 15 million before exploitation by people of European descent and is estimated to have reached 13 million in the 1890s, during the peak commercial catch. If these estimates are roughly correct, then the peak catch was 20 percent of the total population. That is a totally unrealistic catch to sustain over any length of time.

The salmon we catch are the ones returning to spawn; they have survived many dangers and most of their cohort—the individuals of their stock born during the same year—have died. Salmon who spawn are not around to care for their young; either the adults are dead, as is the usual case for these fish, or they have returned to the ocean. Like many fish, salmon overcome lack of parental care by producing huge numbers of eggs, most of which are eaten or otherwise destroyed before they hatch, or they die early in life. The survival of a stock of salmon depends on the chances that, on average, at least two individuals from the eggs of each female, one male and one female, survive all causes of death to return to the stream to spawn again.

It is usual to discuss the growth of a population in any single year as the difference between the number born and the number dying, but so many young salmon die that the key measure is the number of adults that return to spawn at the end of each year compared to the number of adults that returned the previous year. For there to be a surplus population to harvest, this number must be equal to the number that spawned last year plus an excess population, and it is this excess that can be harvested, leaving the population a reasonable chance to sustain itself. If the harvest is less than the excess, then the population may increase. Note that I wrote "may," not "will." The excess adults may not find a place to spawn, as I will discuss later. If the harvest exceeds the excess, then the population will decline. Note that I wrote "will," not "may." But when the numbers of animals returning are as huge as they were in the nineteenth century, and when there are many factors that cause variations from year to year in the number returning, it is hard to know whether the population is in an overall decline, or just in a one-year variation.

As I mentioned earlier, if the estimates for the numbers of adult salmon swimming up the Columbia in the 1920s and 1930s were more or less correct, then there would have been 10 to 15 million of them, and the annual catch would have represented 20 percent of the adult population. For the salmon to sustain that catch, their annual production of adults beyond other causes of death—such as predation by seals and sea lions—would have to equal this number. These adults return when they are three, four, and five years old. Enough young would have to make the swim down the river and then these would have to survive several years in the ocean so that the population returning was 2.5 to 3 million more than required to produce enough young fish to do the whole thing over again, and again, and again. As abundant and productive as these fish are, this is a highly implausible expectation for them, as it is for any medium or large vertebrate. From my study, and the studies of many others, of the long-term histories of animal populations, this seems so unlikely that few would expect, plan for, or advise that such harvests be sustained.

To understand why this is unrealistic, consider the method used to determine the growth of a salmon population and also used to.set the catch. The method still in use was invented in 1839 by a German mathematician name Verhulst, and is known as the Logistic Growth Equation and the Logistic Growth Curve. This is the simplest mathematical expression that includes the idea that a population cannot grow forever in a finite environment. As the simplest such expression, it is highly unrealistic. It assumes that a population of wild animals

190

grows exponentially when there are few individuals, but that, as the population increases, individuals compete for resources, and the growth rate slows down, eventually reaching a point at which the births equal the deaths and the population remains constant. This constant size is called the carrying capacity. In the Logistic equation, all else about the environment is assumed to be constant—ocean currents do not vary, water flow in the river does not change, the number of cormorants that catch young salmon always remains the same, the number and size of debris dams and gravel beds, necessary parts of the salmon habitat, never vary from year to year. If all these things were true, then a population might grow according to the Logistic Curve, but the environment is never constant.

It is my experience over years in studying ecology that most things we observe about nature vary naturally by 10 percent or 20 percent. By this I mean that if you saw two schools of salmon and thought they were identical, they could easily differ from one another by 10 percent or 20 percent. I also mean that the population of a stock could vary up or down from one year to the next by this percentage, as a result of external environmental changes or internal variations in the population. Variations could be greater; in my experience it is unwise to expect it to be much less. Note that I say this is based on my experience, which is an informal statement, not a rigorous, scientifically proven assertion.

Given that the Logistic Equation grossly oversimplifies the real life experience of salmon and that it is dangerous to use the maximum yield obtained from it in practice, then a prudent manager of salmon would harvest some smaller number. What might this be? Surprisingly, in spite of the more than 100 years of commercial harvest of salmon on the Columbia River, in spite of centuries of harvest of salmon around the world where high latitude rivers provide good habitat for these fish, in spite of intense interest by sport fishermen in catching salmon, in spite of a large number of government agencies that have some jurisdiction over the fish and its habitat (we counted 36 separate government agencies that have some jurisdiction over the salmon of western Oregon), we don't know much about the actual growth rate of wild salmon populations or about their maximum potential harvest.

Lacking that information, we can look around for knowledge about the growth rate of other species of medium and large mammals. As with most other ecological knowledge, there are few species for which we have good estimates of growth rates of wild populations. One is the elephant seal, thought to have been brought to extinction by the early 1900s also by harvest—for their furs.

Abandoned by commercial harvesters, elephant seals repopulated their abandoned ecological niche, increasing at an average rate of 8 percent per year. Their habitats—the Pacific Ocean and the islands along the coast where they breed—were in good condition, and their food supply abundant. Even so, their growth rate did not approach even one-half of 20 percent. If salmon could increase at a rate of 8 percent per year, the maximum sustainable catch from a population of 15 million would be 1.2 million, much less than the peak catch taken on the Columbia River.

It is amazing that salmon were able to sustain themselves at all on the Columbia or on most of the other rivers of the Pacific Northwest in the face of the technology mounted against them; early photographs show devices of many kinds forming almost continuous lines across the river during upstream migrations. But salmon are adapted to episodic environments, to change, to variation, and they are robust against these, and they have persisted. Surprisingly, in spite of the onslaught, they have continued to number in the millions in the rivers of Oregon and Washington. Estimates for more recent times are 4.5 million fish swimming upstream in 1977, and between one and three million after 1983.

But these robust fish are not adapted to permanent alterations of their habitats that prevent their return. Floods, storms, droughts, forest fires, and their technological mimics—runoff variations, periods of water removal for irrigation, episodic logging—these they can withstand. But dams that prevent a stock from reaching its spawning grounds for four or five years—enough so that no individual born there can return —ends that stock. Permanent diversions for irrigation that keep the waters forever low and prevent spawning for four or five years also will end that stock. These long-term or permanent alterations of their habitat have, along with intense commercial harvest, decimated some stocks. Coho salmon, important on the Snake River at the time that Lewis and Clark came down that waterway, were eliminated from that river by 1986. So far, there has been no recovery; today there are no known coho on the Snake River; none get to the Lemhi, none to the area of the great Continental Divide.

WHEN EVERYTHING WAS GOING TO BE PLASTIC

There at Priest and Cascade rapids men have labored
day and night,
Matched their strength against the river in its wild
and reckless flight,

Boats and rafts were beat to splinters but it left men
dreams to dream,
Of that day when they would conquer the wild and
wasted stream.

Woody Guthrie, the great American folk song writer and folk singer, is said to have been the first employee of the Bonneville Power Administration (BPA), the federal agency that built the great dams on the Columbia River. Woody Guthrie wrote these words during the Depression, a time when the great social and political movements focused on the plight of the people and on ways to improve their lives. In those times, our streams were "wasted" if they weren't used for economic gain, and it was a social and political—as well as a capitalist— good to conquer the big rivers. Environmental issues were the issues of a small minority. This was during the third period in American history of the relationship between people and the environment, the period of an awakening conservation, when Paul Sears was writing *Deserts on the March*, one of the twentieth century's major works telling of the great effect civilization had had on the environment. But at that time, the needs of a people in the midst of a Depression grabbed public attention with the intensity that environmental problems do today.

Woody Guthrie traveled and knew the Columbia. "I saw the Columbia River and the big Grand Coulee Dam from just about every cliff, mountain, tree, and post from which it can be seen," he wrote. "I made up twenty-six songs about the Columbia and about the dam and about the men, and these songs were recorded by the Department of

194

the Interior, Bonneville Power Administration out in Portland." There was a great public acceptance of his ideas and songs. "The records were played at all sorts and sizes of meetings where people bought bonds to bring the power lines over the fields and hills to their own little places," he wrote. "Electricity to milk the cows, kiss the maid, shoe the old mare, light up the saloon, the chili joint window, the schools, and churches along the way, to run the factories turning out manganese, chrome, bauxite, aluminum and steel."

The first of the great power dams on the Columbia was Rock Island, completed in 1933 in eastern Washington north of Richland, 453 miles from the river's mouth. The next, and perhaps the most famous, was the Bonneville Dam, 146 miles from the mouth of the river, completed in 1938, and built with ladders to allow salmon and ocean-going trout to pass.

The third and largest, in terms of its reservoir, Grand Coulee Dam, was completed in eastern Washington in 1941, 545 miles upstream from the mouth. This dam created a huge reservoir, destroying many miles of spawning areas, and had no passages for fish, so that the salmon could not have reached their spawning grounds if these continued to exist. There are now 18 major dams on the combined Columbia-Snake river systems including their tributaries, extending all the way to the Brownlee on the Snake River, 609 miles from the ocean. One of these, The Dalles Dam, located not far upstream from the Bonneville Dam and above the present town of The Dalles, Oregon, flooded the famous cascades through which the expedition passed.

Much use is made of the water from the reservoirs and dams. Electric power is produced from the 18 dams on the Columbia and the Snake. Without irrigation, this is not the best of climates for farming. Along this part of the Columbia, in the rain shadow of the Cascade

Mountains to the west, the climate is dry, with 4 to 10 inches of precipitation per year, about two-thirds of which falls in the winter. Today's green farm land is the result of irrigation water removed from the Columbia.

The dams have had two detrimental effects on the salmon: they prevented or made more difficult their passage upstream to spawn, so that fewer adults reproduced, and the reservoirs created by the dams flooded streams and destroyed shallow, gravel-bottomed stream habitats where the fish spawned and reared. Large areas were involved. When the Grand Coulee Dam, the biggest of them all, was completed in 1941, 450 miles of the Columbia's main stream was lost to the reservoir, more than one-third of the entire 1,200 miles of the river. When the last of the big dams, the Lower Granite on the Snake River, was completed in 1975, 4,600 miles of river and tributaries had been lost to the Columbia-Snake River basins, 31 percent of the total 14,700 miles available to salmon when Lewis and Clark came down these rivers.

But damming the river has been only part of the story of the effects on the salmon. There are many rivers in the Pacific Northwest where salmon spawn. To the south of the Columbia, there are 32 rivers that flow to the ocean, from Tillamook Bay to the Klamath River in California. Steelhead trout used to be found in Southern California and are still seen today on the Ventura River, less than 90 miles north of Los Angeles. Some of these rivers, which have never had dams, have few fish today.

We know that something went very wrong with that spirited, noble, humanistic, people-centered idea about what to do with the Columbia. Today, the Pacific Northwest is in a white water of controversy over the effects of the BPA's dams. The salmon that lived in and depended on the Columbia and the other rivers of the Pacific Northwest are in trouble; the focus of social and political movements has shifted to the environment, from a people focus to a nature focus; from the fisherman to the fish, from power lines to passage ways.

THE SINGLE-FACTOR APPROACH

Beginning in the fall of 1992, I spent six months in Portland, Oregon, where I discussed the salmon and their habitats with many people as part of the study I have mentioned before that I was conducting for the states of Oregon and California. I heard many simple, single-factor explanations while I was working on that project concerning the salmon of western Oregon and northern California. Not long after we had settled in Portland to work on the study, I had dinner with a locally well-known writer who had lived his life on the Columbia and Willamette rivers, where he built and sailed a variety of boats. "I don't want to hurt your feelings or make you feel bad," he said, "but there is no reason for you to do a study. We already know the answer to the decline of the salmon. Any riverman knows. When loggers clearcut the forests, the bare land erodes and sediments destroy the spawning grounds of the fish. Anybody who knows the rivers knows that's the reason."

A short time later an employee of the U.S. Forest Service told a friend of mine "everybody knows the reason the salmon are disappearing—it's simple—illegal fishing by the Japanese." That incident took place just after the U.S. Customs Service had confiscated a Japanese ship full of illegally caught salmon.

So everybody wants, looks for, and finds a simple answer. We could go back to electricity by the people, of the people, and for the people just as easily as we could stand by the statement that illegal fishing by foreign governments is the cause of the demise of the salmon. All these statements are equally true and untrue. Like gravel in the bed of the Snake River during spring flood, each particle of truth that rises to the surface makes one believe he has seen the entire bed, the whole truth, but as one particle settles back in the turbulent waters, another, of a different size and composition, comes to the surface, telling us a different story, a different aspect of the truth about the salmon. We can, like the river's sediments, go on forever, swirling, spinning, rising, and sinking on the turbulence of our passions and our faith in a simple answer. But these will never bring us passage to the conservation of our natural resources. To find solutions to the apparent decline of the salmon and to find solutions that are consistent with other social and political needs, we must begin to see the world differently, from several perspectives simultaneously.

In the 1930s, our society chose simple approaches to dealing with its natural river resources—choices that concerned a single factor. In the case of the Columbia River, the single factor was water as a resource to produce electricity and for irrigation. In the 1990s, this single-factor approach continues. Today people search for a single factor on which the demise of the salmon can be blamed. But a single-factor approach to these issues can't work, because the systems that support the salmon and that are influenced by the salmon are too complex, and there are many kinds of changes occurring in them all the time. In trying to solve our social and environmental problems, we are swept along by popular currents that look for simple, simplistic solutions. Such a search will continue to fail with systems as complex as the Columbia River and human societies along its shore. And once again, with the salmon, as with the other aspects of nature that Lewis and Clark saw for us for the first time, we must understand what nature was like before the impact of modern, technological civilization. We must come to know the conditions at that time and we must also come to understand how those systems worked—what were the causes and what were the effects, what were the processes that took place within them.

THE COMPLICATED LIVES
OF SALMON

Let us consider the life history of these creatures, whose lives are among the most complex, and who roam among the farthest of all species. A salmon lays its eggs in gravel beds of shallow streams. The conditions are exact and the salmon exacting. A female chooses her place to spawn carefully. She tests the quality of the gravel bed by raising herself into a vertical position in the water and waving her tail vigorously, then inspecting the gravel bed. There must be just the right kind of gravel bed; loose enough to provide space for flowing water to bring oxygen to the eggs, but not so loose that the bed will easily fall apart during flood stages or high water; there must be a mixture of sizes, and the bed must be at least three times her length. If she considers the gravel of the right kind, she lays her eggs.

If gravel in the streams is so important, then the simple thing to do to promote spawning would be to protect the streambeds by preventing any changes from taking place within them. But the natural condition of a river, as we learned from the Missouri and from Lewis and Clark's experiences as they worked their way up that river, is one of change. Rivers and streams of the Pacific Northwest arise in mountains in some of the rainiest countryside in the world, and one of the two or three rainiest temperate climates. Snow builds up during the winter in the mountains. In the spring, warm rains help melt the snow, and the torrents that cascade down the hills wash away boulders and trees and loosen the upper slopes, causing landslides. The waters rush and swirl down to the rivers, moving beds of gravel and transporting sediment to the ocean. At any one location, the gravel is slowly eroded away over the decades by fast flowing water. Eventually, a stream erodes its gravel bed down to bedrock, leaving no habitat at all for a female salmon to spawn. A female salmon swimming through such a bedrock habitat would not even stop to check the area, but would move further upstream.

As the streams rush down toward the sea, they join, one forming the tributary of another, and that larger stream gathering the waters of other tributaries as it flows onward. Hydrologists describe a stream by the number of tributaries that it has. A first-order stream has no tributaries, a second-order stream has tributaries that are first order, and so on. Each tributary carries its gravel to the next higher order stream. The source of the gravel is the upper slopes of the mountains, where land is steepest and most likely to fail and suffer landslides. At the uppermost reaches, the tiny watersheds are too small to create a surface stream. It is these steep-sloped headwaters that provide the gravel to feed all the streams and rivers.

When one of these upper reaches fails and the land slides, there is a small local catastrophe. The first-order stream below is filled with gravel; trees along the sides of the stream are washed away, and the stream is too full of gravel to provide enough water above the beds for the salmon to spawn. For a while, such a stream is out of service for salmon, but the effect is temporary, episodic. Such local catastrophes provide pulses of gravel to second-order streams. But since there are usually a number of first-order streams flowing into a second-order stream, the larger stream has more sources of gravel, and the variation over time is subdued. There are fewer periods without any gravel. The piles of gravel in the small upstream channels take years to erode to the larger downstream channel; this smooths out the pulses as well. It is not all feast or famine for gravel in the larger streams. As a result there are few times when larger streams would be unsuitable for spawning.

Salmon do not spawn in the smallest stream, instead choosing third-order or higher streams, where the gravel supply is more reliable. For a while, a small-order, upper-slope stream that suffers a landslide is ruined as a spawning ground for the fish, and the landscape looks terrible to a casual hiker. But without these local catastrophes, there could be no proper gravel beds downstream, no place for salmon to rear, and no salmon in the rivers. Small disasters are essential for the continuation of this species. Someone who wants to help maintain gravel beds for salmon would have to allow landslides at the upper slopes. An attempt to protect all the mountain forests from change, to keep the steep slopes always and everywhere covered by trees, would lead to a long-term disaster for the salmon.

A similar problem arises when we attempt to suppress fires in prairie preserves. Moreover, a similar story can be told for the supply of food for the fish, but this story is even more complex. When salmon eggs hatch, the small fry stay for a while in the upper reaches of the stream where they were born, feeding on small invertebrate animals and hiding from predators under fallen logs. An intricate food chain is involved in providing their food. At the base are diatoms, microscopic brown algae that, unlike higher plants, can move. The diatoms compete for space to grow, for light, and for nutrients carried by the water with other forms of algae, which cling to rocks and gradually cover them, leaving no room for the diatoms.

Considering that only 10 percent of the newly hatched salmon survive, a seemingly obvious thing a fisherman might do to increase the number of fish would be to help these young fish survive, and one way to do this would be to increase the food supply. What could he do? The obvious thing to do would be to increase the abundance of diatoms. To do that, he would have to understand the requirements and adaptations of these tiny algae.

Diatoms grow well in bright light, and the easiest way to create bright light is to cut down the trees that grow along the stream in the area known as the riparian zone —the land that is outside of the path of the stream and below normal high water, but which receives an abundance of water and is within the flood zone.

Riparian zones, like the upper steep slopes of the mountains, undergo episodic clearings from storms or fire. In the Pacific Northwest, a riparian zone that has just been cleared is reforested first by alder trees whose whitish barks brighten the depths of the dense woodlands. Alders grow well in bright light and in the disturbed but well-watered habitat of the cleared streamside.

Nitrogen-fixing bacteria grow in nodules in alder roots. Alder is the major tree of this habitat with such symbionts. Over time, alders enrich the fertility of the soil by contributing nitrogen-rich leaves, twigs, and roots to the soil. Their nitrogen-rich leaves fall into the stream and provide an important source of food for some invertebrates. When these trees die, their bark and twigs and roots enrich the soil. Alders are comparatively short-lived for trees, lasting not much more than a century, and often much less. Their rapid growth and decay benefit the streams, but this benefit can only occur if the streamside is occasionally disrupted so that light-requiring alder can reseed.

Conifers of various species come into the riparian forest as the alders die and disappear. These live a long time and produce some of the huge trees for which the Pacific Northwest is famous. When the large conifers die and fall over into the streams, they form biological dams behind which other debris collects. These dams can last centuries, especially if the tree falls over with its roots intact, because the big ball of roots helps anchor the tree against the force of water during spring runoff. These debris dams are very important to the salmon. The trees provide places for the young fish to hide. The dams create pools. The stream becomes a pattern of pools and riffles (shallow patches where the water runs fast). The presence of both riffles and pools is important to the salmon.

If we were to take a single-factor approach and decide that the best thing to do would be to help diatoms grow by keeping the forest alongside the river clear of anything but alder, we might cut the streamside every few years. But if the streamside stays brightly lit for about six years, then the diatoms begin to lose in their competition for light to the filamentous, strand-forming algae that retain a better toehold on the rock surfaces. The base of the food for salmon declines. Ironically, the production of food for salmon is greatest during the first six years after the clearing of a streamside forest, but this is also the most unstable time for the food supply. Slowly, conifers start to come into the streamside forest along with the alders, the shade increases, and the diatoms have a hard time getting enough light. For about the next 40 years, the stream produces the least amount of food for the salmon. As the forest gets older and the trees larger, breaks occur that permit moderate light to reach the stream. The production of the diatoms goes up. In the old-growth forest, the production of food for salmon is second best, but the supply is much more stable over time.

A salmon manager who tried to keep the streamside clear of forests would fail to increase the numbers of salmon in his stream. He would not only lose the diatoms that are essential as the base of the food chain, but his stream would never develop the dams formed by large dead conifers. On the other hand, if this manager tried to keep the forest forever in old growth, there would be no nitrogen enrichment from the alders, and the overall fertility of the forest would decline. Change in the streamside forest is necessary, just as change is necessary at the upper slopes for the supply of gravel.

After living and growing in fresh waters, the young fish begin their migration down the river. Along the way, they are vulnerable to many predators: eagles and cormorants, otters, predatory fish. The longer the time spent traveling downstream, the more vulnerable the fish become. Places to hide are important. These hiding places include logs and boulders, as well as the inner recesses of natural meanders and wetlands. Such variation in the stream characteristics over the space through which the stream flows was once the rule. Now with stream channelization, with development near the shores, with water diversion for irrigation, wetlands and meanders are much less common. Another kind of variability, important to the fish, has declined.

Water flow in rivers varies from year to year. The intensity of risks to the fish changes with the amount of water flow; this is especially true during the downstream migration, but the water variation also affects spawning, egg survival, and early fry survival. In low water years, channels narrow and wetlands dry and there are fewer hiding places for young fish. Low water also means that during the summer water temperature can reach levels unhealthy to these northern, ocean-going fish, increasing their mortality. Variations in weather thus affect the survival of the fish, and since weather is always varying, the level of risk due to water flow varies continuously.

Finally, the fish reach the ocean where, depending on species and other factors and events, they spend one to five years—in rare cases a year or two longer for individuals of some species. It is here in the ocean where they put on most of their weight.

Once in the ocean, the fish disperse. Within a single species, some stocks swim north while others swim south. We really don't know where all the fish go. It is believed that most stay along the coast, but in part that is because the only information about the populations is from legal harvests, all of which are within the 200-mile limit. Salmon, like all larger fish, will seek areas where ocean food is abundant, and this occurs where there is an ample supply of chemical elements necessary for life.

Currents in the ocean flow in three dimensions. There are the horizontal currents like the Gulf Stream that flows from south to north, but there are also currents that are upward and others that flow downward. An upwelling is a current that rises vertically; a downwelling flows from the surface to the depths. Upwellings occur under specific conditions that have to do with the relationship between continents, ocean, and atmosphere. Under certain conditions, prevailing winds near a continent are offshore or are otherwise directed so that they drive ocean surface waters away from the continent. Deeper waters rise to replace these surface waters that are driven offshore, and these waters bring with them the nutrients that have sunk to the bottom. Such upwellings are among the best fishing areas in the world. Strong upwelling regions occur along the Pacific Coast. The salmon and ocean-going trout swim into these areas and benefit from their production, which provides some of the prey that make it possible for these fish to put on weight. Because upwellings are caused by prevailing winds, they are subject to the vagaries of climate, and when the winds fail, so do the upwellings. Without a resupply of nutrients, the biological production fails, and the salmon lack food. El Niño is the most famous kind of upwelling failure.

The intensity of upwellings along the Pacific coast varies from year to year, decade to decade. Although scientists do not measure these currents directly—they do not have meters in the ocean that measure the rate of vertical water flow—they infer the intensity of upwellings from air pressure differences between the ocean and the land, from the conditions that create the appropriate wind flows that in turn create the upwellings. Upwellings were strong in the mid 1970s, but since then there has been a peculiar period of weak upwellings along the coast of Oregon. These environmental fluctuations are also likely to influence the size and numbers of fish that return to the rivers. We have little ability to affect upwellings directly, although we might have indirect effects on these currents if the actions of civilization are changing the climate globally. Without any ability to affect upwellings directly, we will always be at the mercy of these variations in the environment as they affect salmon and ocean-going trout. Given all these changing variables, we can never expect the number of fish returning in a given year to be constant; yet this constancy is a premise on which the annual catch of the fish is determined.

THE GLOBAL SIGNIFICANCE OF CONSERVING SALMON IN THE PACIFIC NORTHWEST

Salmon once occurred widely around the northern hemisphere especially in the rivers and streams in areas covered by the past continental

206

ice sheets. They are therefore a species adapted to long-term climatic variation and capable of moving into new rivers and streams as these become available. Many human settlements of these northern areas once depended on these fish. Overfishing and habitat alteration led to declines and elimination of salmon throughout much of their range. Thus the conservation of the fish in the Pacific Northwest, if it succeeds, represents more than a local success. The elimination of salmon has followed in the wake and turbulence of civilization.

The ancestors of salmon can be traced back in the fossil record about 100 million years. Although next to human beings and fruit flies, the genetics of salmon are better known that any other animal, the genealogy and taxonomy of this group are not completely understood or agreed on. The King salmon of the Pacific Northwest and the Siberian huchen of the Danube are the biggest salmonids, individuals exceeding 50 kilograms, about 110 pounds, in weight. Wherever the large salmonids occur, they are of sport and commercial value. Some of the big salmonids live their entire life in freshwater. These include a number of species of trout, as well as the lake char, graylings, and whitefish. Salmonids occur along the Siberian coast and up the rivers of Siberia; they once occurred widely in the coastal rivers of Northern Europe into Scandinavia and in the rivers of Great Britain. Those who know the history of the destruction of these fish, lost one by one in the advancing current of civilization, see the conservation of salmon and ocean-going trout in the Pacific Northwest as a last stand against the forces that are destroying these resources. The conservation of salmon in this area is not merely a local problem; it is the final fortress in the battle against a global loss of these highly valued fish. To understand the motivations and the intensity of concern of those who wish to conserve anadromous fish in Oregon and Washington, where Lewis and Clark found them two centuries ago, we must understand this global

207

concern. As surely as the expedition moved forward foot by foot, portage by portage, just as surely in its wake were the harvest, the exploitation, and the destruction of habitat of these fish.

Across the Atlantic, salmon are in trouble. They are farmed in the fjords of Norway, grown within huge netted pens, provided with food. Like cattle feedlots, these concentrated production areas pollute the environment, but they provide much of the table salmon sold today. Salmon were once abundant on the rivers of the northeastern coast of North America. For the last three decades attempts to reintroduce the fish have failed, except for a small number of salmon that have returned to the Penobscot River in Maine, and for some aquaculture of Atlantic salmon being done near Eastport, Maine.

Recognizing the loss of salmon, people in other parts of the world have begun restoration programs. Salmon were once abundant on the Thames River in England, but were extinct there by 1834. Then in the late 1970s an adult salmon was caught in the screen of a power station, the first salmon seen on the Thames in more than 150 years. The fish, adaptable to variable conditions and capable of reoccupying rivers that were once blocked by ice, appeared able to return to a river once made inhospitable by the action of people. As a result of this single return, a major river restoration program has taken place in the Thames during recent years, with considerable success. There are more than 100 species of fish living in the Thames, but salmon do not complete their life cycle there anymore. The river is stocked every year with 200,000 salmon, but until recently none were able to spawn and provide a second generation. Dams, channelization, habitat alteration, and all the other factors I have described for the Pacific Northwest took place long ago in England. A system of fish ladders and passages is under construction in more than 20 locations to allow salmon to reach potential spawning areas. About a third of the fish that are released are bred from those that have returned to the river. In 1993, 300 salmon that were released in the Thames returned to it. Of these, 30 had been bred from fish that had been released in previous years and returned. The plan is to keep stocking the river with fish bred of those that do return, with the hope that over time the fish will find adequate habitat to spawn and breed without the assistance of people.

SAVING THE RIVER AND OURSELVES

In the 1930s, the engineering development of the Columbia River was part of radical chic, considered by a broad segment of our society to be a public good. To a large extent, attitudes today toward the environment fill the same role. Preservation of the environment has broad support socially and there is a set of radical groups who believe that the defense of the environment is so important as to supersede the well-being of people. To Woody Guthrie, the taming of the river was part of a radical political alteration of our society. To some environmental groups, the reversal of that is part of a radical political alteration of our society. Woody Guthrie's dream did become a benefit to the economic standard of living of the people; but the Bonneville Power Administration, his employer for that time, became a large, entrenched bureaucracy that suffered from the problems typical of such organizations—a focus on its own continuation, on single factors, a lack of flexibility, a slowness to react. What had been radical chic became conservative establishment, unable to respond rapidly to the changing perceptions and needs of the time. Perhaps a major lesson from this history of the Columbia is that, in our enthusiasm to save the environment of the Pacific Northwest, we do not create huge bureaucracies that are unresponsive to the changing and complex needs of the future.

What can we learn from the difference between the idealized societal improvement envisioned in Woody Guthrie's songs and the actual development? We knew too little. Natural systems such as the Columbia River are much more complex than anyone realized half a century ago, and few recognize today. The real lesson is that we should be humble in our approach to both social and environmental engineering. We need to find a way to save both the river and ourselves.

And then there are the salmon—their intricate, complicated life cycle with its many habitats and highly specific demands, yet the great robustness that has enabled this group of fish to not only survive but often to prevail in spite of ice ages and volcanic flows that destroyed habitats for long periods of time. Compare the difference between what appears to be necessary to save buffalo with what is necessary to save salmon. We can grow buffalo on rangeland much as we do cattle. Or we can put them into remnants of native or restored prairie where they can fend for themselves. The buffalo are at one extreme in their requirements in the modern world; salmon, with their intricate requirements, at the opposite extreme. A stream must have just the right combination of many conditions for salmon to breed successfully and return to that stream year after year. If we want salmon in a particular stream, we must provide those conditions. But to make matters even more difficult, the "what" that we must provide is not a thing or group of things, but a set of processes that happen over time, and therefore require changes in the "whats." The salmon have persisted not because there was a single stream that was their home forever, but because some percentage of the salmon enter streams that were not where they spawned and therefore salmon have been able to shift among many rivers and streams as climate and volcanic activity and forest fire changed. If we do not overharvest salmon, and if we allow enough streams and rivers to be available, and make it possible that at least some of these are in the right conditions at any time, the salmon will persist.

We cannot provide this complex set of conditions if we insist that nature is one thing in one condition for all time. Here is the point at which a simplistic ideology, however appealing, just doesn't work— whether it is the ideology of Woody Guthrie's songs, or the contemporary insistence that the streams and rivers be fixed in time and that people be removed from the equation. If political pressures force a situation in which it is either salmon or people, the salmon will almost certainly lose.

Winter and Wood on the Pacific Coast

Takes a flat thousand years for a big tree to grow
So I won't be cutting the next growth or so
A little too long for me to wait 'round;
'Cause Lumber's just King in a Lumbering town.

King Lumber might live for 100 years, too,
If when you cut one tree, you stop to plant two;
But, Boys, if you don't, he's on his way down;
'Cause Lumber's just King in a Lumbering town.

WOODY GUTHRIE, *"LUMBER IS KING"*

A s the expedition neared the Pacific Ocean in November 1805, its forward progress was stopped, the members trapped by heavy rain and high water on narrow shores near the mouth of the Columbia River by Grays Bay, in what is now Pacific and Wahkiakum counties. "We found the swells of waves so high that we thought it imprudent to proceed; we landed, unloaded and drew up our canoes," Clark wrote on November 8, 1805. "We are all wet and disagreeable, as we have been for several days past, and our present situation a very disagreeable one in as much as we have not level land sufficient for an encampment and for our baggage to lie clear of the tide, the high hill jutting is so close and steep that we cannot retreat back."

They were camped on the Washington (northern) shore of the river, about 50 miles downstream from the present site of Portland where the shore is steep and narrow, giving little room between the waves and the woods, a location easily seen from Washington Route 4, which passes right along the shore. The highway is near to the water level and the land rises abruptly to the north. Intense storms, characteristic of that season on that part of the coast, battered the expedition.

In spite of the terrible predicament, the members of the expedition remained "all cheerful and full of anxiety to see further into the ocean," and Clark remained true to the scientific charge of the expedition and measured the drifting logs that threatened the party, finding them huge—some 200 feet long and 4 feet in diameter. The rain lasted for 11 days, and the water rose higher and higher. They could keep dry only by sitting on logs and laying on them to sleep. On the 11th of November 1805, the logs that were their beds began to float in the rising waters. They and their baggage were "scattered on floating logs

213

and such dry spots as can be found on the hill sides and crevices of rocks." "We are all wet as usual," Clark wrote. To add injury to the insult of flood, the rain loosened stones from the hills, and these fell on the members of the expedition. They were immersed in the forest, subject to its conditions; perhaps more than any other time during the expedition, nature was in control, and Lewis and Clark were powerless against her forces.

Forests of one kind or another had been visible along the Columbia River since the expedition had been near the rapids at The Dalles in late October 1805, but during these 11 days the expedition experienced for the first time the fury of severe winter storms of the Pacific Northwest, along with the damage that could be wrought by huge logs of the coastal, temperate rain forests of the Pacific Northwest. At this time, the forest was dangerous to the expedition; at other times in other places, it was beneficial. So it has always been between people and forests; a duality of experiences, a duality of attitudes, a need and love of forests on the one hand, a fear of their darkness and desire to cut them down and let in the light, on the other. For forests are not just a collection of big trees; they are complex systems within whose fabric we have always found it difficult to weave ourselves. With the force of numbers and the powers of technology as basic as the ax and fire, we can cut and burn and clear forests, or we can leave them alone, staying in more open country; but a middle approach has been elusive throughout the history of Western civilization.

To the Indians of the coast, forests were a way of life, providing fuel and structural material; forests have provided all major civilizations with these necessities for thousands of years. The use of forest products by the Indians of the Pacific Northwest was quite sophisticated, as the famous sculptured totem-pole logs from farther north attest, but as was also apparent to the expedition from the look of the native houses.

Clark first visited one of the wooden houses of the Indians who lived along the Columbia River on October 24, 1805, while the expedition was attempting to pass down the dangerous rapids described in the previous chapter. It was the first wooden house inhabited by a Native American that he had seen since he left Illinois. The Indian houses were deep rectangular pits lined with wood planks so that only the roof and the gables were above ground. This construction provided warmth in a region that had cold winters and winds that blasted out of the east, down the Columbia from the mountains. Summers were cool, because of cold onshore winds from the Pacific. The houses were about 30 feet long and 20 feet wide, Clark observed, and were sunk six feet into the ground. Red cedar bark covered the roofs, supported by a "ridge pole resting on three strong pieces of split timber" attached together with cedar strands. Eaves, side walls, and gable ends were covered with split boards and supported internally by "strong pieces of timber."

Construction was similar to that of a simple country wooden house built by people of European descent, except for the lack of brick or stone chimneys and glass windows. "Light is admitted through an opening at top which also serves for the smoke to pass through," Clark observed. There were wooden beds raised above the ground near to the door and a fireplace in the center.

Some of the coastal Indians of the Pacific Northwest encountered by Lewis and Clark lived in larger dwellings with wooden plank walls and plank roofs, housing a number of families. Some were 50 by 55 feet long and had gabled roofs. Among some Indians, huge cedar tree trunks were used for ridge poles and sidebeams to which planks were attached to make walls. The Indians of northwestern California, who built similar houses, used redwood planks.

Wood formed the basis of the Indian way of life; the forests and the rivers were the sources of their most important resources. The Columbia River Indians made dugout canoes from forest trees, and these were their principal means of transportation. They made wooden boxes from red cedar, steaming the wood to make it flexible and then bending it into a box shape. Dishes, spoons, and ladles were made from wood, as were masks and rattles. Much of the woodworking was done with care and skill, with an emphasis on decorations.

From our late-twentieth-century perspective, it is easy to assume that the crafts and skills of the Indians must have been primitive because these people lacked the metal tools and other accoutrements of Western civilization, but the wood craft of the Pacific Coast tribes seem to me to be on a par or better with much of the work of their contemporary country folk of European descent in some of the woodland areas of the United States. Lewis and Clark's descriptions of the living arrangements of the Pacific Coast Indians remind me of a house I visited some years ago in the backwoods of southern New Hampshire belonging to the local elected state representative and her husband. I was helping my father-in-law, Heman Chase, a civil engineer and native New Hampshire man, to survey a disputed boundary between the representative's house and their neighbors, which was the reason that the two families had ceased to speak with each other. It was a midwinter morning, and there was a crackle to the snow as we walked in the woods, and the stillness in the air made it quiet enough to hear a rabbit jump. As we approached the house, quite isolated in second-growth woodlands, we could see that the roof was partially caved in, with a broken ridge pole forming a V-shape rather than a straight line.

216

At first I thought this was an abandoned house that we would pass on the way to the house we were seeking, but it turned out to be the primary residence of one of the state's elected officials.

The main room, about 30 feet long and 20 feet wide, was warmed by a fire glowing in a wood-burning "chunk" stove at one end of the room. More than half of the living room was filled with stacks of wood chunks, among which were several chairs. The representative, a tall, elderly woman whose sunken mouth suggested false teeth, was seated in one at the far inside of the room, and beyond her I could see an open doorway leading to at least one other room. Her husband sat before the stove, opening its door and pushing in chunks of wood as needed. The end of the main room away from the wood stove was crammed with potted plants taking sun from an ample number of windows. It was obvious that the couple spent most of the winter seated before the stove.

When we sat down to talk, the wife, who was the state representative, opened a tin of tobacco. At first I thought that she was going to take a chew, but then she rolled herself a cigarette, placed it in her partially toothless mouth, and began to talk with us about the surveying. Her life, in spite of her importance as an elected official, was not all that different in physical comforts from those of the Native Americans living a century and a half before along the Columbia River. After a brief visit, warming ourselves by the stove, we went outside and surveyed the boundary under dispute, and then left without seeing them again. I never did find out whether the surveyor's map helped resolve the disagreement, or whether the representative and her husband ever talked with their neighbors again, but the image of this elected state representative has remained with me always.

WINTER AT FORT CLATSOP

Lewis and Clark depended on wood during the winter of 1805–1806 as much as did the Pacific Coast Indians. As they had the winter before, Lewis and Clark organized the men and built a wooden fort. They chose a site in early December 1805 that was south of the Columbia along the wide mouth of an estuary, away from the terrible strong winds that poured down the Columbia from the interior mountains, protected by coastal hills and forests from direct exposure to the storms that came in relentlessly from the Pacific. They named the site Fort Clatsop after the local Indians.

The weather at Fort Clatsop had a severe effect on the members of the expedition. They began to build huts on December 11, 1805, in spite of rain. On that day, the journals record that several of the men suffered from "excessive dampness" and that four had very violent colds, one had dysentery, a third "tumors on his legs," and two had injured their limbs. Protection from the weather was desperately needed, and wood was the only resource for such protection. On December 14, working in the rain, they completed the walls of the cabins and recorded that the constant rains spoiled "our last supply of elk" and that "scarcely one man can boast of being one day dry since we landed at this point." The insides of the cabins were finished on December 17, just in time, as their tents had rotted through and tore at the slightest touch, and there was snow and hail the next morning, December 18, which lasted until noon, followed by rain which continued until the next morning. The necessity of wooden shelters and wood fires was clear. On the day after Christmas, the journals record that the men attempted to dry their wet articles in front of fires.

218

Securing food remained difficult for the expedition throughout the winter. The heavy forest cover produced a dense shade near the ground, providing little forage for elk or deer and providing few of the big game animals for the members of the expedition to eat. The Indians survived on a diet of fish dried for the winter, some big game, and some native vegetation.

The dense forests had made obtaining food difficult well before the expedition reached winter camp. On November 11, 1805, Clark sent Joseph Field out to hunt, but he returned shortly and said that the hills were high and steep, the undergrowth and fallen timber so thick that he could not proceed far.

Lewis and Clark wrote frequently during their stay at Fort Clatsop about the lack of food and the difficulty in finding game. On January 6, 1806, Clark left the fort with 12 men on one of the rare clear days of that winter. "The evening was a beautiful clear moon-shiny night and the first fair night which they had enjoyed for two months," he wrote. He went with 12 men in two canoes where they pursued and killed one elk which they ate up entirely. During this time, they were able to find some deer and elk, but the animals were generally lean and the flesh by no means as good as what they had obtained earlier. Elk was a chief food for them when they could find it.

On February 2, Clark observed that "the elk are in much better order in the point near the prairies than they are in the woody country about us, or up the Netul. In the prairies they feed on grass and rushes, considerable quantities of which are still green and succulent. In the woody country, their food is huckleberry bushes, ferns, and an evergreen shrub [*Gaultheria shallon*] which resembles the laurel in some measure. This last, which constitutes the greater part of their food, grows abundantly all through the timbered country, particularly on the hill-sides and other more broken ground."

Replicates of the huts and the surrounding wood fort walls can be seen today at Fort Clatsop National Monument, about 10 miles south of Astoria, Oregon. These seem cruder than the houses of the Indians as Clark described them. Reconstructed Fort Clatsop is a rectangle of huts made of roughly hewn logs not well chinked; the wind seeps through, chilling the air.

I visited the fort twice, once in mid-summer and again near Christmas. The huts are small and dark, and as cold in mid-summer, when the fog drifts in off the Pacific and the rain drips on the wood, as an abandoned New Hampshire farmhouse in October. Even on such a summer day, a fire seemed necessary to take the chill out of the air and make the damp darkness of the interior livable. During my visit in the twilight of December near Christmas, the time of year when the expedition was settling into the fort, it seemed a chilled and dismal existence, one in which the search, cutting, and preparation of wood for fires would be a constant activity.

Reading Clark's accounts of the Indian houses and other wood crafts, one becomes aware that these inhabitants of the forest had the skills to fell big trees, make large boards, and make many utensils from wood. This leads one to wonder if perhaps they had other skills that would give them power over their environment that today we tend not to attribute to such "primitive" people, such as an ability to modify the forest to enhance the production of food and structurally useful timber.

FROM GRASSLANDS TO THE
FOREST

The forests of huge trees occurred over a large area west of the Cascades where the rainfall is high. Lewis and Clark had entered this region of the western coastal forests in late October 1805. After seeing the first interior Indian houses of wood, they continued down the Columbia River and soon entered an ecological transition from grassland to forest. This forested landscape was far different from the countryside to the east, where the expedition first reached the Columbia. There, in eastern Oregon and Washington, the river flowed through dry grassland. The transition from dry grassland to forest occurred rapidly, especially compared to the gradual change from prairie to forest that the expedition had experienced over the many weeks traveling up the Missouri River.

At the Columbia River Cascades, Lewis and Clark saw that "the face of the country of both sides of the river," was "steep, rugged, and rocky, with a very small proportion of herbage, and no timber except a few bushes; the hills to the west, however, have some scattered pine, white oak, and other kinds of trees." Then on October 31, 1805, the expedition came to a huge perpendicular rock in a meadowland along the north shore of the Columbia River, about 50 miles upriver from modern Portland, Oregon. They estimated that rock was "about 800 feet high and 400 yards around the base." Now known as Beacon Rock, after Lewis and Clark's name, and still a famous local landmark, it is a huge volcanic plug believed to have been ejected and thrown across the gorge by an ancient volcanic explosion.

"The low grounds are about three-quarters of a mile wide, rising gradually to the hills, with a rich soil covered with grass, fern, and other small undergrowth," the journals record at Beacon Rock, while the mountains, which approached the river "with steep rugged sides" were "covered with a very thick growth of pine, cedar, cottonwood, and oak." This was a pleasant change for Lewis and Clark. "The country has a handsome appearance." Clark wrote on November 3, 1805, and on the next day wrote, "I walked out [and] found the country fine, an open Prairie for one mile back of which the woodland commences." On the edge of the Prairie he saw white oak, on the hills spruce and pine (his name for Douglas fir) and maple and cottonwood growing near this river. "After being so long accustomed to the dreary nakedness of the country above, the change is as grateful to the eye as it is useful in supplying us with fuel," they wrote. The forests began to provide them, as they have to people before and after, with a major resource on which civilization has always depended: timber for fuel and construction.

Beacon Rock also marked the end of the dangerous rapids through which the expedition had traveled in their boats. Downstream, the river widens. Four miles downstream, Lewis and Clark estimated that the river was about two miles wide, and there they found "a smooth gentle stream." They could feel their approach to the ocean; from the rise and fall of the ocean's tide, whose effect extended all the way to Beacon Rock.

For anyone traveling through this region, Beacon Rock still serves as a good locator of a major environmental transition between the dry region of eastern Oregon and the wet coastal region. This transition is the result of a rain shadow effect from the Cascade Mountains, through which, via the Columbia River Gorge, Lewis and Clark were passing. A rain shadow occurs when a mountain range forces the air to rise as it passes inland from the ocean. Rising air cools and condenses. Such air holds less moisture than warm air, and the moisture it carries condenses and is deposited in the mountains as rain, snow, or as mist in clouds and fogs that intersect trees. Once the air has passed the mountain summits, it descends, warms, and is able to hold more moisture. The little moisture it has retained from its passage over the summit remains with it. In major mountainous regions like the Cascades, the descending air becomes so warm that it can hold more water than it contains, and drinks the eastern land dry, evaporating moisture as it passes by. (A similar process occurs over the Rockies, leading to the relative dryness of the Great Plains.)

The rain shadow effect is as dramatic today along the Columbia River Gorge as it was in 1805. In the short distance between the confluence of the Yakima, Snake, and the Columbia at Pasco, Washington, and Beacon Rock, the country changes climatic zones, from desert to a temperate, wet coastal region. Although the total rainfall is not all that high, the rain falls frequently as light drizzles and occasional heavy storms move through. It is rainy and cloudy for most of the year, except for the summer and early fall.

Anyone who has traveled the countryside of western Washington and western Oregon knows that the forests of the Pacific Northwest are impressive—huge trees tower over the land, darkening the ground, dominating everything, producing huge downed logs taller than a man, almost as tall as a horse, making travel almost impossible. So impressively large and dense are these forests that they seem permanent and unchanging. A hike into one of these ancient forests leaves us with the impression that the Pacific Northwest, prior to human exploitation, must have been a vast, almost mystical, land of dark, giant forests extending over the entire landscape. But was that really the case?

Forests appear permanent to the casual visitor, in contrast to wildlife, which are often difficult to see and move quickly away from human beings. To scientists, forests are much more open to study than wildlife, because trees don't move around, and because in temperate and northern latitudes trees lay down annual growth rings and can be easily aged. As a result, we know more about trees in forests and their interactions with each other and their environment than we do about wildlife.

Forests are an important part of our natural history, not only in the resources and recreation they provide, but symbolically, as they represent the idea of nature to us. It was the immense and seemingly bound-less forests that confronted the first settlers of the eastern United States; the ancestors of Lewis, Clark, and Jefferson as well as the pilgrims and their descendants. Clearing enough of those forests to allow room for crops to grow and towns to be built was a major early activity in North America. Forests have always provided essential resources in North America, just as they have for other civilizations. But compared to most of Europe, we who live in North America have much more direct con-tact with ancient forests, and the clearing of ancient forests over wide areas is much closer to us in time than it is in the European experience.

In recent years, forests have become a major focus of environmental controversies around the world. Much of the controversy has to do with the protection of ancient forests, which are steeped in meaning. In part because of their appearance and the longevity of trees, forests unlogged by human beings seem to symbolize the longevity and persistence of all life. When the early Europeans were settling North America, the forests seemed endless. To clear land in New England, trees were girdled—the bark was cut through to the wood in a circle around the tree so that water and minerals could not get up to the leaves, and sugar could not get down to the roots, a fast and simple way to kill a tree—and the land then burned. From the perspective of the early settlers, there were too many trees to use. Later, when forests became major commercial crops, the people cutting the extensive white pine forests of Michigan and Wisconsin—Paul Bunyan country—thought that they could never run out of trees. They thought it would take so long to cut those forests that by the time the last of the original trees was cut the areas first cut would have regrown to merchantable-sized trees.

Forests have held a special fascination for me. I have spent most of the last 30 years as a professional ecologist trying to understand how forests change over time and what they were like before they were altered by technological civilization. Forests helped shape my own ideas about natural history. Like Lewis and Clark, my first experiences in forests were in the eastern United States, and from there I moved west. My first work in forests began in New Hampshire when I helped Heman Chase survey country land holdings, as I wrote about earlier, and when he and I cut wood for fuel for his modern style wood-burning furnace of his home and for the wood stove and two fireplaces in the house I was renting. Both activities were an education about forests, but the two activities were very different ways to learn about forests. In surveying, you follow a compass line wherever it tells you to go. This meant that we sometimes found ourselves struggling through knee-deep water in marshes. Sometimes we crossed abandoned house sites with their stone cellars ringed by *Vinca minor* and their pathways lined by huge old sugar maples; other times we walked across blueberry barrens on rocky outcrops. Surveying the New Hampshire forests was much like a scientific sampling, forcing us to see the woods as they were, not to meander where we wished to go and see the kind of woods we liked best.

Finding trees to cut for firewood was just the opposite activity; we sought out the trees that made the best firewood and looked for stands of trees dominated by those species. Heman kept 60 acres of his own land as a woodlot so that he could concentrate his cutting in one part of his land and leave the rest for other uses. His woodlot was on low flatland, seldom visited, and in an area that did not interfere with the views from ridgetops.

The trees of New England differ greatly in their quality as firewood, with sugar maple by far the best, lasting the longest and giving off the most heat. In a house heated only by wood, this quality becomes very important during cold long winter nights when fires must be kept going. If you had good sugar maple, you only had to get up once during the night, about three in the morning, to add fuel and bank the fire again. Sometimes, if the weather wasn't too cold and the wood was especially good, you could sleep the entire night and find coals still red and the rooms still warm in the morning. Red oak was usually second best, but it took two years to dry and was hard to split when wet. Elm burnt well but had grain that twisted as the tree grew, making it the hardest tree of all to split. Outside my house was an elm that had just died from Dutch elm disease, and I split chunks of it when I had time. One two-foot-long chunk had four wedges forced into it before it yielded. Ash had such straight grain that it almost jumped apart with the slightest blow from an ax—it is that fine straight grain that makes it the wood of choice for baseball bats. Yellow and white birch were pretty good firewood, too, but white pine and other soft woods were terrible for fires, burning quickly with much smoke. Heman burned about 10 cords of wood a year to keep his house warm, and tossing that many wood chunks from soil to truck and truck to woodpile and woodpile to house was a keen lesson in identifying tree species by their bark. Surveying the woods and searching for good firewood formed my first education about forest ecology and provided the basis for my own natural history.

Heman's 60-acre woodlot, which he had been cutting selectively for the best firewood species for about 30 years, had changed from a maple and birch woodland to a stand dominated by trembling aspen, which Heman called "junk wood" because it was quite poor as firewood and not very useful for boards either.

Heman's land also included Prentice Hill, a small rise of granite bedrock from which there was a grand view of the countryside. In 1938 a hurricane that passed through much of New England had cleared much of Heman's woodland. It knocked down almost all the trees around Prentice Hill, and for many years after the view from the top was wonderful. But white pine grew back quickly in what had been pastures near the summit and these soon obscured the scenery. Heman, himself a lover of woodlands, countryside, and beautiful views, made it a practice to have summer picnics when everybody pitched in to cut down some of the white pine that obscured the view of Warren's Pond, the watermill, the white houses of the villages around, and the surrounding hilltops with their bright reds, oranges, yellows, and greens of fall foliage.

A casual visitor from a city or midwestern farmland or western desert, unused to these eastern forests, would have passed through much of these different kinds of woodlands without realizing how much they had been changed by Heman and how purposeful and localized his forest practices were. White pine grew fast on the deep soils downslope from Prentice Hill, and my guess is that many such visitors would think they were in virgin forests because of the size of those 50-year-old trees.

The more time I spent in the woods, the more I became curious about how forests changed over time and at what rate. I discovered that there were few studies with hard data about the condition of the land at specific times that went back more than a decade or two. Over the years I spent in New Hampshire, Heman and his wife, Edith, told me many stories about each part of their land. Heman remembered what land was open fields when he first moved there as a young boy around 1910. For many parts of their land, Edith remembered the year that a field was last cut for hay or pastured.

One early fall day, she and I walked over much of their 250 acres. I had a map of the property in one hand and a camera in the other. Edith told me the year that each field had been allowed to go back to forest, and from this I was able to make a map of the gradual reforestation of this patch of New Hampshire and photograph the process of changes in vegetation that took place over 60 years. The field across from their house had been abandoned for pasture a year before. Just beyond was a stand of young but tall white pine growing in a field that had been pastured until the day of the 1938 hurricane. And so on. Some of the older woodlands had many species of trees and some of the trees were more than a foot or a foot and a half in diameter. We all loved the woods and saw the use of them and their protection as one and the same activity. I learned the skill of reading a forest to guess its age, and also learned to be cautious in attributing too old an age to forests that looked mature.

It was about this time that I began to read the journals of Lewis and Clark. My own experiences in eastern forests brought life to their travel. I sympathized with their struggle to interpret the countryside as Jefferson had asked them to do, given only brief glances of much of it as they hurried westward. Knowing the difficulty of cross-country travel through forests, I was impressed with the time they were able to devote to writing their observations of natural history.

It was also from these first experiences in the Chase's woodlots that I became curious about the real condition of the original landscape of North America. I began to explore that original landscape as best I could. About this time, one of my ecological colleagues, Bill Reiners, who was teaching at that time at Dartmouth College, worked with another botanist and wrote a little pamphlet listing all the known never-cut forest areas in New England. In New Hampshire there were just two—one called "The Bowl," a low-lying area in northern New Hampshire on forest service land, and the other, called "Nancy Pond" at

228

about 3,000 feet in the White Mountains. In about two centuries, set-tlers in New England had cut all but two tiny areas at least once, and much of the state had been cut over several times.

Along with a few friends from the forest service, I visited both of the uncut areas and measured out square plots within which I recorded the species, height, and diameter of every tree inside so that I could have a quantitative characterization of old-growth forests. Neither site was what we imagined it would be. The bowl was a series of patches of species that looked somewhat strange to us. Moosewood, a kind of maple that we knew only as a small tree that grew underneath the tall trees of New Hampshire's forests, grew to more than a foot in diameter and raised its leaves to the canopy of the forest in the bowl.

The woods around Nancy Pond were dense stands of red spruce that were small in diameter and height, hardly resembling anyone's idea of ancient forests except in the density of the shade. A much younger grove of white pine, which could reach much larger sizes quickly, matched our ideal of old-growth forests much better than what we saw at either of the actual uncut stands. So much for our myths and beliefs about old forests, I thought. Perhaps I could discover more about the real quality of our ancient forests from historical journals like those of Lewis and Clark.

OLD-GROWTH FORESTS AND NATIVE AMERICANS

The contact between Lewis and Clark and the Indians along the Co-lumbia River who used wood extensively, and the experiences of the expedition in the forests of the Pacific Northwest lend valuable insight for us to apply today, when we debate the future of the forests of the Pacific Northwest.

Not many years ago only a few citizens paid much attention to the forests except as places for occasional recreation, where few ventured far from well-marked trails. Most conservationists focused on individual species of large birds and mammals. But today, forests have become one of the major concerns among conservationists and loom large as a symbol of our natural history. These societal concerns are having an affect on state and federal agencies that manage forests. There is a shift from the traditional concern of these agencies from a single-factor goal of providing a maximum supply of timber to much broader goals under the name of "ecosystem management." This term and its companion, "sustainability," have become the main jargon in the discussion of forests. Unfortunately, there are many meanings attached to these terms.

The forests of the Pacific Northwest are famous for huge trees valuable for timber, especially Douglas fir, used widely in house construction in the West. On the one hand, timber companies and the U.S. Forest Service see these forests as major resources to be used, and private landowners, believing that they have fundamental property rights to the resources on the forest lands they own, resist government regulation. On the other hand, we find many environmental groups and tourists traveling through these areas, who are shocked to see how large the areas are that have been clearcut, creating great rectangular barren slopes of brown rock and soil which appear abruptly next to some of the densest forests in the world. Whatever the real effect of these large clearcuts on the long-term persistence of the forests, this checkerboard effect gives a devastated look to the countryside, a look very different from the one seen by Lewis and Clark.

Conservation groups have lobbied for the conservation of the ancient forests, with a concern that most or all of the original giant forest trees will be cut if there is no regulation. This controversy raises several fundamental questions about wild, living resources. While these questions form a particular focus in the Pacific Northwest, they have become worldwide: what is necessary to sustain these forests? How much timber can be removed and at what rate so that the forests continue to sustain themselves? These questions lead in turn to another: how much old-growth forests are necessary to prevent extinction of any of the species now found in them, to sustain production, and to sustain the larger and vaguer qualities referred to under the rubric of "ecosystem"?

THE GLOBAL CONTEXT FOR THE CONSERVATION OF FORESTS

What Americans decide to do with and for the forests of northern California, Oregon, Washington, and Canadians with those of British Columbia, is more than a regional issue limited to the events of today or last year or next year; it is more than one nation's issue. It is part of several global issues.

There is a global context behind the concern with the use of forest resources: where in the future can the peoples of the world obtain the forest products they want or need? Throughout the history of civilization, forests have provided fuel and a primary structural material; since the time of the printing press, forests have supplied the bulk of the world's paper. We can imagine some substitutes; we talk about a paperless office where people use only computer screens, files, disks, and modems. We can produce paper from linen and rice and other herbaceous plants. We can even produce it from oil. We can suggest other sources of fuels. But the reality is that for today and for a long time in the future, forests will continue to be the source of fuel for many peoples, especially those of undeveloped nations, houses will continue to be built of wood, wood will continue to be a major component of decorative interiors, and we will continue to write on paper.

We cannot plan correctly for the conservation and use of our forests in a geographic and historic vacuum. In the previous chapter I explained the global context within which we must view the present situation of the fish harvests of the Pacific Northwest. Salmon and their close relatives, the ocean-going trout, have disappeared from many of the rivers of mid and high latitudes throughout the northern hemisphere. People who recognize this can readily adopt a "fortress mentality," in which it appears imperative to preserve all existing stocks of these fish, because otherwise there seems an historical imperative for people to destroy them and their habitats. This global perspective is an unspoken agenda among conservation groups. To miss this is to leave one wondering what all the fuss is about. It is about the potential loss of the last remnant of what was once a global resource.

Forests of the Pacific Northwest are among the most productive in the world. If we do not obtain timber from these forests, where will it come from? There are a limited number of regions in the world where there is likely to be a major excess of forest production in the future—an excess above local use: the North American boreal forest; the Siberian boreal forest; tropical rain forests; temperate deciduous forests of North America; southern pines in North America; and plantations in western Europe, including Scandinavia. The boreal forests are the northern coniferous or "Christmas tree" forests. In North America, these extend from Minnesota to near Hudson Bay, and from New Brunswick and Maine to the eastern slopes of the Alaskan Rockies.

232

Which of these are most likely to provide a continuing source of timber? Although currently there is much harvest in tropical rain forests, there is little to tell us such forests can be managed to provide sustainable supplies. For many tropical forests, there are theoretical reasons to believe that they are unlikely to be sustainable for high yield timber production. And because tropical rain forests house so many kinds of species, this is not a kind of forest we would like to banish from the Earth or reduce to very small remnants. Strong arguments can be made that the tropics, although heavily forested today, cannot be relied on as a source of timber in the future.

The less we allow ourselves to use forest resources from one part of the world, the greater the pressure will be to use those from others. A policy that prevented harvesting timber in the Pacific Northwest would put greater pressure on other areas. This in turn suggests that we need to know the minimum amount of each kind of forest that must be conserved in order to retain all the properties of each of its ecosystems, including sustaining all the species of trees, other plants, and wildlife native to these forests so that we do not allow any of these kinds of forests to be constrained to a smaller size than that minimum. We also need to know the minimum size of each of these forests so that we could obtain a reasonable fraction of the world's timber resources from each on a sustainable basis. Of course, we hope that we can sustain much more of each of these forests than some minimum area.

How can we answer the question: what is the minimum size of forests required to sustain this kind of ecosystem? Some believe that the answer lies in knowing the conditions of these forests before European settlement and exploitation. These forests seem to have persisted for thousands of years, so one way to maintain their sustainability would be to reproduce the conditions they were in before European settlement.

To many, this seems the surest way. This approach to the question is especially appealing if you believe in the constancy of nature and believe that the forests of the Pacific Northwest prior to European influence were in a single, uniform condition that persisted indefinitely on the landscape. Scientists who studied forests in the early part of the twentieth century believed in this kind of forest. They believed that forests developed after a disturbance such as a fire or storm through a clearly identifiable and repeatable pattern of changes called forest succession to an old-age stand. They believed that old-age stands were the ones that could persist indefinitely on the landscape, and they called them the climax stage in forest succession. This belief in the constancy and fixed balance of nature is one of the heritages of the natural history of European civilization. This idea contradicts the message of the Missouri River that I discussed in earlier chapters—that nature is changing and depends on change. But it is still a common popular belief, one that my own experiences in the forests of New England clearly ran counter to.

Throughout this book I have written about the difference between the conditions of nature as observed by Lewis and Clark and the present conditions. But our natural history differs not only in the "what" of the forests, prairies, rivers, and mountains, but also in our scientific understanding of how forests work. During the almost two centuries since Lewis and Clark wintered in Fort Clatsop, we have learned much about forests as ecosystems, and some important parts of this understanding has occurred in the last 20 years in the forests of the Pacific Northwest, not far from where Lewis and Clark spent their second winter.

There are three paths open to us to try to understand what leads to a sustainable forest and its ecosystem. One way is to learn what these forests were like prior to European settlement, under the assumption that they had persisted for thousands of years before this happened and therefore were sustainable. A second way is to study modern forests and subject them to experiments; to find areas that have been disturbed and measure how they change over time, or to create experimental disturbances and see what happens. A third way is to develop a scientific theory and models of how forests grow, based on understanding of individual trees, and see how these model forests sustain themselves in a computer. Ecologists try all three ways. Lewis and Clark's experiences help us with the first. Groups of twentieth-century ecologists have done much research on the second—in fact, great strides have been made during the past 20 years through experimental studies in understanding the processes that take place in small watersheds and their streams following clearings. This work is one of the fields of study that ecologists in North America can be the proudest of. But the implications of that research for the practical questions I am writing about here have only begun to be addressed. My own work has emphasized the third approach, as I will explain later.

CONTINUOUS FOREST OR A PATCHWORK LANDSCAPE?

How much old-growth forest was there before European settlement? One school of thought holds that the region from the western slopes of the Cascades to the Pacific Ocean—in Lewis and Clark's terms, more or less from Beacon Rock to Fort Clatsop—was one continuous forest of huge trees, unbroken except for occasional dead and fallen ancient trees whose place would be occupied through the natural process of small-scale ecological succession by a sequence of species, ending with trees of the same species as that which had died and fallen over.

A required assumption, usually unstated, of this school of thought is that the Indians who lived along the Columbia and elsewhere along the coasts and streams of Oregon and Washington had essentially no impact on the forests, that either by choice or because of technological inabilities, or both, they did not or could not alter these forests in any significant way. This seems a strange assumption when one considers the importance of wood to these people, their skill in crafting utensils, totems, and buildings from wood, and their dependence on big game animals that thrive in young forests or in grassy areas.

A second school of thought believes that the presettlement forests were not continuous, because variations in soils, bedrock, topography, and climate would benefit forests in some areas, grasslands and treeless swamps in others. However, this school believes that, where conditions allowed forests to grow, old growth forests would have occupied the entire region—the forested land would have been a carpet of continuous ancient, huge trees, these carpets interspersed with throw-rugs of prairie and wetlands. Again, the Indians would have had essentially no effect on such a forested region.

A third school believes that the forests were a mosaic of many stands of many different stages in development, because natural fire and storm damage were the rule and were dominant factors, and these were supplemented by the actions of the Indians, especially intentionally lit forest fires. Some argue further that the forests of the Pacific Northwest as seen by Lewis and Clark were very much the product of intentional actions by the Indians, and that their character was primarily the result of Indian management, and that this management led to more open conditions than would have otherwise occurred.

236

The condition of the presettlement forests of the Pacific Northwest is much more than a curiosity for naturalists; it represents a lot more than the observation, say, of a single spotted owl that a bird-watcher could add to his life list. Timber harvest in the Pacific Northwest is a multi-billion dollar a year business, so the answers matter economically; jobs are at stake. By law, our society is required to protect endangered species and maintain their habitats. The usual assumption is that presettlement conditions represented optimum habitats for all species, and that the way to save an endangered species is to restore its habitat to that condition. Many groups want to conserve the ancient forests in their presettlement condition. Given these goals, if the presettlement condition was one of continuous trees, then little logging or other land clearing can be done. If the presettlement condition was a mosaic, broken by prairie and wetlands, and within the forests a patchwork of stands of many different ages and stages in development, and if disturbance was the rule, then much more opening of the land would be consistent with these conditions, and logging could take place at a higher level. If these presettlement conditions were heavily influenced by the Indians, then to achieve those conditions again we might have to carry out the same kind and level of human actions.

The forests of the Pacific Northwest within which Lewis and Clark spent the winter of 1805–1806 contain some of the largest trees and the greatest density of wood per unit of land area found anywhere in the world. These magnificent forests are a bounty of rich soil and persistent rain, together providing wonderful growing conditions for trees. Individual Douglas fir trees have been found to be 600 years old. But was the land of western Oregon and western Washington one continuous ancient forest? Some of the accounts from Lewis and Clark suggest large areas of continuous, dense forests, consistent with the first school of thought. For example, on November 9, 1805, when the expedition was caught in the storms and between the waters of the river and the logs of the forest, Lewis and Clark recorded that the loosened and drifting logs were "very thick on the shores."

On November 13, the expedition was still caught in the terrible storm, camped along the steep shore of the Columbia described at the beginning of this chapter. For a short time the weather broke, however, and Clark could see Sitka spruce on nearby high mountains. Intrigued and curious about the mountains and the forests, Clark hiked about three miles to the top of one mountain "with much fatigue." That night he wrote that "the whole lower country was covered with almost impenetrable thickets of small pine," a term he applied to many of the conifers, so we are not certain which collection of species he saw. These, he wrote, made travel "almost impossible." On the hills he found many trees 8 and 10 feet in diameter and more than 100 feet tall. He measured one Sitka spruce to be 14 feet in circumference.

About a week later, on November 18, Clark and 11 men traveled north to Cape Disappointment, named by earlier ship explorers who arrived offshore at this point that extends from the Washington side of the Columbia out into the ocean, only to find that they were unable to find a passage through the sand bars into the Columbia River. The country was "low, open, and marshy interspersed with some high pine and a thick undergrowth," Clark wrote. On November 12, 1805, Clark found some conifers that he estimated were 7 to 8 feet in diameter and 200 feet high. Arriving at the Chinook River, he found low hills "very thickly covered" with several species of conifers, many of which were "three or four feet through" and some of these huge trees were "growing on the bodies of large trees which had fallen down, and covered with moss and yet part sound." On the coast, they found waterbirds and "dined" on some brant and plover. The Cape is now a park with a

238

display marking the completion of the westward travel of Lewis and Clark, and from the park building a visitor can look out onto the same rough waters and dense forests that Clark observed.

Clark's observations on that day are consistent with the school of thought that the presettlement forests formed a continuous cover of huge, ancient trees. On that day and in that location, Clark had reached the interior of one of the Earth's most impressive and amazing forests, the temperate coniferous rain forests of the Pacific Northwest, the product of an unusual combination of environmental conditions: one of the wettest climates in any temperate latitude, a fertile soil, and species of trees capable of reaching immense sizes. The rain was a consequence of the proximity to the ocean and of prevailing climate patterns along the Pacific Northwest, which carry ocean-evaporated moisture to the shore. The fertile soils are a result of the long, often violent, volcanic history of the region, which produced some of the largest lava flows anywhere in the world, creating the erosion-resistant rock that forms the Columbia gorge and its difficult rapids. These flows also provide the foundation for fertile soils.

There are only a few places around the world where similar temperate-rainy conditions exist. The west coast of the southern island of New Zealand is another such area, famous also for its temperate rain forests and for glaciers. But in New Zealand the rains are much heavier and the soils less fertile. The forests that develop, although diverse in numbers of species, are smaller in stature.

Some other records from the journals of the expedition are consistent with the second and third schools of thought, that the forests were not continuous, but were broken by grasslands and shrub areas, and influenced by Indian actions. For example, on November 6, 1805, the expedition passed by cliffs at what is known now as Green's Point where Lewis and Clark saw "a beautiful extensive plain." Then they

239

passed two islands in the river—Grims Island, which they estimated to be a mile wide and three miles long, and Gull, a smaller island downstream. They saw "high rugged hills, thickly covered with timber," on the north side of the river, ending in low wetlands covered with rushes, grasses, and nettles," along with bulrushes and flags. In short, the edge of the river was a large wetland that would not support trees.

Later, when they had settled for the winter at Fort Clatsop, the members of the expedition made regular trips to the ocean, where they kept fires burning to evaporate sea water and make salt for the homeward journey. They explored the countryside for considerable distances from the bay where their camp was located. On December 8, 1805, a Sunday, Clark left camp with five men to find a place to make salt. First they passed over a ridge through "thick pine timber," much of which had fallen. After crossing two small streams, they passed through swampy land through which they waded to their knees. Then they came to "an open ridgy prairie," covered with bearberry, suggesting comparatively wet soils. They located a large herd of elk, an indication that they were in more open country. Pursuing the elk, they crossed wetlands covered with mosses and cranberries, and composed of hummocks and deep water in which they sunk to their hips.

In other places they found upland prairies—drier areas dominated not by trees or by swamp shrubs, but by grasses. On December 28, taking a route to the coast, they went five miles through thick woods that they found varied with hills, ravines, and quaking bogs filled with cranberry crossing through "water and thick brush for half a mile" and then reached a "prairie which wavers, covered with grass." Although these observations from the journals tell us that there were open, grassy areas among the forests, especially to the south of the Columbia, and such openings might be the result of soil condition or of Indian

240

actions, they do not provide us with any clear insights as to the role of Indians.

RECONSTRUCTIONS OF FOREST HISTORY

Additional insights into the conditions of the forests before European settlement are being obtained today from modern archeological studies of the Indians of the Pacific Northwest, from studies of the forests themselves, and from historic records made after the Lewis and Clark expedition about the forests. Since these studies are new, there is so far not much agreement about their implications.

Geological studies show that the forests of western Oregon experienced regional catastrophic events at various times in the past. During the last ice age, the coastal areas were not covered by ice; they seem to have been a refuge for many species of plants and animals. At the end of the last ice age, between 15,000 and 12,800 years ago, there were a total of 100 large floods on the Columbia River, so large that the flood waters spilled over into the Willamette Valley and filled it with water, ice, and sediments.

Indians seem to have arrived not long after, about 11,000 years ago, after which fires appear to become more common. The first contact of coastal Indians with Europeans occurred in the 1770s when Spanish trading ships visited the area, but Captain James Cook's voyage later in that decade began the major introduction of European goods and diseases. There is some evidence that, as disease killed many of the Indians, there was a decrease in the frequency of forest fires and a subsequent decrease in the amount of land in prairies and an increase in the amount of forested land.

One area for which such a history has been reconstructed is the Siletz River Basin in Lincoln and Polk counties, Oregon, about 10 to 15 miles inland from the present town of Newport and about halfway down the Oregon coast between the Columbia River and California. The first modern sawmill was built in this basin about 1856, but logging was light until after World War I.

Perhaps the earliest written observations of the forests in the Siletz River Basin were made in 1788 by Robert Haswell, who kept a journal while on board the trading ship of Captain Robert Gray. On Tuesday, October 5, 1788, Haswell wrote that he saw many fires during the night and many columns of smoke. From this he surmised that the land must be "thickly inhabited." He wrote also that "the land was beautifully diversified with forests and green verdant lawns which must give shelter and forage to vast numbers of wild beasts."

A newspaper report of September 7, 1848, describes mountainous countryside heavy with timber and interspersed with small prairies "covered with fern" as well as larger prairies and a large burned area. There, the timber was "not very good, having been badly burnt for some miles around." Another account, made in the following year, 1849, in the journals of Lieutenant Theodore Talbot, describes mountains "covered with forests of pine and fir" and "enveloped with such a dense mass of smoke, occasioned by some large fires to the south of us, that we could see but little of the surrounding countryside." One day he passed through "one tract of burnt forest several miles in extent." On the next day he passed through a "handsome prairie, extending several miles." He camped in such a prairie "about a mile long and a half mile in width" surrounded by tall forests. There were also areas with many downed logs that made travel difficult.

242

Such studies suggest that the Indians had a major effect on the forests, especially through fire and much more of the land may have been open prairie or recently burned forests than occurred after European settlement. As I explained earlier, when I began the study of salmon and the relative effects of forest practices on them and their habitats, we could find no maps of forests conditions, present or past, except for two maps that attempted to show the location of remaining old-growth forests on federal lands, one done by the Wilderness Society and one by the U.S. Forest Service. But slowly, during the two years of this project, maps have begun to appear. First, the Oregon Department of Forestry produced a map of forest conditions from 1988 Landsat satellite imagery, which we could use to represent present conditions and which I described earlier. Then the 1914 map which had been thrown out but recovered from the trash, was relocated, a story I also told earlier. When I wrote the first draft of this chapter, that was the state of our knowledge of maps of forest conditions in western Oregon. But after I wrote that draft, we learned from the Bureau of Land Management that they had a set of maps made by the U.S. Geological Survey from field transects for 1850, 1890, 1920, and 1940. The maps were made from ground surveys in which people went cross country with surveying equipment, much as Heman Chase and I had done in the woods of New Hampshire. The countryside of western Oregon is rough; the bedrock tends to form blocklike hills, one after another. Susan Day, who works with me on the Oregon project and is a native of that state, knows an old man who participated in the more recent surveys. The methods seem good and the maps seem reliable. This has been a great find for that study, and for our attempt here to learn what the forests of the Pacific Northwest were like before they were altered by Western civilization.

The maps divide the landscape into five categories: forests 200 years or older; 100–199 years old; 50–100 years old; 0–49 years; and recently burned areas. Although the distinction between "recently burned" and "0–49 years" is not completely clear in the material supplied with the maps, it seems that the "0–49 years" means areas that were logged, not burned. According to these maps, forests older than 200 years, which we can take to represent old-growth forests, covered 40 percent of the Oregon Coast Range in 1850, 46 percent in 1890, 50 percent in 1920, declining to 19 percent in 1940. Forests older than 100 years covered 62 percent in the 1850 map; 52 percent in the 1890 map; approximately 70 percent in 1920; and approximately 50 percent in 1940. Both the percentage older than 200 years and the percentage older than 100 are useful to us, because some consider a 100-year-old forest to have characteristics that can be considered "mature" while others believe that old-growth forests must be 200 years or older. These maps tell us that western Oregon south of the Columbia River was not wall-to-wall ancient forests that was unchanging in time. Instead, the percentage of the forest in old-growth varied over time, but was at least 40 percent and no more than 50 percent before the turn of the twentieth century. They tell us that the big change in the percentage of older stands began around the time of the Second World War. Finally, we are beginning to be able to characterize the forests where Lewis and Clark spent their second winter and which are so much discussed today.

SUSTAINABILITY AND RECOVERY
OF FORESTS FROM DISRUPTIONS

The capacity of forests to recover and form dense stands of large and old trees is well known and has been a focus of ecological research since the beginning of the twentieth century. Ideas about the character of forests undisturbed by human actions have undergone major changes in recent years. Earlier in the twentieth century, ecologists believed that forests went through a process of development from clearing to old-growth, and that the ancient stages were the only "natural" ones, believed to be capable of persisting indefinitely as long as storms, fires, and landslides did not disturb them. It was believed that the seeds of the trees that dominated these ancient stands could germinate and the saplings grow in the deep forest shade; that these ancient forests not only contained a huge amount of organic matter, but also had the greatest diversity of species. The stages that occurred early were seen as important as the mechanisms by which a forest healed itself, but were merely transitory and not required for the continuation of the forests or the wildlife that lived within them. In this way, these forests were perceived to be intrinsically static except when altered by external disruptions.

Mount St. Helens, a mountain visible on a clear day to Lewis and Clark to the north as they traveled down the Columbia River, is a famous case of a forested area subjected recently to a catastrophic disturbance. Before its eruption on May 18, 1980, this mountain had been a pleasant, wooded area. There were patterns in the forests on this mountain. One pattern was the change with altitudes of which species of trees were most important. Hiking up Mount St. Helens before the eruption, you would have found at the lower altitudes—below 3,600 feet (or 1,200 meters) above sea level—a rough landscape covered by forests of Douglas fir and western hemlock, while above this altitude mountain hemlock and western firs grew.

But on that May morning, the trees and animals were devastated by a rapid series of events. First, a large earthquake produced a massive debris avalanche, moving the entire upper part of the mountain. Then superheated water and steam blasted the area. Mudflows spread downward to the valleys, and volcanic ash rained on other areas of the mountain. Finally, lava began to flow down the slopes. In all, 151,000 acres or 61,000 hectares of land were damaged; forests were completely flattened on 52,000 acres or 21,000 hectares; much of the soil was lost.

The landscape was devastated and seemed without life. It was believed that all animals above the ground at the time were killed, including 1,600 elk. Stream habitats were destroyed and fish almost disappeared from the streams. But to the surprise of almost everyone, including ecologists, life returned rapidly. Where the debris was not too thick above the original soil, fireweed and other plants common in clearcut forest areas sprouted. Around fallen trees, spring flowers like trillium appeared. Even trees sprouted in areas protected from the blast and heat. Four years later, by 1984, the return of wildlife was well under way. After the eruption, stream habitats were destroyed and fish almost disappeared, but four years later, steelhead had increased to an amount 10 times the abundance found soon after the eruption. More than 600 elk were living in the area, and the streams were populated by 20 times as many steelhead trout as there had been after the eruption. Life was returning, and the process of ecological succession—the establishment of an ecosystem and its ecological community—had begun on the mountain. Trees began to return and eventually the slopes of Mount St. Helens will appear as heavily forested and peaceful again, until the next "disturbance."

COMPUTER GAMES AND ANCIENT FORESTS

These results of a spectacular event are helpful to us in trying to understand the process that sustains forests, but volcanic eruptions are rare

246

and we have few examples of forest recovery on volcanic slopes. In the past 20 years, a number of excellent studies have been made of the ancient forests of the Pacific Northwest. One of these is on U.S. Forest Service land in the Andrews Experimental Forest of western Oregon, about a hundred miles south of the Columbia River. There entire small watersheds have been cut and the effects on water flow, erosion, soil fertility, and regeneration of the forests have been studied. Much has been learned that is yet to be applied.

These studies tell us much about specific places. The question remains how much we can generalize from them. Another approach remains, one that is part of the tradition of the scientific method. This is to develop a theory and connect that theory to observations. At the time Lewis and Clark set out on their journey, modern science was comparatively young, and the best theories at that time—in the combination of elegant mathematical theory tested against observation—was in physics. The kind of mathematics developed and used by Newton, differential and integral calculus, did an excellent job of explaining the motion of physical objects. But the complexity of life seemed then and for a long time after, indeed still seems to many today, to be beyond such theory. The theory of biological evolution was two generations in the future when Lewis and Clark set out on their journey, and the term *ecological succession* had to wait for Thoreau, who first used it in print, 30 years after Lewis and Clark returned.

Today, we live in a computer world where children play complicated games that involve chance and skill and adults play Simcity, where the player gets a chance to be mayor of a growing town. In that computer town catastrophies happen and the game simulates in a crude way the effects of government decisions. When I first started out in ecology there were no explicit mathematical models for forests. Computers were just beginning to be used in scientific research and the idea of creating a computer model of a forest seemed farfetched and silly to most scientists.

The work I did in the woods in New Hampshire, which I wrote about earlier in this chapter, persuaded me that I wanted to study forests and learn how they really changed over time. I went back to college and began to study plant ecology with Professor Murray Buell, one of the few experts in that field in those days.

When I was a graduate student at Rutgers University, I was involved in field work about forest ecosystems. Several circumstances led to my interest in developing a computer model of forest growth. My experience with computers was one. My thesis research was done in the "Irradiated Forest" of Brookhaven National Laboratory, where one of the first digital recording systems ever applied in forest field research was employed. Digital information at that time was recorded on paper tape and transferred from a system in the field to a mainframe computer for analysis. My thesis forced me to spend many hours in the woods trying to measure photosynthesis, light, and temperature, while also learning to deal with digital equipment and mainframe computers. Computers in biological research were novel at that time and extremely novel in ecology, and I was fortunate to obtain an early acquaintance with these devices.

I was also fortunate at that time to be working under as excellent a field naturalist as Murray Buell. As his teaching assistant and as the caretaker of the Hutchinson Memorial Forest, the research preserve of Rutgers, 65 acres of woods never logged, I spent many hours on walks through the forest with Murray. As we walked in the woods, we stopped at many trees and tried to answer the question: why does this tree grow here while a tree of a different species grew somewhere else?

One early fall morning we were in the back part of Hutchinson forest, in a mainly upland area dominated by red, white, and black oaks in the forest canopy and with an understory of saplings that were mainly sugar and Norway maple, along with typical understory shrubs of the oak-hickory forests of the Atlantic Coastal states—viburnums, flowering dogwood. In that corner of the woods we came across a single American walnut, somewhat north of its general range. Murray and I stood in front of that tree for a while, talking about how its seeds might have gotten there and how it had managed to persist where no others of that species could be found. We talked about the relative openness of the site which allowed more light to penetrate, making conditions favorable to this relatively shade-intolerant species. We talked about the local soil and how that might be particularly advantageous to the tree. Providing the background for this discussion was Murray Buell's long experience in the field as well as his knowledge of plant taxonomy, physiology, and anatomy; my acquaintance with these subjects was more recent. The information from these fields provided a foundation in causal mechanisms that helped us "explain" what we observed.

However, I was bothered by our inability to test if our insights were justified about why a walnut tree grew where it did. The lessons of my undergraduate major in physics, with its problem-solving approach and the importance physicists attached to theory strongly connected to observation, were much in my mind. We could not do experiments that would take 40 or more years, such as planting seeds of walnut and waiting to see how they did in various sites. How could we test the implications of our assumptions, understanding, and information?

I began to think that computer programming might provide a way to test the implications of beliefs that Murray Buell and I had reached on our walks in the woods. I thought that it might be possible to set down in computer code the assumptions that he and I were making about the relationship between an individual tree and its environment, and then see the implications of these assumptions—whether these assumptions were sufficient to explain the natural history of a forest: how forests grew and changed over time; how forests differed when grown on different soils and in different climates.

How then to create a computer model of forest growth? Others were exploring the same question, and it was unclear at that time what would be an effective approach. Some argued for the application of engineering systems analysis and for taking a "top-down" approach, modeling an entire forest as composed of highly aggregated compartments, such as a single unit representing all trees, another all soil organic matter, connected by simple differential equations. If this were true, the natural history of our forests could be explained as if trees were machines. Others pursued an approach involving great detail, trying to grow trees from each leaf positioned in three-dimensions, but this went way beyond our knowledge of nature.

One of the main ways our natural history differs from that of Lewis and Clark is in our advances in scientific understanding. We know much about trees and forests that were not clear in the early nineteenth century, and this gives us a chance to develop a new natural history, consistent with our own understanding.

During the first half of the twentieth century, there were hundreds of studies of individual plants in greenhouses, including some tree seedlings. Much of this research was related to agriculture, in attempts to improve crop yields, and much was just out of curiosity. Certain useful generalizations became clear about trees, others about vegetation in general, and some about all life. But these laboratory studies had not been applied very much to trying to understand the natural history of forests.

Scientists had learned that the growth of a tree is directly related to the amount of leaves on the tree. On the other hand, growth slows down with the amount of non-photosynthetic tissue that must be supported. In a tree, this non-photosynthetic tissue exists mainly in the inner bark. Hundreds of experiments over several decades had established that the rate of photosynthesis increased with light intensity following a saturation curve—photosynthesis increases rapidly with increases in light at low light intensities, but the rate of increase declines as light becomes brighter. Although there is one general saturation curve for all vegetation, the exact shape of the curve differs for different kinds of trees. Trees tolerant of deep shade have higher rates of photosynthesis at low light intensities than shade-intolerant species, but the curves cross, and shade-intolerant species grow faster in bright light than shade-tolerant species.

Much was also learned about the connection between temperature and living things. Every chemical reaction in a cell, every cell, and every individual organism has an optimal temperature—a temperature at which metabolic rates take place most rapidly. Above and below that optimum temperature the rates of growth decrease.

With generalizations such as these, there seemed to be a basis for the development of a model and theory for a natural history of forests. By the time I had worked this much out, I was teaching at the Yale School of Forestry and Environmental Studies. In 1970, IBM sponsored a summer research program to support development of computer software for socially useful projects, and I was fortunate to be able to participate in that program. I had the extraordinary opportunity to cooperate with Dr. James Janak and Dr. James Wallis of the IBM Thomas J. Watson Research Laboratory. Work began with informal discussions in which Janak, Wallis, and I discovered a common interest and began to work together. They brought their own interests and expertise to the discussion. Wallis was an expert in hydrology and statistical analysis and Janak was a theoretical physicist with an interest in ecology.

The initial ideas I presented were improved and clarified through our discussions and converted by Janak and Wallis to mathematical statements. Then we cooperated in writing the initial computer code. We proceeded to build a model that began with the simplest case and added complexity. First we developed a model of a single tree, then of trees competing under constant environmental conditions, then of trees competing in an environment in which we could change the temperature and moisture conditions. We followed the classic scientific approach, including the idea that we should develop a model no more complex than needed to explain observations. By the end of the summer we had a working model that seemed to reproduce realistically what was known about the dynamics of forest communities.

When we ran this model we found the results contrary to the prevailing theory about forests. Rather than create a forest that remained in a single condition, the computer forest varied over time. The old idea of a climax forest also included the belief that this forest had the greatest amount of wood in it and the greatest biological diversity. But the computer forest reached a peak in both of these partway through succession. The old-growth forest predicted by the model had a much smaller amount of timber and fewer kinds of trees. The same year that we published these results a study of real forest stands of many different ages in Wisconsin was published by Orie Loucks, an ecologist then at the University of Wisconsin. His analysis showed the same thing that the computer suggested—that diversity reached a maximum partway through succession.

I was surprised by these initial projections and went back to the assumptions in the model to try to understand what was happening.

252

This is one of the great advantages of a computer model—the computer faithfully tells you the exact implications of your assumptions, whether you like them or not. I found that the reason the amount of wood and the biological diversity reached a maximum partway through succession was because at that time the fast growing, early successional trees had reached their largest size, while the tree species typical of old-age forests, able to grow in the deep shade of the forest, were abundant enough to also contribute to the amount of wood and the diversity. Later, the trees characteristic of the early stages in succession died out, and fewer species—only those that could persist in deep shade—continued to grow.

The forest continued to vary in all characteristics because there was inherent risk in the model. Just as in a real forest, there was always a chance that a tree would be struck by lightning or attacked by disease or insects and die. Just as in a real forest, there was chance involved in whether a seed would fall onto the kind of soil in which it could sprout and survive. With these kinds of variations built into the model, the computer forest varied widely but never went completely extinct or reached levels of wood or diversity beyond those observed in nature. The computer model was more like the Missouri River I talked about in the early chapters of this book than it was like the static, fixed forest of early-twentieth-century ecological theory.

Some attempts have been made to develop versions of this model and some other kinds of models for the forests of the Pacific Northwest, but not enough has been done yet to give us the kind of insight we need to resolve the major questions about the importance of old growth in these forests. With computers as tools, and with the next generation becoming familiar with complex computer games, we have a chance to find a new kind of natural history, one that is consistent with all the complicated things that go on in a forest. This is one of the ways our natural history has changed since the time of Lewis and Clark.

LEWIS AND CLARK AND FORESTS

Considering the amount of time that the expedition spent within the great forests of the Pacific Northwest—one of the two longest periods of the journey—and considering the detail with which Lewis and Clark describe many aspects of the natural history on their way up the Missouri and down the Columbia, their journals comment surprisingly little about the forests. Perhaps the struggle to survive the cool and persistently rainy winter at Fort Clatsop, where food was scarce and the men often ill, was too much for them to maintain the curiosity that they had sustained through the time of westward travel. Perhaps the task of writing up the notes from the outward journey was too absorbing, for this was the primary work of Lewis and of Clark during that winter. Perhaps their eyes and hopes were on the ocean, searching the horizon for sailing ships that might take them home in comparative ease. Perhaps the forests were just too imposing, too impenetrable, too wet and rainy. Whatever the reason, their experiences are a metaphor for our own conflicts and dilemmas. Like Lewis and Clark, we have spent little effort until recently on forests issues; we know too little of the real history of these forests, of the role of the Indians in forming the character of these forests, and of the conditions under which these forests can produce a sustainable supply of timber. Perhaps like Lewis and Clark we have found these forests too dark and imposing, too mysterious, or perhaps, like them, we have been too busy with other tasks.

We haven't spent the time that we need on exploring real forest history, the real dynamics of the forests of the Pacific Northwest, or on computer models of these forests. Now, faced with major dilemmas about these forests, we find ourselves still unable to resolve them.

CHAPTER ELEVEN

The Return Through Prairie Country

Space, Time, and Environmental Heritage

Prairies are quiescent . . . looked at for any length of time, they begin to impose their awful perfection on the observer's mind. . . .

The drama of this landscape is in the sky, pouring with light and always moving.

WALLACE STEGNER, *IN WOLF-WILLOW*

THE CORNER OF 144ᵀᴴ
AND STATE STREETS

It was in the prairies that Lewis and Clark began the transition from the civilization they knew to the land unsettled by people of European descent, and it was through the prairies, on their return, that they re-entered their civilization. It is therefore a useful place for us to consider the connections between human society and the natural landscape.

Because it was diminished so early in the development of North America, the prairie was gone before the rise of environmentalism as a major social and political movement. As a result, comparatively little attention has been paid to its conservation until recently. Today environmentalists tend to focus on conservation of the remaining large areas not yet so disrupted as the American Prairies—tropical rain forests and forests of the Northwest of the United States, on species often far from our homes, the black rhinoceros and elephant of Africa, the sea turtles of Costa Rica and the Caribbean. The prairie is important to us in three ways: its soils continue to provide the basis for much of America's agriculture; it contains considerable biological diversity; and like the Missouri River, the prairie contains messages for us about how we can approach solutions to environmental issues today. It tells us about patterns in space as well as in time.

At the time of the Lewis and Clark expedition, the prairies occupied more land area than any other kind of ecosystem in North America. Prairies extended in one vast continuous sheet, west from Indiana to the Rocky Mountains. They reached north to the tundra in Canada, covered much of Saskatchewan and Alberta, covered eastern Montana, the Dakotas, Minnesota, Nebraska, Iowa, western Illinois and Ohio, eastern Wyoming and Colorado, Kansas, western Missouri, the eastern edge of New Mexico, and spread into Oklahoma and Texas, ending at the edge of the desert in Arizona. Separate outliers—prairie islands—extended into the far West: the Palouse grasslands of Washington and the grasslands of California's Great Central Valley. These vast and often seemingly empty lands were the home of the Apaches, Assiniboines, and Cheyennes; the Chippewas, Comanches, and Crows; the Kiowas, Mandans, Omahas, Osages, the Otos, Pawnees, Poncas, Sioux, and Wichita and many other tribes, about thirty, depending on how they are enumerated. These prairies were part of grasslands that had covered one-fourth of the Earth's land: the steppes of Asia, the pampas of South America, the veld of South Africa.

In my attempt to understand the environment through which Lewis and Clark passed and to understand how that environment had changed, I began a search for original prairie. I contacted my colleagues, both those who were experts on prairie vegetation and those who were experts on the Lewis and Clark expedition.

As a result of my inquiries, on August 10, 1992, my wife and I were standing on the corner of 144th and State Streets in Omaha, Nebraska, looking for a prairie. Lewis and Clark had searched for a road in the wilderness of Montana. We were searching for one of the last remnants of the Great American Prairie which, we had been told, we would find within this city's limits. Across the street, we saw a barbed wire fence with signs at regular intervals: "Nature Preserve, No Trespassing." At an entrance a short way down 144th Street, a sign explained, "This is the Allwine Prairie Preserve, a research area of the University of Nebraska, Omaha." We had come to Nebraska to see remnants of the prairie through which Lewis and Clark had spent more than a year of their outward-bound travel, from the start of their trip on May 14, 1804, through their first winter with the Mandans in what is now North Dakota, until they reached the Rocky Mountains and left the plains, near the end of July 1805. They had passed through more than 700 miles, as the jet airplane flies, of prairie land. We were having troubling locating any of that prairie. This was the last day of a week of travel, searching for prairie in Nebraska, Iowa, and the southern edge of South Dakota.

We had sought the Allwine Prairie on the advice of Tom Bragg, a botanist at the University of Nebraska, at Omaha, and the local expert on prairies. I had called him that morning and said that I would like to see some areas of original prairie—areas that had never been plowed and that retained the original prairie vegetation.

We walked around the small preserve to get a feel for prairie countryside, as much as it was possible in this situation. It was a bright, sunny, late summer afternoon. Except for a farmer driving a tractor and cutting hay in a field to the north, no one else was visible. On this pleasant summer afternoon, no one else sought to find this rare remnant of the oceans of grass that had once covered more land area than any other kind of landscape in North America, more than the great eastern forests of sugar maple and basswood, oak and chestnut; more than the great northern forests of spruce, fir, and birch; more than the deserts; more than the mountains.

We walked along the edge of the prairie. Behind us, the diesel engine of the tractor baling hay droned, snorted, and grumbled. Wind whispered in the chest-deep grasses. The restored prairie was a series of patches, unlike the hay field to our north, which was smoothly uniform. Coarse forbs grew densely in one small area reaching six feet high, next to a patch of grass. Upslope grasses cast the reddish hue of little bluestem; halfway down the slope were grasses of a brighter green. A stream and wetland separated the eastern edge of the restored prairie from the hayfield. Approaching the wetland, we saw standing water covered with the dense green of floating plants, duckweed, and algae. The rich green suggested some pollution from runoff of agricultural fertilizers from the hayfield. One of the first features of the prairie that we observed was a complexity of patterns on a small scale, quite different from the uniform green of the adjacent hay field. The patterns were scruffy and irregular, not like a French Renaissance garden, perhaps more in the style of eighteenth- and nineteenth-century English gardens, which retained an intentional aspect of variety. But even those gardens were much neater in appearance.

I began this book with Lewis and Clark's search for a road through the wilderness, and I end it with my own search for the original American Prairie, one of the few remnants of which I found protected by high fences at the corner of 144th and State Streets in Omaha, Nebraska. This is as much a story of the loss of our sense of environmental heritage and the loss of our collective memory of environmental history as it is the story of the destruction of the prairie. This lack of heritage was brought home to my wife and myself during our attempt to find remnants of the prairie. It was illustrated perhaps as well as anywhere in our visit to the Spirit Mound in South Dakota.

THE SPIRIT MOUND AND ENVIRONMENTAL HERITAGE

On August 25, 1804, Captains Lewis and Clark, along with 10 of their men, traveled on foot north from the Missouri River for four miles to see an isolated hill on the prairie that the neighboring Indians called the Spirit Mound. The local tribes of Indians in this region believed the mound to be "the residence of devils" which "are in human form with remarkable large heads about 18 inches high." The Indians believed these devils were "armed with sharp arrows with which they could kill at a great distance" and that they "killed all persons who are so hardy as to attempt to approach the hill."

After crossing a creek they estimated to be 23 yards wide and recording that it watered "an extensive valley," they saw "a large mound in the midst of the plain," rising about 65 or 70 feet, with a level top about 90 feet by 12 feet. They described the base as forming a regular parallelogram with the longest side about 300 yards long, the shorter side 60 or 70. "The only characteristic of this hill . . . is that it is insulated or separated a considerable distance from any other," Clark wrote. The regular form of this hill would in some measure justify a belief that it owed its origin to human beings, "but as the earth and the loose pebbles and other substances of which it was composed bare an exact resemblence to the steep ground which border on the creek in its neighborhood, we concluded it was most probably the production of nature." Once again, Lewis and Clark reveal themselves as careful observers and insightful thinkers about the origin of the landscape and the causes of the patterns they saw. They reminded me of my own curiosity about natural areas, and the puzzles that were there to solve about why a hill persisted where it did, and why one kind of plant or animal lived on that hill.

"From the top of this mound we beheld a most beautiful landscape," Clark wrote, with "numerous herds of buffalo" which were "feeding in various directions." The plains extended from northeast to northwest "without interruption as far as can be seen." The soil of the prairie surrounding the mound was "delightful," he wrote, always on the lookout for areas to settle.

"The plains country which surrounds this mound has contributed

261

not a little to its bad reputation," the journal continues, "the wind driving from every quarter . . . . drives with unusual force over the naked plains and against this hill; the insects of various kinds are thus unvoluntarily driven to the mound . . . or fly to its leeward side for shelter. The small birds, whose food they are, consequently resort in great numbers to this place in search of them. The Indians believed that large numbers of birds near the mound was evidence of it being the residence of some unusual spirits. Among the birds they saw were many brown martins looking for insects, and these were "so gentle that they did not quit the place until we had arrived within a few feet of them." They also saw other birds typical of the plains, the blackbird, the wren or prairie-bird, and lark "about the size of a partridge, with a short tail."

They stayed on the Spirit Mound for quite a while, enjoying the view, but then left about one o'clock. "The excessive heat and thirst forced us from the hill . . . to the nearest water," Clark noted, "which we found in the creek at three miles' distance, and remained an hour and a half." Following the creek downstream toward the Missouri, they entered a wetland about a mile wide that they had passed on their way north that morning. "Here we gathered some delicious plums, grapes, and blue currants, and afterward arrived at the mouth of the river about sunset."

On August 9, 1992, we drove from South Sioux City toward Yankton, South Dakota, to find the Spirit Mound. We expected it to be well visited, perhaps a popular spot. People enjoy a mysterious place, and the Spirit Mound is noted on the National Park Service Lewis and Clark map, a guide to travelers who want to revisit the route of the expedition, as one of only 80 landmarks on the entire route.

In the early morning there were many small, low cumulus clouds in the sky above well-tended farmland. North of the Big Sioux River, we

262

passed a huge cattle feedlot filling the air with a strong smell of manure. Farms looked prosperous in this river valley, each a cluster of buildings, appearing from a distance to be a small hamlet: a house, a main barn, a storage building for big machinery, chicken houses, corn storage structures, silos.

We headed west on Route 50 and entered the town of Vermillion, then turned north onto Route 19 to find the Spirit Mound. Route 19 traverses the flood plain, and is built on a kind of dike above the farm fields. It took us across the floodplain and onto and into the low bluffs that seemed to mark the north border of the flood plain. The bluffs were pastured, and many of the pastures had a line of trees forming a windbreak, composed mainly of cottonwoods with some volunteer red cedars and occasional exotic trees, including Norway spruce. Among the pastures were fields of beans. In addition to the windbreaks, there were occasional planted groves of cottonwoods that are unlike natural forests, lacking humus and woody litter and having instead a grass understory that was neatly mown, kept the way European plantations and groves of trees around large houses in America are maintained.

We arrived at the Spirit Mound by a small roadside historic marker on which was written: "This hill was visited by Meriwether Lewis and William Clark and seven other members of the famous expedition on August 25, 1804, after a four hour walk from the Missouri River," a trip that had taken us about ten minutes. Although it was easy to find the historic marker by the roadside, the marker stood in a wayside that would allow only one or two cars to park at the same time. Weeds were abundant, suggesting that this was not a well-trod tourist attraction.

The mound was clearly visible as an isolated hill just to the west, but there was no public access in view—no path or roadway and no sign indicating how one might reach the top. Just up the road from the sign was a driveway leading to a farmhouse. The Spirit Mound seemed to be on private property. We turned in the driveway and parked next to the farmhouse. I knocked on the door and a young farmer came out. He was bearded, in stocking feet and new bluejeans, accompanied by his dog. I asked if there was a way to get to the top of the Spirit Mound. I was concerned that he would be annoyed with frequent repetitions of that question, but he responded in a friendly and pleasant fashion. He said we were welcome to climb up it on his land, and told us how to reach it, which required that we walk through his garden patch in a field behind the house, climb under the barbed wire fence separating the house from pastures, and then follow along a line of mulberries and red cedars.

I thanked him and we started out. After climbing through the barbed wire fence, we found ourselves in a cattle wallow full of manure. Crossing that, we climbed uphill through the cedars until we were parallel to the summit of the mound. Then we climbed under and over the barbed wire fence again and hiked through knee-high grass to the top.

We were now on the top of the Spirit Mound with a pretty view in all directions—farmhouses, neat fields, small streams, and beyond, in the haze, the floodplain of the Missouri River and the blue cast of the bluffs beyond that. The steady breeze, blowing uphill, was warm and carried with it the scents of hay and plowed soil; insects buzzed in the knee-high grass and birds swirled above them. No cars approached or retreated on the highway we had just traveled, which was a still, straight dusty line. Little in this view was reminiscent of the scene that Lewis and Clark would have experienced—no patch of original prairie. Even the Vermillion River had been channelized and straightened. Only trees along the Vermillion River floodplain had a resemblance to the original landscape.

Hidden in the grass at the top of the Spirit Mound was a stone marker on which a brass plate explained, "This spot was visited in 1804 by members of the Lewis and Clark expedition. Placed by Paha Wakan Chapter, Daughters of the American Revolution, 1921." The grass grew against the rock. We cleared the vegetation to read the sign. We seemed to be the only people or large mammal to have come up here in a while. Passage of any other large mammal would have been indicated by flattened grass.

The grass around the Spirit Mound appeared to be orchard grass, which is of European origin. Here was a place that could have been a beautiful bit of natural prairie. Even so, I hasten to add, even in its present condition, the mound is pleasant to visit and offers a beautiful view of heavily settled, prosperous farmland.

The mound stands by itself in miles of otherwise flat landscape, and it is composed of a deep soil without clear outcropping of bedrock. No wonder the Indians attached some mystical significance to it. The day was clear and sunny, and we saw beautiful farms on the river valley all around. The scene was like a children's book drawing of what farmland should be.

We returned to our car and left the driveway of the farmer who had so kindly given us permission to walk to the top of the Spirit Mound. Clearly, this was not a place that could be visited by many tourists without some kind of change in access—through land purchase or through an easement accompanied by the construction of a footpath to the top. Perhaps this was just as well for the conservation of the hill, but it surprised us that a site listed on the National Park map as one of 80 locations to visit on the entire route of the expedition seemed isolated and little visited. We returned to Route 19 and turned south, thinking about the lonely hill and its lonely condition as we returned to the busy highway on the floodplain.

As we drove south, I imagined another Spirit Mound in another time, made into a wayside park, restored to prairie, with a footpath to the top and made part of our prairie heritage. Those thoughts were jarred a bit when we passed a sign that proclaimed proudly that we were passing "Kayeville: Hay Capital of the World."

THE PLATTE AND NEBRASKA COUNTRYSIDE

On July 21, 1804, Lewis and Clark reached the point where the Platte River flowed into the Missouri. They were in the midst of the tall grass prairie. Although smaller than the Missouri, the Platte is one of the major rivers of America, draining 90,000 square miles. Even today when most of its waters are diverted for agriculture, during spring run-off the Platte can be almost a mile wide in some places. The Platte drains the Rockies and western and central Nebraska, whose sediments are rich in sand, so that the river carries a sandy load through flat country. The Missouri, also known as the Big Muddy, passes through glaciated terrain, through fine wind-blown deposits on the loess hills, and carries a finer, silty load. Lewis noticed the difference between the two rivers immediately, writing that the "boiling motion" of the Platte's sand left "no doubt" about the material that made the Platte streamload and bed.

The expedition camped for five days not far north of the confluence of the Platte and the Missouri. Men sent out to hunt game found open plains intersected by a "small beautiful river" and other small streams. They saw wolves, grouse, deer, and beaver, but thought the game scarce. On July 26, a windstorm blew clouds of sand that filtered into the tents, but the storm let up by nightfall and Clark wrote that "this evening we found very pleasant."

I had remembered the Platte, from visits years before, as a river of the prairie. In the summer, when the water was low, downed cottonwood snags lay exposed across the shallow riverbed through open country. I looked forward to seeing that river again, to compare my impressions with those of Lewis and Clark. We started our search for other prairie remnants, leaving Lincoln on Interstate 80 headed toward the Missouri River, following near the Platte.

Like the land on the outskirts of the city, the wide strip on both sides of the Interstate was planted in lawn, and we passed mowing machines keeping the lawn trim. We passed a construction site for a new interchange and saw the deep, black prairie soil where the bulldozers had cut into the soil, yielding the only clue that we were on land that was once the Great American Prairie, and reminding us also that these strips could be planted in prairie, reflecting the heritage of the countryside and probably requiring less intensive care than lawns.

We had hoped to find a place where we could rent a canoe or rowboat on the Platte or the Missouri, to get a feel for the rivers. Ty Harrison, the botanist who was advising Gary Moulton, the editor of the new edition of the Lewis and Clark journals, about the plants identified by Lewis and Clark, gave us extensive and useful suggestions about our trip. He told us that the Platte retained more of the quality of the original Missouri River than did the Missouri near Omaha, and he suggested that we stop at several of the Nebraska State Parks right along the Platte where we might be able to rent a boat. A boat ride on the Platte would give us a feel of the rivers of the Midwest as Lewis and Clark had experienced them, he told us.

I called ahead to each of the parks that seemed to border the Platte and learned that the railroad separated each park from the river, and none had river access or boats to rent. We decided to stop and see one of the parks anyway, and took the turnoff from I-80 to Nebraska Route 66 to Eugene Mahoney State Park. We found a new, well-kept park with a pleasant lodge and many kinds of recreation for adults and children. The main building faced toward the river. From its porches, rooms, and restaurant one had a pleasant view of the Platte, but the building sat on a high point and obscured the river from view for those outside. There were swings and places to play golf and tennis, but none of the recreation that we could find hinted at the location or the heritage—of the river and the prairie.

We left Mahoney State Park and took several side roads that the map suggested would lead us to the Platte. We found a bridge over the Platte near a sand quarry, where big trucks threw dust on the countryside. Crossing the bridge, we turned around in a small park filled with trailers and motor homes. Although the park was next to the river, the Platte was obscured by trees and vehicles, as if it were an afterthought and unimportant to the purposes of the campers. This piece of prairie heritage, the Platte River, seemed ignored also.

THE MESSAGE OF THE LOST PRAIRIE

"The scenery needed no foreign aid," the historian of the American frontier, Francis Parkman, had written of his visit to the prairies near Fort Leavenworth in 1847. "Nature had done enough for it; and the alteration of rich green prairies and groves that stood in clusters, or lined the banks of the numerous little streams had all the softened and

polished beauty of a region that has been for centuries under the hand
of man . . . the green swells of the prairie were thickly studded with
blossoms."

The great prairie ocean with its patterns in space and time is gone;
only puddles, meanders, and small backwaters remain. One of the great
heritages of America has almost disappeared. In a week of searching for
prairie, we came to feel that this part of the country—the prairie states
—had cut itself off from its past. Without familiarity with its environmental heritage, how could a country understand how to deal with the
confusing array of newly arising environmental issues?

It wasn't that we were being sentimental about the disappearance of
a single species; it wasn't that we were lamenting the rise of people
against the spread of the prairie. It was the loss to our own humanity,
our sense of ourselves, that seemed sad. It was as if the Midwest had cut
off its feet and no longer knew where it had walked. For in searching for
the prairie, we were searching for ourselves, for our heritage, for our
understanding of where we had come in our landscapes. Without that
view of the past from which our country had come, how could we
move ahead wisely into the future? And how could we be comfortable
with our place in that landscape if we did not know what it had been
and had no good idea of what it could become? We might be becalmed
today in the steady, modern agricultural production that seemed to
auger only fair weather, but at a deeper level we were adrift in a land of
possibly changing climate and eroding soils. With only the present as
our perspective, we tend to seek simple, single-purpose answers to the
complex questions about how to live over the long-term with the un-
steady state of our modern environment. No wonder we try to solve
environmental problems as if they were as simple as fixing the old wind-
mill, a familiar landmark on old midwestern farms.

The prairie through which Lewis and Clark passed was the product of many events over a long geological history. Some of these events would seem catastrophic if there had been people to observe them—the continental glaciations, the production of volcanic ash from eruptions. These two processes provided much of the primary material for the fertility of the soil of the Great Plains. With this soil as its pallet, the Missouri painted the countryside with fertile land. Our alterations of the prairie leave us without large stretches of prairie land in which we can see the larger patterns, so that we no longer have direct contact, a direct feel for these aspects of our environment.

We tend to think that solutions to environmental problems are simply a matter of an accumulation of facts, simply a technical inquiry; we leave it to laboratory technicians to tell us what river is polluted or what species is disappearing. But in my work attempting to help solve environmental issues, I had become convinced that the way that we deal with our environment has a lot to do with our cultural heritage and our myths about nature. As we become an increasingly urbanized and suburbanized people, more and more of us lose our direct contact with the land. As we remove the remnants of our natural environment, we lose contact with an important part of our heritage. We try to solve environmental problems from myths that seem to make sense from both the farmhouse and the apartment house. It is as if we were trying to navigate the prairie ocean without knowing where we had started, without a compass, or a path.

It was the loss to our own humanity that seemed sad to me as we traveled near to the Missouri, seeking the Spirit Mound, the Allwine Prairie, and a boat landing on the Platte River.

On August 12, 1806, the expedition returned to Fort Mandan near Bismarck, North Dakota, where they had spent the first winter. The journals note that "since we passed in 1804, a very obvious change has taken place in the current and appearance of the Missouri." Lewis and Clark once again confronted the variableness of the Missouri. "In places where at that time there were sand-bars, the current of the river now passes, and the former channel of the river is in turn a bank of sand," they wrote. Not only had they become well acquainted with nature's variation on the outward bound journey, they observed and reflected on this quality once again as they neared the end of their trip. When, at noon on September 23, 1806, they reached St. Louis, successfully completing their journey, they had come to know the countryside and written about it in a way that no one had before and in many ways no one has since. They had searched for and found nature, observing it as it was, describing it with great accuracy and detail, seeing its beauty, experiencing its dangers, knowing its changeableness. Theirs was a knowledge of nature most important to us as we face the effects we have had on the environment of the American West as well as the environment of the entire planet.

The day after we visited the Allwine Prairie, we drove to the Fontenelle Forest Preserve in Bellevue, Nebraska, a city along the Missouri River on the opposite side of Omaha, the southeast. Tom Bragg had told us we should by all means visit the Fontenelle Forest Association, which owned two tracts, a shoreline woodlands in Bellevue, and another area that included some restored prairie to the north of the city. "Visit with Gary Garabrandt," he said, the Association's chief ranger and naturalist. "He knows all about the prairie and riverside woodlands."

It was a clear and pleasant August day, not too hot and not humid. The Association's headquarters were in a pleasant and neatly kept modern building with several displays about the woodlands and prairie.

Gary came out to greet us and, although he knew no more about who I was or what I was doing than I had explained over the phone, he took us on an hour's tour of the woodlands that clung to a bluff along the river. Thin, wiry, and dressed in a standard brown ranger uniform, Gary gave a soft-spoken but enthusiastic and detailed account of the area's natural history. This land and its woodlands and prairie were the focus of his life. Here, in Gary, was the sense of prairie heritage that seemed missing throughout the rest of our trip that summer. He had worked here for a quarter century and wrote his master's thesis about the vegetation of the forest.

A local publication, "Plants of Fontenelle Forest," published in 1959 by the Omaha Botany Club, calls the woodlands a "virgin forest," but the forest does not exhibit the classic balance of nature—a primeval forest that never changes, Gary told us. Over the years he has been able to locate about 20 acres that appear never to have been logged, pastured, or otherwise farmed on the entire 1,300 acres of the preserve. The rest were used in varying degrees beginning with the first settlement of Bellevue, Nebraska, in 1823 when Joshua Pilcher established a trading post for the Missouri Fur Company. The locale was well known. George Catlin sketched Bellevue from the Iowa shore in 1832. Carl Bodmer painted the agency buildings and the bluffs along the river in 1833 when he accompanied Prince Maximilan on a trip that followed the first year of Lewis and Clark's journey.

Gary said that the main kind of big, old trees in Fontenelle forest were bur oak, but these are not regenerating. They are favored by fire, and fire has been suppressed for years. Deer eat the bur oak seedlings and a recent increase in the deer population had put added pressure on the vegetation. The situation reminded me of other natural preserves I had visited and worked in over the years, where land casually believed to be virgin forest had experienced a long and complex history of different uses.

Bur oak grows on the drier sites. The moist ravines are dominated by Linden and red oak, but at the time we visited, red oak was suffering from a blight. Gary showed us several middle-sized bur oak that had died because they were shaded by surrounding trees—openings that would have occurred from forest fire would have favored them.

The forest grows on loess soil, the wind-blown soil formed during the ice ages as I will explain, and in this way the forests that thrive along the river bluffs are a product of change. Today's Fontenelle Forest is different from the nature we had sought; from a distance it would resemble the wooded riverside bluff seen by Lewis and Clark, but up close the forest is closed—with dense shade and leaves of one tree brushing against those of it neighbors, rather than open, with trees standing in groves above prairie grasses, forbs, and shrubs. Along the river there is much more forest now than at the beginning of the nineteenth century and less prairie and oak openings.

In the fall a year later, I returned to Omaha to give a talk to the members of the Fontenelle Forest Association, where I was fortunate to stay at the home of one of its primary supporters, Dr. Neal Ratzlaff, a retired physician, and his wife, Izen. Neal and I spent many hours talking about the prairie and its conservation. Thin and of medium height, Neal spoke quietly and shyly about his work and interests in conservation of the prairie lands of southern Nebraska. He has been active in prairie conservation and is an example of the kind of person badly needed—a locally active person of influence who devotes time to help purchase and conserve natural areas. He owns 40 acres in the loess hills of Iowa which he is managing as a natural area. He is on the board of the Iowa division of the Nature Conservancy. He bought 30 acres of prairie, which he donated to the Prairie/Plains Resource Institute in Aurora, Nebraska, a small non-profit organization devoted to prairie conservation.

The day I arrived, Gary drove me to Neale Woods northeast of Omaha, which is another property held by the Fontenelle Forest Association. There he showed me farmlands that the Association, under his direction, was converting back to prairie. It was a lazy Indian summer day; the sun shown weakly through thin clouds, augering a change in weather.

I stayed over the weekend so that I could go on several field trips with Neal and Gary. Neal, Gary, Gary's young son, and I drove north on the east side of the Missouri River and then crossed the river and visited the DeSoto National Wildlife Refuge, where I had been several years before with my colleagues from Iowa State University, as I mentioned in an earlier chapter. The weather had changed severely. The snow blew past us, whipped horizontally by the powerful prairie winter winds. Gary, his little boy, and Neal walked along a path at DeSoto National Wildlife Refuge to a bird blind. Peering through holes from which wind and flakes of snow brushed into our eyes, we watched snow geese rise from the backwaters of the Missouri and climb overhead, moving white forms gracefully balancing themselves in the settling and driven snow. It was bitterly cold, but beautiful in the blacks and grays of the leafless trees and whites of the snow and birds.

From the DeSoto National Wildlife Refuge we drove south along the east side of the Missouri and then took some side roads that went through loess hills. Here these soils were laid down between 30,000 and 17,000 years ago. Loess began as silt transported from the mountains to the plains by the Missouri and Platte rivers. Big rivers, whose waters travel at different speeds in different locations, separate the material they carry by sizes. The bigger the particle, the greater the velocity of water required to move it, so the biggest and heaviest materials are deposited first. The heaviest materials—stones and pebbles—are dropped as the rivers leave the steep slopes of the mountains and the water loses velocity. Sands are deposited next, but as Lewis and Clark found at the mouth of the Platte, sands can be transported for quite a long distance from their sources. Silts, which are finer materials than sands, are carried farther and deposited when a river floods and, after the floods, the quiet back waters allow the fine particles to settle out.

Spread over a wide area by the raging waters during the last ice age, the silts were then moved eastward by intense winds that were created along the southern edge of the glaciers. These formed a rolling country of fine, uniform material without apparent layers. In Iowa, where we were driving that morning, the loess soils, formed during the most recent glaciation, known as the Wisconsin, sit on top of glacial till from an earlier glaciation known as the Kansian glacier, which dropped material here 750,000 years ago, and covered all of Iowa. Below these deposits are bedrock of sandstones and limestones which were laid down in ancient oceans and which form a deep bowl that rises far to the west as the mountains are approached.

The loess forms small, rounded, but steeped-sided hills. On July 16, 1804, Lewis and Clark passed by the area Gary and I were driving through, and they saw these strange, small hills. At that time they were covered by extensive prairies and Clark called them "bald pated prairies" because the grasses and forbs gave the hills the look of a bald-headed person. Water filters comparatively quickly through the loess soils, and the upper slopes of the loess hills are dry compared to the land along the river floodplain. When fires were common, prior to European settlement, the hills were covered by drought-tolerant vegetation, especially on the steep southwestern slopes, which intercept the intense and drying westerly winds. It was these slopes that were readily visible to Lewis and Clark as they traveled up the river.

To remain covered by prairie grasses and forbs, the bald-pated hills require occasional fire, and since fires have been suppressed since European settlement, prairie preserves have slowly converted to woodlands. Red cedar, a small tree common in old fields from Iowa east to New Jersey, was abundant in the loess hills that had not been burned. These shade and crowd out the prairie grasses. Near to where Gary and I drove was the Loess Hills State Recreation Area near the small town of Castana, Iowa. There, a program is underway to use controlled fires to restore the native prairie.

We drove through the cold, gray country, stopping occasionally at local preserves like the 40 acres owned by Neal. We talked about conservation of the prairie. Neal said that the Nature Conservancy, on whose state board he served, was concentrating its activities to help save prairie lands north of Sioux City, Iowa—in other words, north of Iowa and Nebraska. This makes sense from a national perspective, because so much of Iowa and Nebraska is actively farmed, while there is more unused land to the north in the Dakotas. But it also means that a huge part of the original prairie has few champions. Fontenelle Forest Association, Gary said, is one of the few membership organizations devoted to prairie conservation—or any local biological conservation for that matter—in all of Nebraska, and its membership is about 4,000 people out of the state's 1.6 million residents, and out of 335,000 residents of Omaha and 30,000 of Bellevue. Of Nebraska's 77,000 square miles, less than 150 are state parks and recreation areas. Private holdings— Audubon, The Nature Conservancy, Prairie Plains Institute—add considerably. Those who head up the Fontenelle Forest Association and its staff represent the kind of effort so badly needed for our prairies—important not only for the land, but for ourselves, to reconnect us with our environmental heritage. We stopped along the western edge of one of the loess hills and I took out my camera to photograph the hills and the Missouri River and Nebraska's biggest city in the distance. The metal on the camera felt like ice to my fingers, and the wind dried my eyes as I tried to focus the lens. But in spite of the icy wind, falling snow, and drab, gray clouds, I was happier that day than I had been at any other visit to the prairie countryside, for with me were two people who loved the land and shared the sense of natural history and nature's heritage, as it really was and is, not as we imagine it to be.

And so I left Omaha the next day, believing that useful solutions to environmental problems are possible, but that they require that we understand how nature really works, and therefore we understand the rivers, the mountains, and the prairie—in the case of the prairie, how the collection of animals and plants, fungi and bacteria, have persisted for thousands of years; why this collection occupied more land area in the United States than any other. We need more Fontenelle Forest Associations and more people like Gary Garabrandt and Neal Ratzlaff—local people with a stake in the future of the local land and its resources, open to learn about it, devoted to it.

My visits to the remnants of the great American prairie were brief and few. An occasional visit to a nature preserve is not, generally speaking, enough to create the bonding, the contact, the feel, of our relationship with nature. It is that environmental heritage that we have lost, which we must regain in the spirit of the expedition of Lewis and Clark, whose loss I found myself mourning that summer day at the corner of 144th and State Street in Omaha, Nebraska, and whose future I began to hope for in the wind and snow on the loess hills.

Afterword

When I began work on *Our Natural History* in the early 1990s, few cared about Lewis and Clark or their expedition. In fact, few that I met in my travels even knew about it. I had chosen to write about Lewis and Clark not because they were popular, which they were not, but because I had been fascinated by their journals. These personal writings revealed them as to be excellent naturalists with exceptional abilities of observation and interpretation of the nature around them, and gave insight into the realities of nature in the American West, a countryside that has entered our folklore and is filled with myths. It seemed to me that no other story could dramatize as well as these journals what a landscape unaffected by modern technology was really like. No other explorers could tell us so accurately, with such amazing tales, how to think about, observe, and come to terms with nature.

By the end of the 1990s, Lewis and Clark had become popular, due in part to the excellent new edition of their journals edited by Gary Moulton, and Steven Ambrose's book *Undaunted Courage*, as well as the approach of the bicentennial of the expedition. In the past decade, Lewis and Clark's fame has grown, and so this new publication of *Our Natural History* takes place at a very different time in terms of the appreciation of their expedition.

Ironically, not that much has changed in the way we approach nature and in what we believe to be true about it. We need to understand all the more how Lewis and Clark survived and prevailed in their difficult journey. Their survival and success demanded an understanding of the nature and the peoples they met along the way, whose help was essential.

When I wrote *Our Natural History*, I was living in Oregon, working on a project for the state about the effects of forest practices on salmon. On weekends I would drive to Lewis and Clark sites, read their journal entries, and look at the countryside they had once seen. They measured every inch of the land they covered, and always knew where they were. They approached nature like the best of modern ecologists. At the same time, they greatly appreciated the beauty of the countryside. Nothing illustrates this better than Lewis's attempts to describe the Great Falls on the Missouri River, where he spent several days trying to find just the right way to detail the beauty he observed.

During the week, I pursued modern facts about salmon and forestry. The contrast could not have been greater. The state of Oregon's water and fish and game departments did not know the length of the rivers they were in charge of managing, nor the size of those rivers' watersheds. The state counted salmon in only two rivers south of the Columbia River, and therefore knew little about those salmon. At the start of my project, the state did not have a map of forest conditions. Logging permits were given out by counties, which did not record the location, area, or method of logging. How then could one analyze, scientifically, the effects of forest practices on salmon? Oregon did not know how many dams it had, nor which had fish ladders. Some scientists claimed that ocean currents and upwellings had specific effects on the abundance of salmon, but our review of the data showed these claims as empty handwaving. It was shocking to me that in the supposed age of science and information, when it came to environment we lagged behind those intrepid explorers of the early nineteenth century. All I could think was woe to us!

Sadly, the situation has not improved. I have spent much of the last decade working to help save the salmon in the Pacific Northwest. In the spring of 2003, I traveled to northern California where, the previous summer, 33,000 chinook salmon had died on the Klamath River. It seemed a great disaster for the salmon run on that river, but how big a loss actually was it? When I tried to find out what percentage of the total run of salmon 33,000 represented, I could not. No one counted the salmon on the Klamath. What we needed was not more modern technology but the clear thinking of Lewis and Clark.

And so as I view our society at the beginning of the twenty-first century, I fear for its future. Those who do not measure do not know. In taking a new look at the Lewis and Clark's expedition, we need to view it as more than a great adventure (which it was); we need to see it as a path to clear thinking about people and nature, the kind of thinking that is essential for the survival of both in this century.

Daniel B. Botkin
San Francisco, CA

281

Notes

There are two editions of the Lewis and Clark journals used in this book. The primary and definitive one is the new edition, still in progress, edited by Gary Moulton. The complete reference to this edition, with eight volumes published, is: Moulton, G. E. (ed.), *The Journals of the Lewis and Clark Expedition*, University of Nebraska Press, Lincoln. Each of the eight volumes has its own publication date. In the notes that follow, for the sake of brevity, references to this edition are given as GM: volume number: page number.

The other edition used is the classic one edited by Elliott Coues, originally published in 1893 by Francis P. Harper in four volumes. It was a reprint with explanatory notes of Nicholas Biddle's first edition of the Lewis and Clark journals of 1814. The edition I have used is the three-volume Dover reprint of Coues, the complete reference to which is: Coues, E. (ed.), 1965, *History of the Expedition under the Command of Lewis and Clark*, Dover Books, N. Y., three volumes. For brevity, references to this edition are given as C:volume number: page number. Unless otherwise noted, short quotes not specifically referenced are from the Moulton edition, which can be located in that edition by the date of reference.

Biddle (and Coues) combined the various journals into a paraphrase as one continuous narrative. Wherever possible, I have relied on Moulton's edition, which is completely true to the original. However, because I began this project as a long-standing interest in the expedition, my earlier notes were made before Moulton's editions were available, and therefore some references are cited from Coues's edition. I recommend Moulton's edition to anyone interested in the expedition, not only because of the accuracy of the text but because of the excellent notes, including identification of plants by T. Harrison. In quoting from the journals, I have modernized the grammar and spelling.

P R E F A C E :   P P .   x i i i – x i x

xiv *"A recent survey"*: Environmental Opinion Study, Inc., Washington, D.C.

C H A P T E R   O N E :   P P .   1 – 1 9

1 *"Lewis was blessed"*: Moulton, G. E. 1991, *American Encounters: Lewis and Clark*, the People and the Land, Center for the Great Plains Studies, University of Nebraska, Lincoln, 32 pp.

2 *"all communication"*: Coues, Elliott (ed.), 1893, *History of the Expedition under the Command of Lewis and Clark*. Originally published by Francis P. Harper, N.Y., reprinted in three volumes by Dover, Publications, N.Y., 1965.

3 *"Record the mineral production"*: C:I:27, letter by Jefferson regarding Lewis.

4 *"Accept no soft-palmed gentlemen"*: Dillon, R. 1965. *Meriwether Lewis: A Biography*, Coward-McCann, Inc., N.Y., 58.

4 *"He also designed a rifle"*: Dillon, R. *Meriwether Lewis*, 39–48 contains a detailed discussion of the equipment taken on the expedition, and upon which my discussion is based.

5 *"He brought bandages"*: Additional notes about the medicine brought on the expedition: calomel is mercurous chloride (Hg_2Cl_2), a white, tasteless powder which has been used as a fungicide as well as a purgative. Camphor is a terpene ketone ($C_{10}H_{12}O$), a whitish and translucent crystalline from the camphor tree. Copperas, ferrous sulfate ($FeSO_4 7H_2O$) is a bluish-green crystal, salty-tasting material. It was also called green vitriol. Ipecac comes from *Cephaelis ipecacuanha*, a plant of the madder family. Niter, also known as saltpeter, is potassium

nitrate (KNO₃). It is a white, salty-tasting solid, found naturally in limestone deposits and was once mined in limestone caves.

5   *"On Tuesday, June 17, 1806"*:   An excellent discussion about the members of the expedition can be found in GM:2:509–529 (Appendix A). For the purposes of this book, the following summary is helpful. The expedition included Lewis and Clark, 9 men from Kentucky, 14 U.S. soldiers, 2 French watermen (Cruzatte and Labiche), an interpreter and hunter (Drouillard), a black servant (York). All except York were appointed as privates in the Army and then 3 were made sergeants (Floyd, Ordway, Pryor). Later, with the death of Floyd, Patrick Gass, a private, was made sergeant. In addition, a corporal and 6 soldiers and 9 watermen were employed to accompany the expedition to the Mandan Indians. Thus there were 45 people, of which 16 were engaged only to go as far as the Mandan Indians. The names are somewhat obscure of the 16 who traveled only to the Mandans except for a Corporal Warfington. Only one, Charles Floyd, died on the expedition. In addition, the expedition was later joined by an Indian woman interpreter, Sacagawea. Thirty-three people left Fort Mandan for the major part of the journey, counting the baby, Jean Baptiste Charbonneau. [C:I:3:note 3.]   Journals were kept by Lewis, Clark, and by each of the sergeants, the most notable of which is that by Sergeant Patrick Gass, whose journal was published first in 1807 (before the publication of the journals of Lewis and Clark) under the title *A Journey of the Voyages and Travels of a Corps of Discovery Under the command of Capt. Lewis and Capt. Clarke of the Army of the United States, from the mouth of the River Missouri through the interior parts of North America to the Pacific Ocean, during the years 1804, 1805, & 1806. Containing An authentic relation of the most interesting transactions, during the expedition—A description of the country—And an account of its inhabitants, soil, climate, curiosities, and vegetable and animal productions.* Zadok Cramer, Pittsburgh. 262 pp. [C:I:cxviii-cxiv].

6   *"there was not the appearance"*:   C:III:1047.

8   *"After their discussions"*:   C:III:1047.

9   *"The next morning, June 18,"*:   C:III:1047.

9   *"and we had great difficulty"*:   C:III:1048.

9   *"thick underbrush"*:   C:III:1049.

9   *"The mortification of being obliged"*:   C:III:1051.

10   *"They found three Indians,"*:   "Three Indians, who promised to go with us to the falls of the Missouri, for the compensation of two guns. One of them is the brother of Cut-nose, and the other two had each given us a horse, at the house of Broken-arm; and as they are men of good character, respected in the nation, we had the best prospect of being well served" (C:III:1053).

10   *"Crossed abruptly steep hills . . ."*:   Our route lay on the ridgy mountains which separate the waters of the Kooskooskee and the Chopunnish, above the heads of all the streams, so that we met no running water. The whole country was completely covered with snow, except that occasionally we saw a few square feet of earth, at the roots of some trees around which the snow had dissolved" (C:III:1055).

10 "A commanding view": C:III:1056-57.
11 "so well beaten": C:III:1069.
11 "an extensive, beautiful,": C:III:1073.
12 "Who cannot wonder": Cicero, Marcus Tullius. 1972 translation. The Nature of the Gods. Penguin Book, Aylesbury, Great Britain (trans. H. C. P. McGregor), 278.

CHAPTER TWO : PP . 2 0 - 3 8

20 "I spent a year": Vestal, S. 1945. The Missouri. Farrar & Rinehart, N.Y., 14.
20 "Going up that river": Conrad, Joseph. 1977. Heart of Darkness. Penguin, London, 48.
21 "On Saturday, August 11, 1804": C:I:73.
23 "are washing away,": C:I:67.
23 "Judging from the customary": C:I:68.
24 "Nearly three-quarters": GM:1986: 2:391.
25 "Set out this morning": GM:4:139–140.
25 "The banks of the Missouri": C:I:68.
25 "hurried by this impetuous torrent,": GM: 2:400.
28 "The river runs crooked": Steward, C. D. "A Race on the Missouri." The Century Magazine, LEX (4) February 1907, 588. Quoted in Vestal. The Missouri, 13.
28 "eating all the time": Vestal. The Missouri, 13.
29 "The records suggest": Vestal. The Missouri, 13.
29 "The Independence,": Vestal. The Missouri, 52.
29 "In spite of meanders,": Vestal. The Missouri, 53.
30 "So treacherous was the Missouri": Vestal. The Missouri, 44.
30 "About 11 wrecks": One of the more famous wrecks occurred at the location of what is now DeSoto Wildlife Refuge. The wreck has been excavated and a museum of its contents developed at the headquarters of the Refuge. Here a visitor can see the materials that early travelers took with them on their journeys to settle in the countryside originally explored by Lewis and Clark.
31 "The vast Missouri river system": Facts about the Missouri are from the Encyclopaedia Britannica, 15th edition (1992) 8:190–191.
32 "The low grounds": C:1:53.
34 "The rivers rose": Allen, William H. 1993. The Great flood of 1993. BioScience 43: 732–733, Number 11.
34 "As much as 17,000": Church, George L. 1993. Untitled, Time Magazine, July 26, 1993, 27.
34 "This summer's war": Price, Richard. 1989. "Some Never Will Get Over the Flood." USA Today, August 9, 1993, 1.

34 "*While about 7 percent,*": Hoversten, Paul. 1993. "Flood-Control System Under a Microscope." *USA Today*, August 9, 1993, 2.

35 "*Geology Professor George C.B. Belt, Jr*": Tumulty, Karen, and J. Michael Kennedy. 1993. "In River Battle, Some View Levees as Most Dangerous Enemy." *Los Angeles Times*, Saturday July 17, 1993, A16.

35 "*The Los Angeles Times reported*": Tumulty and Kennedy. "In River Battle," A16.

35 "*It's time to prevent*": Allen, William H. Great flood, 734.

35 "*People have created*": Tumulty and Kennedy. "In River Battle," A16.

36 "*We have the opportunity*": Tumulty and Kennedy. "In River Battle," A16.

36 "*Locating homes*": Tumulty and Kennedy. "In River Battle," A16.

36 "*Richard E. Stuart*": "Racing to Rebuild as the Lost Summer Ends." *The Washington Post*, Monday, September 20, 1993.

36 "*Instead of paying*": Allen, William H. Great flood, 735.

37 "*The flood did not*": Allen, William H. Great flood, p. 732.

37 "*On July 8, 1993*": Allen, William H. Great flood, 733.

CHAPTER THREE: PP. 39 – 58

39 "*When something is suggested*": *Los Angeles Times*, Sunday March 7, 1993, A21.

39 "*We were cut off*": Conrad, Joseph. *Heart of Darkness*, 51.

40 "*On June 3, 1805*": GM:4:246–250. All quotes from this day come from these pages.

44 "*a most disagreeable night*": GM:4:262.

44 "*The clay soil*": This clay is so described in a note by Moulton (and R. Bergantino) in GM:4:264, note 1.

44 "*God, Captain*": GM:4:262–263. The entire episode with Windsor is accounted on these pages.

46 "*The notes of Lewis*": There is a long debate among philosophers and scientists about the fundamental character of nature and the universe in regard to chance and predictability. Some of the world's greatest thinkers have refused to accept the idea of chance as a fundamental property of nature. As Einstein once said, "God doesn't play dice," thereby placing himself clearly in the philosophical camp that believes that ultimately every event has a deterministic cause and it is only our lack of knowledge about details that make events seem to involve true chance.

Thus some philosophers would argue that each detail in Lewis and Clark's experiences was determined exactly, and that if we only knew enough we could predict exactly what would happen to a person of exactly Windsor's characteristics—his weight, his mental attitudes, his coordination, etc. Mathematicians would call this a set of deterministic processes, meaning that each event was completely and precisely determined by prior causes. In a deterministic process, each and every event in the future is exactly, completely predictable, more predictable than the flow of the channelized Missouri at DeSoto Wildlife Refuge. The rotation of the paddle wheel on one of the early steamboats to float the Missouri, as long as the machinery remained functional, is deterministic in this sense.

I discussed this philosophical issue in my previous book *Discordant Harmonies*, where I made the point that, philosophical discussions aside, in the world as observed and sensed by living things, we and other creatures have no ability to distinguish between real chance and pseudo chance events. Therefore the world within which life has evolved is a world that for all intents and purposes involves and is characterized by chance. In the case of Lewis and Clark, the real world of struggling up the Marias River, a highly complex but completely determined world, would be indistinguishable to any person or any other living creature from a true chance event. For this reason, the world that we observe, the world in which we struggle, is, to our senses a world of chance, of luck, and, as in the fact that Windsor slid only halfway over the edge—as well as the fact that he had a leader with the calmness, presence of mind, and intelligence of Lewis—, a matter of fortune.

46 *"predictable or"*: Mathematicians refer to processes that involve chance as "stochastic" processes. While stochastic processes involve chance, they can have aspects of predictability. It is possible to predict the probability of an event—how often it will occur. It is also possible to predict the strength or amplitude of an event, based on past experiences. That Lewis and Windsor encountered rain on the day of their return was a matter of environmental risk —an event with certain probabilities that it might occur; informally, we would call it a matter of luck or fortune. The fact that Windsor slipped in such a way as to almost fall over the cliff is philosophically a more difficult issue. If one had prior knowledge of the characteristics of gumbo clay and knew that it was on the bluffs, then the situation might have been avoided (a problem of uncertainty). The probabilities of slipping increase greatly on wet gumbo soil than on dry, and so with the knowledge that this soil was present, we could predict that the chances of slipping over the edge would go up considerably once the rain began. But whether Lewis or Windsor would slip at the exact spot that they did, and whether they would slip near to the edge but not over it, as did Lewis, or half way over it, as did Windsor, seems a matter of chance. Perhaps a slight distraction of one's eye from a foothold, or a chance difference in a bend in one's foot or shift in weight, could cause a difference in luck. These two kinds of uncertainty—uncertainty about a fact that already exists, and uncertainty about a chance of something happening—confronted Lewis on his exploration of the Marias River.

47 *"In Glendive, Montana"*:   Hart, H. C. 1957. *The Dark Missouri*. University of Wisconsin Press, Madison, 10.

47 *"Countryside of wind"*:   Hart. *Dark Missouri*, 10.

47 *"Mitchell and Scottsbluff"*:   Hart. *Dark Missouri*, 10.

48 *"the most exhaustive study"*:   Hart. *Dark Missouri*, 12.

53 *"map from the trash"*: Zybach, R. 1993. The Future of Oregon's forest could be historical data. *Forest Log:* 6–9, Oregon Dept. of Forestry, May–June 1993.

53 *"a second copy"*: Walter Schutt, Oregon Department of Forestry, pers. comm.

CHAPTER FOUR: PP. 59–86

60 *"Provability is"*: Hofstadter, Douglas R. 1979. *Gödel, Escher, Bach: An Eternal Golden Braid*, Vintage Books, N.Y. 19.

60 *"May 11, 1805"*: GM:4:141.

60 *"These bear"*: C:1: 307 (for May 11, 1805).

60 *"renders them"*: C:1: 307 (for May 11, 1805).

61 *"Each shot seemed"*: C: 1: 307 (for May 11, 1805).

61 *"There is no chance"*: Lewis and Clark were the first to provide a written scientific description of the grizzly, although it did not receive its scientific name, *Ursus horribilis*, until 1815. C: 1: 307 (for May 11, 1805).

61 *"which is also thick"*: C: 1: 307 (for May 11, 1805).

63 *"The country abounds"*: GM:II:306.

63 *"The Indians give"*: GM:4:31.

64 *"burning sulfur"*: GM:4:21, note 3.

64 *"very troublesome"*: GM:4:19–20.

65 *"tracks of bear"*: GM:7:127.

65 *"Like frost"*: GM:4:81.

65 *"first scientific record"*: GM:4:84.

66 *"The largest"*: GM:4:113.

66 *"before he fell"*: GM:4:168.

66 *"The man's gun"*: GM:4:256.

69 *"To my surprise"*: Burt, W. H. 1964. *A Field Guide to the Mammals*. Houghton Mifflin, Boston, 49.

70 *"A little further"*: Servheen, C. 1985. "The Grizzly Bear." 401–415, in *The Audubon Wildlife Report 1985*.

70 *"Historical Perspective"*: *The Audubon Wildlife Report, 1985*, cites for this information Storer, T. I., and L. P. Tevis, *California Grizzly* (Lincoln and London: University of Nebraska Press, 1955).

73 *"I found another estimate"*: See Craighead, F.C. 1979. "Track of the Grizzly," Sierra Club Books, San Francisco; and Craighead, F.C. 1982. *A Definitive system for analysis of grizzly bear habitat and other wilderness resources utilizing LANDSAT multispectral imagery and computer technology*, University of Montana: Missoula.

75 *"with the sole exception"*: The study of the density of grizzlies might seem something that would have been done long ago, archived today in some dusty shelves in the back room of a natural history museum. But on the contrary, knowledge of grizzlies is on the increase, and scientists attempting to estimate their abundance are using modern technology. In the midst of writing this book, I gave a talk at Cornell University, hosted by the graduate students in the

School of Natural Resources. Shawn Riley, a graduate student who was my primary host, had worked in Montana on wildlife and gave me a just-published article about estimating the density of grizzlies using automatic cameras. This work was done in heavily forested, rugged terrain with rock outcrops, avalanches, and dense forests in the Swan Mountain Range in western Montana, in an area bounded to the south by the Bob Marshall Wilderness and on the north by Highway 2. Bears were captured using tranquilizers, tagged and released in 1988 and 1989. Automatic cameras, with flash and infrared sensors to detect the bears against the background, were placed within the area according to a statistically determined sampling scheme. The camera stations were baited, and the cameras photographed the bears when they came in to feed. Even with these elaborate methods, they snared only 27 bears in 3 years, and estimated the density between 6.5 and 17.4 bears per 100 square mile, a number considerably higher than what I obtained from the Lewis and Clark journals. This seems to be a better technique, especially because it allows for a calculation of the sampling error, but the use of baiting to bring in the bears could bias the sample, and would tend to lead to a high estimate of the density, and so it is difficult to compare this method with others. The reference is Mace, R. D., S. C. Minta, T. L. Manley and K. E. Aune. 1994. "Estimating Grizzly Bear Population Size Using Camera Sightings," *Wildlife Society Bulletin*, 22:74–83.

81 *"Based on genetic factors"*: This discussion is based on Soule, M. E., 1980. "Thresholds for survival: Maintaining fitness and evolutionary potential.: 151–169, in Soule, M. E. and B. A. Wilcox, eds. *Conservation Biology*. Sutherland, Mass.: Sinauer. See also Ehrenfeld, D. W. 1972. *Conserving Life on Earth*. Oxford University Press, N.Y., and Council On Environmental Quality And the Department of State, 1980. *The global 2000 report to the President: Entering the twenty-first century*.

82 *"It is a risk"*: Dennis, B., P. L. Munholland, and J. M. Scott. 1991. Estimation of growth and extinction parameters for endangered species, *Ecological Monographs* 61(2): 115–143.

82 *"population of butterflies"*: Ehrlich, P., and A. Ehrlich. 1981. *Extinction: The Causes and Consequences of the Disappearance of Species*. New York: Random House.

83 *"extinction of the heath hen"*: Soule, M. E. 1980. "Thresholds," 159–169.

84 *"The species is"*: Soule, M. E. "Thresholds."

85 *"On June 28, 1805,"*: GM:4:338

CHAPTER FIVE: PP. 87–100

87 *"When you can measure"*: Williams, L. Pearce, 1978. *Album of Science, The Nineteenth Century*. New York: Scribners & Sons.

88   *"Lewis and Clark"*:   In Jefferson's words, the goals were "to explore the Missouri river, and such principal streams of it, as by its course and communication with the waters of the Pacific ocean, whether the Columbia, Oregon [*sic*], Colorado, or any other river, may offer the most direct and practicable water-communication across the continent, for the purposes of commerce." Coues, *History of the Expedition*, p xxvi, letter by Jefferson regarding Lewis.

88   *"the soil and face"*:   Jefferson's letter of June 20, 1803, to Lewis, quoted by Coues, (C:I:xxviii).

88   *"Perhaps no traveler's"*:   C:I:Introduction.

88   *"As a captain"*:   Letter by Thomas Jefferson, a memoir of Meriwether Lewis, in Coues,(C:I:16 ff). Of Lewis, Jefferson wrote (C:I:22): "Of courage undaunted; possessing a firmness and perseverance of purpose which nothing but impossibilities could divert from its direction; careful as a father of those committed to his charge, yet steady in the maintenance of order and discipline; intimate with the Indian character, customs, and principles; habituated to the hunting life; guarded, by exact observation of the vegetables and animals of his own country . . . honest, disinterested, liberal, of sound understanding, and a fidelity to truth so scrupulous that whatever he should report would be as certain as if seen by ourselves—with all these qualifications, as if selected and implanted by nature in one body for this express purpose, I could have not hesitation in confiding the enterprise to him."

91   *"20,000 bowheads"*:   For those familiar with statistical methods, it will be useful to know that the mean value is 20,000; the 95% confidence error is 10,000.

92   *"Every April"*:   The following information about the modern monitoring of the bowhead whale is from Burns, J. J., J. J. Montague, and C. J. Cowles, eds. 1992. *The Bowhead Whale*, Special Publication #2, The Society of Marine Mammalogy, Allen Press, Lawrence, Kansas.

C H A P T E R   S I X :   P P .   1 0 1 – 1 2 7

101   *"On the high plains"*:   Moulton, G. E. 1991. *American Encounters: Lewis and Clark, the People, and the Land*. Center for Great Plains Studies, University of Nebraska, Lincoln, p. 15.

101   *"Last night"*:   GM:4:215.

103   *"Its first buffalo"*:   GM:2:282.

103   *"Buffalo were sighted"*:   C:I:34.

103   *"with great method"*:   C:2:403, (for July 5, 1805).

103   *"The men of the expedition"*:   GM:2:283, note 6.

103   *"shoot a buffalo"*:   GM:2:502.

103   *"From the top"*:   GM:3:11.

105   *"Leaves are falling"*:   GM:3:180.

106   *"Winter had approached"*:   GM: 3:221–222. Henceforth, unless otherwise

noted, short quotes from the journals about the buffalo are from the GM
edition, volume 4, for each date mentioned.

107 *"32 deer"*: GM:3:238.
110 *"lighting of the fire"*: There are other explanations for these fires, however (see
GM:2:400, note 11; for July 20, 1804).
110 *"Few Indians"*: GM:3:321.
110 *"John McDonnell"*: Haines F. 1970. *The Buffalo.* Thomas Y. Crowell, N.Y., 24.
111 *"Little Muddy River"*: GM:4:59.
113 *"a most beautiful"*: GM:4:283.
117 *"encapsulated by Mari Sandoz"*: Sandoz, Mari. 1954. *The Buffalo Hunters.* University of Nebraska press, Lincoln. Her book is perhaps the most eloquent
account of the history of the demise of the buffalo, and in many aspects seems
to be the best documented.
117 *"General Isaac I. Stevens"*: Quoted in Haines. *The Buffalo,* 33.
117 *"Colonel R. I. Dodge"*: Sandoz. *Buffalo Hunters,* 34.
117 *"always buffalo somewhere"*: Sandoz. *Buffalo Hunters,* 83.
119 *"40 to 50 million"*: Haines. *The Buffalo,* 3.
119 *"15 million"*: Sandoz. *Buffalo Hunters,* 34.
119 *"Buffalo Hunt"*: Sandoz. *Buffalo Hunters,* 83.
121 *"Cabeza de Vaca"*: Haines. *The Buffalo,* 73.
121 *"Near Roanaoke"*: Haines. *The Buffalo,* 74.
121 *"One herd"*: Haines. *The Buffalo,* 32.
122 *"Fossils of bison"*: Haines. *The Buffalo,* 11.
122 *"The Buffalo"*: Haines. *The Buffalo,* 190.
123 *"25 cents"*: Haines. *The Buffalo,* 191.
123 *"In 1873"*: Haines. *The Buffalo,* 197.
124 *"Estimates range"*: Sandoz. *Buffalo Hunters,* 50.
124 *"General Mitchell"*: Sandoz. *Buffalo Hunters,* 48.
124 *"Colonel R. I. Dodge"*: Sandoz. *Buffalo Hunters,* 88.
124 *"this excellent beast."*: Sandoz. *Buffalo Hunters,* 99.
124 *"Laws were passed"*: Sandoz. *Buffalo Hunters,* 127.
124 *"would not last long"*: Sandoz. *Buffalo Hunters,* 127.
124 *"fewer than 5,000"*: Sandoz. *Buffalo Hunters,* 349.
125 *"abundance of elk"*: Thomas, J. W., and L. D. Bryant. 1987. "The Elk." 495–
508, in Di Silvestro, R. L., W. L. Ch., K. Barton, and L. Labate. Eds. *Audubon
Wildlife Reports,* Academic Press, N.Y.

CHAPTER   SEVEN: PP.   128–158

128 *"about wolves"*: Federal Writers Project, "Idaho Lore," Varis Fisher, American
Guide Series, 121. Quoted in B. A. Botkin. 1944. *A Treasury of American
Folklore.* Crown Pub., N.Y., 622.

130 *"white streak"*: GM:2:428–429 (Clark's entry for July 30, 1804).

130 *"Parrot Queets,"*: GM:2:325.

131 *"no known case"*: L. M. Talbot, pers. comm.

132 *"wolf clans"*: Young, S. P. 1970. *The Last of the Loners.* MacMillan, London.

134 *"Snowshoe Thompson"*: De Quille, Dan. 1886. "Snowshoe Thompson." *The Overland Monthly*, VIII (second series), 428–429, quoted in B. A. Botkin. *A Treasury of Western Folklore*, 150–151.

135 *"Sergeant Floyd"*: Sergeant Floyd was the only member of the expedition to die on the journey, and his symptoms appear to be those of appendicitis, which at that time would have killed him wherever he was located. His story has been told many times in other books about the Lewis and Clark expedition. After his death, Lewis appointed Gass, whose journals later became so important, as a sergeant to replace Floyd.

136 *"Wolves follow"*: C:1:172–174.

136 *"Whatever is left"*: C:1:208–209.

137 *"Buffalo, elk, and goats"*: GM:4:111.

137 *"immense herds"*: GM:4:124–128.

138 *"The beaver"*: Burroughs, R. D. 1961. *The Natural History of the Lewis and Clark Expedition.* Michigan State University Press, East Lansing, 107.

139 *"yellow root"*: GM 3:453, a note written while at the Mandan village in the winter.

140 *"Yellowstone National Park"*: July 3, 1993, *The New York Times.*

147 *"Although a pack of wolves"*: Talbot, L. M. 1978. "The Role of Predators in Ecosystem Management." 307–321, in Holdgate, M. W., and M. J. Woodman. Eds. *The Breakdown and Restoration of Ecosystems.*

153 *"wolves on Isle Royale"*: Mech, L. D. 1966. The Wolves of Isle Royale. U.S. . National Park Service Fauna Series Number 7, 210, and Jordan, Peter, pers. comm.

CHAPTER EIGHT: PP. 159–175

159 *"Cabeza de Vaca"*: Long, H. 1972. *The Marvelous Adventures of Cabeza de Vaca.* Condor Books, London, 20.

161 *"On that Saturday"*: GM:4:436–437.

161 *"Sacagawea was"*: "Her services . . . among the Shoshonean-speaking people in the Rockies were indispensable, while her presence with a baby calmed the fears of many tribes that the party was a war expedition. She did provide valuable assistance as a guide in the region of southwestern Montana in which she had spent her childhood. Clark seems to have had a high opinion of her, as he did of Charbonneau and the couple's son, but romantic fantasies concerning the two have no foundation in the record . . . The best evidence is that she died at Manuel Lisa's trading post, Fort Manuel, on the Missouri River in Cor-

son County, South Dakota, in 1812 . . . Certainly Clark recorded her as having died by 1825–28. Assertions that she lived to be nearly one hundred, dying in 1883 on the Wind River Shoshone Reservation in Wyoming, rest on Shaky evidence" [GM:3:229 (note 2)].

161   *"Jean Baptiste Charbonneau"*:   GM:3:291 (note 1). Jean Baptiste Charbonneau later became a mountain man, a fur trader, and a guide for Frémont and other explorers, finally settling in California and dying in Oregon in 1866.

161   *"cheered the spirits"*:   GM:4:416.

162   *"August 5,"*:   GM:5:47.

162   *"August 6"*:   GM:5:52–3.

162   *"This peak"*:   GM:5:61 (note 6).

163   *"mortification and disappointment"*:   GM:5:70.

163   *"Crossing the Continental Divide"*:   GM:5:74.

164   *"he might shoot me"*:   GM:5:104–105.

165   *"secrete themselves"*:   GM:5:105–106.

165   *"Sacagawea's relatives"*:   GM:5:116 (note 2).

165   *"the Clearwater River"*:   C:iii:1263: (note 2).

165   *"the Bitterroots"*:   Moulton. *American Encounters*, 21.

166   *"even Lewis's dog"*:   GM:5:112.

167   *"Linneaus's book"*:   Dillon, R. 1965. *Meriwether Lewis*.

168   *"The compass was lost"*:   GM:4:342–343.

168   *"found the compass"*:   GM:4:345.

169   *"observed fires"*:   GM:2:398.

169   *"on August 15th"*:   GM:2:484.

170   *"a hundred carcasses,"*:   GM:4:216.

170   *"The part of the decoy"*:   GM: 4:216–217.

170   *"over the precipice"*:   It has been known for more than hundred years, since the observations of the English naturalist and biologist, Wallace, that since the end of the last Ice Age the biggest of the large mammals have disappeared from North America. Some attribute these extinctions to climatic change, but others, most notably the anthropologist Paul Martin, have observed that these extinctions coincided more or less with the arrival of Indians in North America, and that it might have been possible for groups of Indians, approaching a prey, to have caused the decline and possibly the extinction of species. Lewis observed the ability of the Indians to kill large numbers of buffalo, more than they could use at one time; Martin extends this ability to suggest that it could have caused extinctions. Whether extinctions were entirely or partially the result of such hunting, the observations of Lewis tell us that Native Americans could have major impacts on large herds.

171   *"Do them No Harm"*:   Swayne, Z. L. 1990. *Do Them No Harm!*. Legacy House, Orofino, Idaho.

171   *"Lolo Trail"*:   GM:5:222.

172   *"They saw men"*:   Swayne. *Do Them No Harm!*, 16.

172 *"Some Indians stole"*: GM:5:230.
173 *"Wat-ku-ese could not sleep"*: Swayne. *Do Them No Harm!*.
175 *"lone horseman"*: C:3:1244.

CHAPTER NINE: PP. 176–211

176 *"Thousand years"*: Murlin, B. ed. 1991. *Woody Guthrie Roll On Columbia: The Columbia River Collection.* Sing Out Pubs., Bethlehem, Pa., 17.
177 *"In the West"*: *The Wall Street Journal,* April, 2, 1993.
180 *"Chief Cameahwait"*: GM:5:83.
181 *"fish either perishes"*: GM:5:122.
182 *"August 23"*: GM:5:153.
182 *"The incredible abundance"*: C:II:657.
183 *"the Indians dried salmon"*: GM:5:331.
184 *"The Dalles"*: Alt, D. D., and D. W. Hyndman. *Roadside Geology of Oregon.* Mountain Press Pub. Co., Missoula, Mont., 179.
184 *"view the rapids"*: GM:7:336 (note 6).
185 *"10,000 pounds of fish"*: GM:7:355. This is given as 10,000 w. of neet fish.
185 *"a beautiful gentle stream"*: GM:7:339.
185 *"sockeye and chinook salmon"*: Kadera, J. 1993. "Plan Aims to Restore Declining Salmon." *The Oregonian.* Thursday, October 21, 1993, A1 and A15.
188 *"commercial exploitation"*: Kaczynski V. W., and J. F. Palmisano. 1992. *A Review of the management and environmental factors responsible for the decline and lack of recovery of Oregon's wild anadromous Salmonids.* Technical Report, Oregon Forest Industries Council, Portland, Oregon, 202–204.
193 *"4.5 million fish"*: Kaczynski and Palmisano. Environmental factors, 205.
193 *"Coho salmon"*: Kaczynski and Palmisano. Environmental factors, 211.
193 *"There at Priest"*: Murlin, B. *Woody Guthrie,* 17.
194 *"Paul Sears"*: Sears, P. 1935. *Deserts on the March.* University of Oklahoma Press, Norman.
194 *"I saw the Columbia River"*: Murlin, B. *Woody Guthrie,* 40.
207 *"The ancestors of salmon"*: Allendorf, F. W., and R. S. Waples. 1994. "Conservation and Genetics of Salmonid Fishes," in Avise and Hammick. Eds. Conservation Guidelines, Chapman and Hall, N.Y. (in press).
208 *"Recognizing the loss"*: Waite, T. L. 1993. "Effort to Nurture Salmon in Thames Advances." *The New York Times.* Tuesday, November 16, 1993.

CHAPTER TEN: PP. 212–255

212 *"Takes a flat thousand years"*: Murlin, B. *Woody Guthrie.*
213 *"In spite of"*: GM:6:37–38.

213 *"They and their baggage"*:   GM:6:41.
215 *"Construction was similar"*:   GM:7: 333, 335.
216 *"Wood formed the basis"*:   *Encyclopaedia Britannica* (1992) 13:324.
218 *"The weather at Fort Clatsop"*:   GM:6:125.
219 *"Lewis and Clark wrote"*:   GM:6:172.
219 *"the elk are"*:   GM:6:276: There they recorded the latitude to 46° 10′ 16″3‴ N.
221 *"The low grounds"*:   C:II:688.
221 *"The country has"*:   GM:6:10.
221 *"On the edge"*:   GM:6:15.
222 *"After being so long"*:   C:II:687.
222 *"Beacon Rock"*:   GM:6:9.
233 *"For many tropical forests"*:   Botkin, D. B., and L. M. Talbot. 1992. Biological diversity and forests. 47–74, in N. Sharma, ed. *Managing the World's Forests: Looking for Balance Between Conservation and Development.* The World Bank, Washington, D. C.
238 *"impenetrable thickets"*:   GM:6:45 (note 2 points out that this may have been *Pinus contorta.*)
238 *"Sitka spruce"*:   GM:6:44.
238 *"Clark found some conifers"*:   GM:6:42.
238 *"some of these huge trees"*:   GM:6:70 (November 19, 1805).
238 *"brant and plover"*:   C:II:712.
240 *"to make salt"*:   GM:6:116.
240 *"On December 28"*:   GM:6:116–117.
242 *"first modern sawmill"*:   Zybach, R. 1993. A general forest harvest history of the Upper Siletz River Basin, Oregon, above the mouth of Sunshine Creek. Unpublished report to The Center For the Study of the Environment, Santa Barbara, CA.
242 *"earliest written observations"*:   Zybach, R. 1994. Early historical peoples, plants and animals of the Siletz River, Oregon (1788–1849). Unpublished report to The Center For the Study of the Environment, Santa Barbara, CA.
242 *"large burned area"*:   Albert, September 7, 1848. Quoted in Zybach. Early Historical Peoples.
242 *"He camped"*:   Zybach. Early Historical Peoples.
243 *"set of maps"*:   Teensma, P. D. A., J. T. Rienstra, and M. A. Yelter. 1991. Preliminary reconstruction and analysis of change in forest stand age classes of the Oregon Coast Range from 1850 to 1940. U. S. Dept. of Interior, Bureau of Land Management, Technical Note T/N OR-9, Portland, Oregon, 9 pp.
246 *"soil was lost"*:   Franklin, J. F., J. A. MacMahon, F. Swanson, and J. R. Sedell. 1985. Ecosystem responses to the eruption of Mount St. Helens. *National Geographic Research* 1 (2): 217–235.
246 *"After the eruption"*:   Lucas, R. E. 1986. Recovery of game fish populations impacted by the May 18, 1980, eruption of Mount St. Helens: Winter-run steelhead in the Toutle River watershed. 276–292 in S. A. C. Keller. Ed. *Mount St.*

NOTES

Helens: Five Years Later. Eastern Washington University Press, Cheney, Washington.

246 *"600 elk"*: Merrill, E. H., K. J. Raedeke, K. L. Knoutson, and R. D. Taber. 1986. 359–368, in Keller. *Mount St. Helens: Five years later.* Eastern Washington University Press, Cheney, Washington.

246 *"steelhead trout"*: Lucas, R. E. 1986. Recovery of game fish populations.

C H A P T E R   E L E V E N :   P P .   2 5 6 – 2 7 7

256 *"Prairies are quiescent"*: Stegner, Wallace. 1980. *Wolf Willow: a History, a Story, and a Memory of the Last Plains Frontier.* University of Nebraska Press, Lincoln, 7.

257 *"Prairies extended"*: Garrett, W. E., and J. B. Garver, Jr., 1988. *The Historical Atlas of the United States.* Centennial Edition, National Geographic Society, Washington, 68.

261 *"The regular form of this hill"*: GM:3:10.

261 *"From the top"*: GM:3:11.

262 *"Among the birds"*: GM:3:10.

269 *"the green swells"*: Quoted in Botkin, D. B. 1977. The vegetation of the West. 1216–1224, in H. R. Lamar. Ed. *The Reader's Encyclopedia of the American West*, Crowell, N.Y., 1218.

271 *"the variableness of the Missouri"*: C III:1187.

272 *"virgin forest,"*: "Plants of Fontenelle Forest." Published in 1959 by the Omaha Botany Club, 1.

275 *"bald pated prairie"*: GM: 2:383 and note 5, p 386.

276 *"native prairie"*: I had been taken to the Loess Hills State Recreation Area to see the experimental burning in 1991 by my friends and colleagues from Iowa State University, Tom Jurik and David Glenn-Lewin.

Index

distribution and abundance, 103, 116–19
drowning of, 110
exploitation of, 121–25
herd size, 115–16, 117–18
hunting, 108–15, 121–25
population estimates, 118–19
range of, 122
The Buffalo (Haines), 122
The Buffalo Hunters (Sandoz), 117
Bureau of Land Management, 243
Bur oak, 272–73

Cabeza de Vaca, Alvar, 121
Ca-me-ah-wait (Shoshone Indian), 164–65, 180
Canoes, 216
Cape Disappointment, 238–39
Carbon dioxide, 53–54, 97–99
Caribou, 141
Carolina parakeet, 130
Carrying capacity, 77, 78, 190–91
Cascades Mountains, 222
Catastrophe, natural, 83
Catlin, George, 272
Cattle ranching, 132
Chance. *See* Probability
Charbonneau (French-Canadian trader), 161, 167–68
Chase, Edith, 227–28
Chase, Heman, 216–17, 225–28
Chinooks (winds), 47
Chinook salmon, 185, 187–88
Chippeway Indians, 181
Chum salmon, 188
Cicero, 12
Civil War, 123
Clark, William, 1–2, 3, 65–66, 167–68, 184–85
See also Lewis and Clark expedition
Clatsop Indians, 174
Clean Water Act (1970), 120
Clearcuts, 230
Clearwater River, 165, 182
Climax stage forests, 234, 252
Clothing, 4–5
Cody, Buffalo Bill, 123
Coho salmon, 178–79, 188, 193

Columbia River, 90, 180, 181, 182, 183, 184, 198, 213–14, 241
grassland to forest transition, 220–23
power dams on, 195–96
Columbia River Cascades, 221
Compass, 167–68
Computers, 246–54
Condor, 84
Conifers, 202–3
Conservation, 130, 186, 194
of forests, 230–35
and grizzly bears, 75–80
justifications for, 138–39
aesthetic, 153–58
mechanistic, 140, 142, 156, 157
utilitarian, 138–40, 155–56
and original population estimate, 75–76
and planning time period, 85
and resource exploitation, 120
of salmon, 206–9
species recovery, 79
and viable populations, 79–80, 81–85
of wolves, 133, 138–48
See also Environmentalism
Continental Divide, 2, 163
Costa Rica, 126
Coues, Elliott, 88
Coyote, 131
Cultural heritage, 270

The Dalles (Columbia River rapids), 184
The Dalles Dam, 195
Dams, 31, 193, 194–96
See also Debris dams
Day, Susan, 243
Debris dams, 203
Depression (economic), 194
Deserts on the March (Sears), 194
DeSoto National Wildlife Refuge, 32, 37, 274
Diatoms, 201–2
Dicks, Norm, 186
Dieffenbach, Bill, 35
Disaster payments, 36
Divine-order myth, 12–13
Dodge, R. I., 117, 124
Do Them No Harm! (Swayne), 171
Douglas fir, 230